Before you start to read this book, take this moment to think about making a donation to punctum books, an independent non-profit press

@ https://punctumbooks.com/support

If you're reading the e-book, you can click on the image below to go directly to our donations site. Any amount, no matter the size, is appreciated and will help us to keep our ship of fools afloat. Contributions from dedicated readers will also help us to keep our commons open and to cultivate new work that can't find a welcoming port elsewhere. Our adventure is not possible without your support.
Vive la open-access.

Fig. 1. Hieronymus Bosch, *Ship of Fools* (1490–1500)

First published in 2017 by dead letter office, BABEL Working Group
an imprint of punctum books, Earth, Milky Way.
https://punctumbooks.com

The BABEL Working Group is a collective and desiring-assemblage of scholar–gypsies with no leaders or followers, no top and no bottom, and only a middle. BABEL roams and stalks the ruins of the post-historical university as a multiplicity, a pack, looking for other roaming packs with which to cohabit and build temporary shelters for intellectual vagabonds. We also take in strays.

ISBN-13: 978-0-9985318-4-7
ISBN-10: 0-9985318-4-7
Library of Congress Cataloging Data is available from the Library of Congress

Book design: Vincent W.J. van Gerven Oei

Elisabeth Weber

KILL
BOXES

Facing the Legacy of
US-Sponsored Torture,
Indefinite Detention,
and Drone Warfare

TABLE OF CONTENTS

ACKNOWLEDGMENTS

Early versions of some of the chapters gathered in this volume were presented at different conferences and seminars, among them the Graduiertenkolleg "Mediale Historiographien" of the Universität Erfurt, Germany; the University of Macau; Johns Hopkins University; Yale University; Cornell University; the University of Manitoba, Winnipeg; the Deutsche Forschungsgesellschaft Symposium on "Allegory" at the Villa Vigoni, Italy; and my own institution, the University of California, Santa Barbara. I am grateful to the colleagues and students at these institutions for the lively discussions that have helped shape the arguments of this book.

I thank Gil Anidjar, Cathy Caruth, Wolf Kittler, Christian Kläui and Bettine Menke for their critique, inspiration, and encouragement.

I thank Eileen Joy for inviting me to punctum books and Vincent W.J. van Gerven Oei for his invaluable help in the preparation of the manuscript.

I thank Julie Carlson, my friend and colleague, for our deeply inspiring exchanges and for her unwavering generosity in reading and responding to my work.

My profound gratitude goes to my American–Armenian–German–Afghan family here and abroad for countless conversations and for their love, especially to Helga Weber for teaching me so much, to David and Ruben Saatjian for moving me, and to Mark Saatjian — for everything.

Shocks of Recognition

In late April 2004, photographs taken in the Iraqi Abu Ghraib prison and electronically shared among American troops were leaked, causing outrage around the world. The images showed American military personnel torturing, humiliating, and sexually abusing Iraqi detainees, in some cases to the point of murder, in flagrant violation of the Geneva Conventions. Among all the photographs, one of a hooded Iraqi man standing on a box with extended arms, his hands attached to wires indicating the imminent danger of electrocution, became an icon for the gross human rights violations and war crimes committed by the US military in Iraq and in other "theaters of war," as was discovered after the Abu Ghraib revelations.

As Peter Selz notes, this image "has for many people around the world replaced the Statue of Liberty as the symbol of what the United States stands for."[1] In a now-famous mural in Sadr City, the largest Shiite neighborhood of Baghdad, the Iraqi artist Sallah Edine Sallat juxtaposes the hooded man on the box with a Statue of Liberty portrayed as a "Klansman/torturer." Instead of holding the torch of freedom, the latter reaches up to "pull the electrical switch" that activates the wires attached to the hooded prisoner of Abu Ghraib (fig. 1).[2]

---

1   Peter Selz, *Art of Engagement: Visual Politics in California and Beyond* (Berkeley: University of California Press, 2006), 71.

2   W.J.T. Mitchell, *Cloning Terror: The War of Images, 9/11 to the Present* (Chicago: University of Chicago Press, 2011), 116. For Mitchell, "the inscription on the mural, 'That Freedom for Bush,' is perhaps redundant, insofar as the metonymic juxtaposition of the Hooded Man and the Statue of Liberty be-

Fig. 1: Iraqi boys in front of Sallah Edine Sallat's Baghdad Mural.
Photo by Awad Awad/AFP/Getty.

Far beyond the countries of the Middle East, the Abu Ghraib photograph has achieved worldwide notoriety. The reasons for this fact converge, I contend, in the shock of recognition the image causes in the viewer. On the one hand, there is the recognition by scholars like Alfred McCoy, eminent historian of the CIA and its torture programs, who immediately recognized the CIA's signature in the photo. It is equally significant, that the photo's global resonance responds to a subconscious or even unconscious recognition: the uncanny resemblance of the victim with the crucified Christ. I will return to this point shortly.

I open this book with a reflection on this image, because it haunts the illegal or extralegal practices addressed in the chapters that follow. Thus, acknowledging and analyzing the shock of recognition face to face, as it were, with the hooded man from Abu Ghraib opens the way for registering similar shocks of recognition in other scenes of massive violation of individuals' rights. We cannot think these extralegal practices, if we assume them to be occurring in a faraway world against a faraway enemy, who by his hostile actions, often portrayed as "barbaric" and utterly alien, has provoked such retaliation, as illegal as it may be. The readings of literary, philosophical, and artistic texts that follow draw on what Jacques Derrida calls the two "ages of cruelty," one that is scientifically and technologically sophisticated, allegedly surgical and precise, the other that is characterized as archaic, indiscriminate, and bloody. They set out to explore a mutual implication not only in these "ages of cruelty," but also in the suffering caused by both cruelties. In other words, the chapters of this book attempt to register and explore shocks of recognition in the "other's" cruelty and the "other's" suffering. To initiate and explore such shocks of recognition is, I maintain, one of the major responsibilities but also one of the major promises of the practice called "the humanities."

However, to acknowledge recognition, there needs first to be the acknowledgement of an address. The cultural (literary, philosophical, artistic) strategies explored here start from a fundamental given, as banal as it is complex: we are addressed, and we have been addressed long before being able to respond, as Emmanuel Levinas and Jacques Lacan didn't tire of recalling, coming from two vastly different (if intersecting) traditions.[3] We are addressed, and fiercely addressed, in the photo of the hooded man, all the more so as he was brutally prevented, in our name, from returning the camera's (and thus our) gaze. We are addressed in the screams that turn a person, tortured in our name, into howling flesh. We are addressed in poems written in the Guantánamo Prison camp, however much American authorities try to censor them, in our name. We are addressed by the victims of the US drone wars, however little American citi-

---

came a kind of slang condensation for Iraqis, so that they reportedly began to refer to the Bagman himself as the Statue of Liberty, a powerful occasion for jokes about the American promise to bring electricity to Iraq along with freedom" (103-4).

3 In my *Verfolgung und Trauma: Zu Emmanuel Levinas' Autrement qu'être ou au-delà de l'essence* (Vienna: Passagen Verlag, 1990), I have tried to develop this common preoccupation in Levinas's and Lacan's œuvres.

zens may have heard the names of the places obliterated by the bombs for which their taxes pay.

I would contend that we know well that we are addressed, in spite of all the talk of the "clash of civilizations" and in spite of a number of strategies of brutal refusal of heeding those calls. Strategies of refusal include the acceptance of the knowledge that people are locked up without trial in cages that in any other context would be reserved for animals, the acceptance of their imprisonment in metal containers for weeks, months, or years of solitary confinement, the justifications for shackling them to the ground in freezing or overheated cubicles while subjecting them to deafening music and strobe lights, or the tacit or explicit consent to locking them up in virtual kill boxes whose lethal walls move with the prey. Kill boxes, I argue, in addition to their definition by the US military, come in many shapes.

I take as paradigmatic the resonance arising from the very peculiar address by a hooded man threatened with death by electrocution upon the slightest movement. It is well documented that the torture practices of Abu Ghraib were exported from the Guantánamo Bay detention camp.[4] The hooded man's conscious and unconscious recognizability is thus a critical factor not only in the discussion on torture, but also in the discussions on indefinite detention without trial, as practiced in Guantánamo, and in debates on the strategies to circumvent the latter altogether, as practiced in drone warfare and its extrajudicial assassination program.

For these reasons I have chosen to open the present volume with an analysis of this image, especially as seen through W.J.T. Mitchell's eye-opening reading. As mentioned already, the image's iconic quality is owed to the viewer's "uncanny sense of recognition," which Mitchell explored first in an op-ed on June 27, 2004, in *The Chicago Tribune* and later in depth in his book

---

4   Alfred McCoy, *A Question of Torture* (New York: Holt, 2006), 133–39; Jason Leopold, "How Guantanamo Became America's Interrogation 'Battle Lab,'" *Vice News*, Jan. 12, 2012, among a number of important pieces Leopold has dedicated to what one official called "the legal equivalent of outer space."

Cloning Terror.[5] The title of the op-ed, "Echoes of a Christian Symbol: Photo Reverberates with Raw Power of Christ on Cross," summarizes why the photo's symbolic and "iconographic resonance" transformed it, above all the other photos coming out of Abu Ghraib's torture chambers, into the "icon" of the Abu Ghraib scandal, figuring both as the "icon of the moment," and at the same time, "possibly" as a "historical marker." Evoking the "long history of images that unite figures of torture and sacredness or divinity," Mitchell deciphers the image of the hooded man as what used to be called a "Christ figure."[6]

As Thomas Lentes has noted, no other body has "informed the history of Western iconography as deeply as the martyred and wounded body of Christ."[7] This iconography and the theology that informs it are deeply marked by the practice of torture. Alfred McCoy explains in the introductory chapter to his groundbreaking book *A Question of Torture* that

> the impact of judicial torture on European culture went far beyond the dungeon, coinciding with a subtle shift in theological emphasis from the life of Jesus to the death of the Christ — a change reflected in artistic representations, both painting and sculpture, of his body being scourged, tortured, and crucified. From limited details of Christ's agonies in the Gospels, medieval artists, in the words of one scholar "approximated these grisly violations with the unerring eye of a forensic pathologist," creating an image of the pain inflicted on his battered body that mimed, and may have legitimated,

---

5   W.J.T. Mitchell, "Echoes of a Christian Symbol: Photo Reverberates with Raw Power of Christ on Cross," *The Chicago Tribune,* June 27, 2004; Mitchell, *Cloning Terror,* 144.

6   Mitchell, "Echoes of a Christian Symbol."

7   Thomas Lentes, "Der Blick auf den Durchbohrten: Die Wunden Christi im späten Mittelalter," in *Deine Wunden: Passionsimaginationen in christlicher Bildtradition und Bildkonzepte in der Kunst der Moderne,* eds. Reinhard Hoeps, Richard Hoppe-Seiler, and Thomas Lentes (Bielefeld: Kerber, 2014), 43.

the increasingly gruesome legal spectacle of torture and public execution.[8]

What then are the specific reasons why this one photograph, rather than any of the many others that surfaced at the same time, became the "icon" for Abu Ghraib? Why, otherwise put, did its "iconographic resonance" go "beyond this immediate event to touch on the contemporary world system" during the era of the War on Terror? The answer to these questions can be found in the fact that the image of the Abu Ghraib Man is, as Mitchell elaborates,

> a "world picture" in three senses of that phrase: 1) as a globally circulated and instantly recognizable icon, which requires only minimal cues, visual or verbal, to be called to mind; 2) [as] a symbol of a planetary conflict (the Global War on Terror) that is not confined to the present moment of the early twenty-first century, but resonates deeply within a long history of figures of power and abjection in the repertoire of Christian iconography and beyond; and 3) as a symptom of a new world order of image-production and circulation made possible by bio-digital technologies, the era of "cloning." The fact that the image goes beyond the specific echoes of the Passion of Christ to evoke medieval and Renaissance images of the human body (and Christ's body in particular) as an *imago mundi* or microcosm of the world helps to reinforce the uncanny sense that this image was already, in some sense, quite familiar as an icon, even at the first moment of its appearance in April 2004.[9]

---

8   McCoy, *A Question of Torture*, 16. McCoy quotes Mitchell B. Merback's book *The Thief, the Cross, and the Wheel: Pain and the Spectacle of Punishment in Medieval and Renaissance Europe* (Chicago: University of Chicago Press, 1999).

9   Mitchell, *Cloning Terror*, 142–43. (Date changed from April 2003 to April 2004, the date when the photographs were aired on CBS's *60 Minutes*).

Mitchell relies for his analysis on Meyer Schapiro's 1960 essay "Words and Pictures," which explores the relations between Jewish and Christian icons, and, specifically, the "genealogy that links the figure of a victorious Moses to a crucified Christ." Schapiro's "formal distinction between frontal and profile renderings of the human figure" is here of particular relevance, given their "association with the implied 'address' of the image as an 'I' facing the spectator as a 'you.'" The formal difference between frontal and profile views corresponds in Schapiro's analysis to the distinction between "themes of state" and "themes of action": the former are found in images that confront the viewer "directly with a static, frontally posed figure," while the latter characterize images depicting a "self-contained action seen beyond the picture plane."[10] Owing its iconic potential at least partly to the "static, frontally posed figure," the photograph of the hooded man from Abu Ghraib resonates so powerfully with a Western viewer because the image "remembers," "recuperates," and "transforms" representations of Christ "with his arms raised, either at the Crucifixion or the resurrection, or in scenes of prayer and blessing." And those representations, Mitchell continues, already remembered and recuperated the "figure of Moses raising his arms at the battle of the Israelites with the Amalekites," absorbing it retrospectively into Christian iconography as a "prefiguration" of Christ crucified, which in turn became the "prototype for gestures of both sacred and secular sovereignty throughout Christendom, including the gesture of the priest celebrating mass, or the monarch addressing his subjects."[11]

Three main features, then, turned the figure of the Hooded Man into the "universally recognizable icon" of the Abu Ghraib scandal. First, the image "recuperates" and "transforms" the crucified Christ, whose image already "remembered" Moses. Second, this frontally posed figure "faces the viewer directly,

---

10 Ibid., 144. Mitchell continues: "a contrast strangely reminiscent of Michael Fried's distinction between images of theatricality and absorption."

11 Ibid., 144–47. See also Klaus Mladek, "Folter und Scham," in *Wahrheit und Gewalt. Der Diskurs der Folter in Europa und den USA*, ed. Thomas Weitin (Bielefeld: Transcript, 2010), 262.

hailing the viewer as the 'you' who is addressed by an 'I.'" And third, the "theme of state" is reinforced by the man's positioning on a pedestal, which precludes any action or movement: "absolute stillness was required to maintain this position."[12]

If later versions of an image "remember" earlier versions, the same applies to the actual torture practice employed. Indeed, experts like McCoy, who has studied the torture practices of the CIA and US military for more than two decades, "believe that the procedure suffered by the 'hooded man' is a standard torture method the CIA has been using for years."[13] Moreover, Darius Rejali has shown that this particular form of positional torture, forced standing, is an old technique used by many countries (including the US, several European countries, Israel, and a number of Middle Eastern countries) and in many varieties. The Nazis, for example, used a variety called the "standing cell" (*Stehzelle*). By 1970, the Brazilian variety in which the victim was forced to stand on tiptoes while holding four telephone books in each outstretched hand was referred to as "Christ the Redeemer." The version that includes electric wires attached to the prisoners was called "The Vietnam."[14]

One of the facets of the shock of recognition, then, is that Abu Ghraib "remembers" globally applied torture methods, including torture perpetrated by the Nazis, which is evinced not only through the one image referred to here. At the Belgian Fortress Prison in Breendonk, the Gestapo routinely practiced hooding and suspending prisoners from a hook-and-pulley system while their hands were tied in the back.[15] The writer Jean Améry, who was subjected to torture at Breendonk, reflected on his experience in a seminal philosophical essay that still proves extremely

---

12 Ibid., 145–47.

13 Ralf Hoppe and Marian Blasberg, "Photos from Abu Ghraib: The Hooded Men," *Der Spiegel*, March 22, 2006. Hoppe and Blasberg continue: "Jamie Fellner, Director of Human Rights Watch, also believes that other prisoners were tortured in the same manner."

14 Darius Rejali, *Torture and Democracy* (Princeton: Princeton University Press, 2007), 313, 320, 333.

15 Ibid., 101, 333.

productive today, because it lays out with unflinching clarity the devastation inflicted by torture.

The first chapter of this book therefore offers an approach to the question of torture through close attention to the textual fabric of Améry's essay, especially in the original German. Torture, Améry asserts categorically, was "the essence of National-Socialism." Linguistic creations by the Bush administration such as "ghost detainee" and "ghosting," while intended to refer to the victims' invisibility from public witnessing or scrutiny, contain an unintended but revealing proposition about torture that is central to Améry's reflection: torture subjects the victim to an experience of death while still alive. Part alive, part dead, neither dead, nor alive, the torture victim occupies a zone in-between in which torture never ends. My reading of Améry's text explores how it traces the connection not between torture and destruction, but between torture and a heightened form of destruction: annihilation. Améry's remapping of the semantic field of the German word *Verfleischlichung* bespeaks the "fleshization" of the experience of torture and how the torturer's perversion of language confirms and underscores the apocalyptic totality of annihilation. This is one reason why in the early modern period in Northern German cities, anybody who had undergone torture lost his or her right to residency forever, even if he/she was able to prove his/her innocence.[16] The mere suspicion of being guilty of an infamy so great that it warranted torture in the eyes of the juridical system was sufficient for an expulsion from civil society. Torture threatens to radically destroy the social fabric and thus confronts us with the most urgent question of what it means to live together, especially with the enemy. Recognizing a long iconographic heritage in the hooded man of Abu Ghraib also calls for the recognition of the subterranean levels on which this violence operates in order to make its long history addressable.

---

16 Werner Riess, "Die historische Entwicklung der römischen Folter- und Hinrichtungspraxis in kulturvergleichender Perspektive," *Historia: Zeitschrift für Alte Geschichte* 51, no. 2 (2002): 215n50.

The question of "living together" in an age of torture, and thus "with" torture, is central to Chapter Two. Taking as its point of departure the recognition of a shared vulnerability of the flesh through Rejali's reading of a scene uniting a Jewish guerrilla fighter, tortured by the British CID in Palestine and an old Arab man bringing him food, the chapter offers a close reading of Jacques Derrida's essay "Avowing — The Impossible," a text the philosopher describes as a "lesson" on "living together." Placing particular emphasis on the language of the heart, Derrida explores a "fundamental mode" of living together: compassion.[17] It is now well documented that some of the torture methods used by American interrogators in Guantánamo, Iraq, and Afghanistan aimed precisely at the destruction of compassion for the torture victim, including in the presumed enemy's own community. The relentless use of euphemisms such as "enhanced interrogation," the application of "no-touch" or "stealth" torture methods, combined with the persistent use of the singular "the enemy" in the government's statements about detainees in Guantánamo and other American-run prisons overseas, hollow out the potential for what Frans de Waal calls "the synchronization of bodies," where empathy and sympathy start, not to form a whole, a totality, but to bridge (not overcome) irreducible differences.[18] Compassion as a visceral response, attested in its Hebrew name, *rachamim,* the plural of *rechem,* "the womb," and in its Arabic relative *rahma,* is also systematically undermined in the dichotomies that Derrida scrutinized and deconstructed throughout his career, including the dichotomy between "human" and "animal," and, as the public debate on torture has evidenced all too clearly, the related dichotomy between "friend" and "enemy." However, even if the "enemy" is locked away in faraway offshore detention camps such as Guantánamo and in

---

17 Jacques Derrida, "Avowing — The Impossible: 'Returns,' Repentance, and Reconciliation," trans. Gil Anidjar, in *Living Together: Jacques Derrida's Communities of Violence and Peace,* ed. Elisabeth Weber (New York: Fordham University Press, 2013), 30.

18 Frans de Waal, *The Age of Empathy* (New York: Three Rivers Press, 2009), 48.

overseas prisons such as Abu Ghraib and Bagram in order to deny him a hearing in American courts, one must still live together and, as Derrida underscores, "one must do so well, one must well do so [*et il le faut bien*]," "one has no choice."[19] For Derrida, it is not only a responsibility but a necessity to think the "war over the matter of pity" that "we find ourselves waging."

Almost sixty years prior to Cesare Beccaria's famous indictment of torture, Christian Thomasius's *On the Torture That Needs to be Banned from Christian Courts,* published in 1705, castigated the practice of torture as a "godless perversity" exacerbated by the fact that it forces victims to abdicate any pity with themselves. For Thomasius, such "self-betrayal" is *constitutive* of torture, and its injustice cannot be surpassed by any other punishment. Thomasius insists that the Bible "abhors" torture, and he expresses unending perplexity at the fact that crucifixion is, alongside other "pagan things," defended "doggedly" as "the holiest."[20] The shock of recognition between the hooded Muslim of Abu Ghraib and the central symbol of Christianity receives here another deeply disturbing trait: the abuse at Abu Ghraib was done by agents of not only the most powerful Western country in the world, but also of a country that, with all its guarantees of religious freedom and its assertion of the separation of church and state, remains deeply anchored in the Christian faith. In a believer's perspective, the central symbol of Christianity declares Jesus's radical and revolutionary solidarity with the least of the least and declares those expelled from the human community as not only human, but also as belonging to God's kingdom. Addressing the forgotten or repressed memory of this symbol ought to elicit this shock of recognition.

Like Mitchell, Stephen Eisenman has shown that the photographs of torture at Abu Ghraib prison need to be inscribed into the long tradition of Western art indebted to the "Pathos formu-

---

19 Derrida, "Avowing — The Impossible," 23.

20 Christian Thomasius, *Über die Folter: Untersuchungen zur Geschichte der Folter,* ed. and trans. Rolf Lieberwirth (Weimar: Hermann Böhlaus Nachfolger, 1960), 176–77.

la" that has allowed "images of torture, power and domination" to be "passed down from one generation to the next" in such a way that they "come to be widely embedded in both visual memory and the physical body." This is what makes these photos "at once disturbing and familiar in their form and content, demanding yet somehow denying interpretation," conjuring "a perceptual and imaginative realm that Sigmund Freud called *unheimlich,* or uncanny."[21] In short, for Eisenman the Abu Ghraib photos "can be seen as the product, in the words of Warburg, of a 'heritage stored in the memory.'"[22] Warburg's formulation, together with Walter Benjamin's "optical unconscious," alluded to by Mitchell, allows us to see the photos in much needed relief, especially in the context of the massive attempt by government officials to downplay the "Abu Ghraib archive" by invoking the "bad apples" hypothesis.[23]

Chapter Three turns to another aspect of that heritage stored in memory, or, in this case, rather embellishingly disfigured, idealized in memory to circumvent shocks of recognition. I propose a close reading of Shoshana Felman's concept of "literary justice" and examine her assertion that the "promised exercise of legal justice" is a "pattern inherited from the great catastrophes and the collective traumas of the twentieth century."[24] Not only

---

21 Stephen Eisenman, *The Abu Ghraib Effect* (London: Reaktion, 2007), 15.

22 Ibid., 17. For the hooded man of Abu Ghraib, Eisenman invokes a similarity with a drawing by Francisco Goya of a victim of the Inquisition. The hood thus recalls the *carochas* "worn by victims of the Spanish *auto-da-fé* and typically decorated with flames and devils," in addition to "'dunces' caps once used to punish schoolchildren, the hoods worn by members of the Ku Klux Klan and subsequent American racist organizations, and the hoods worn both by executioners and their victims" (13). But Eisenman also underlines that already a brief reflection on the two images reveals the similarity between them as "only superficial." He recalls that not the similarity, but the "fundamental distinctions between modern artworks and the torture images" were often the "reason for making the comparison." By contrast, Eisenman's goal is to show the photos' indebtedness to classical paintings and sculptures (14, 15, and passim).

23 Mitchell, *Cloning Terror,* 117, 140.

24 Shoshana Felman, *The Juridical Unconscious: Trials and Traumas in the Twentieth Century* (Cambridge: Harvard University Press, 2002), 3.

has the War on Terror betrayed this promise time and again, but over the twentieth and twenty-first centuries, "Western civilization" has been directly responsible or massively complicit in many of those catastrophes. Analyzing Felman's distinction between "legal" and "literary" justice, I put it to the test in the context of the utter denial of justice to hundreds of men imprisoned without due process in Guantánamo Bay, and the massive censorship of poems written by some of the prisoners. The fact that, as the Pentagon asserts, poetry "presents a special risk" to national security because of its "content and format" ought to be of great interest to anybody invested in the role of the humanities in our day and age. Like their "legally unnameable and unclassifiable" authors, most of the poems are considered too dangerous for release. The silencing of legal justice here goes hand in hand with the silencing of literary justice. Censorship by the US authorities targeted poems in Arabic and Pashto but also, in at least one case, a well-known counting verse in English. Such censoring zeal reveals that the singularity of the verbal body is invincible not only in foreign languages and their translation, but also in the most familiar of idioms. The medium *nursery rhyme* captures *in nuce* the mediation of community and of language necessary for the organization of the infant's fragmented body into a fictive integrity. The assessment of this medium as intolerable security risk is highly significant, insofar as it indicates that torture is intimately bound up with the elimination of the victims' language, and, just as intimately, with the attack on their "be-longing" to a community. The shock of recognition in the case of these poems lies in the realization that the address of language (and language is, at heart, *address*) is inherently subversive. Once language is suspected to be dangerous "code" in one of its forms, for example in poetry, its danger, in principle, cannot be reined in. Rather all of language, *in principle*, becomes tainted with suspicion.

The subversiveness of language is, however, also its vulnerability. Chapter Four returns to Guantánamo poems, first in a close reading of Paul Muldoon's poem "Hedge School," through which I show how Guantánamo leaves its mark on language, and how it has changed language. This is so not only because the policies responsible for and resulting from the prison camp have given rise to hundreds of euphemisms of which Fred Halliday's book *Shocked and Awed: A Dictionary of the War on Terror* offers a painstaking account.[25] More insidiously, as Muldoon's poem suggests, Guantánamo may "force" students to conjugate differently verbs such as the Latin *amare,* to love. Guantánamo leaves its mark on the thesaurus of language, but, more perniciously, it may affect the grammar, the structural rules that govern the use of language. Turning to the poems written within the prison camp, the chapter examines the frequency of the motif of compassion the prisoners employ. Far from exhausting itself in convention, the invocation of the Qur'anic call to compassion in the Guantánamo poems may provide a way to make suffering sharable without drowning in shame. In spite of its very modest volume (only twenty-two from among possibly hundreds), the corpus of poems cleared by the American authorities for publication, after scrutiny and translation by "linguists with security clearance" rather than literary translators, gives an indication of what the censoring agencies might fear more than "code," namely the shock of recognition that might occur here through the invocation of compassion, and in the realization of a shared vulnerability of the flesh.

Chapter Five approaches the iconographic memory stored in the photograph of the hooded man from Abu Ghraib from yet another angle. As mentioned above, despite the temporal and political specificity of the photograph, it reactivates images widely and deeply "embedded in both visual memory and the physical body" through a number of crucial characteristics the man shares with other images well-known enough to have an iconic status in the Western tradition.[26] Mitchell recalls that for Schapiro the "theme of state" was "not merely a formal matter of figural 'stasis' and frontality in the address of the image," but

---

25 Fred Halliday, *Shocked and Awed: A Dictionary of the War on Terror* (Berkeley: University of California Press, 2011).

26 Eisenman, *The Abu Ghraib Effect,* 15.

a "key resource for the iconic representation of religious and political sovereignty."[27] The figural "stasis" of the image thus activates the memory, conscious or unconscious, of the Crucified on the one hand, and of the Sovereign on the other. A reflection on the shock of recognition between the hooded Muslim of Abu Ghraib and Christ as victim of the most abject torture thus needs to be paired with a reflection on the other side of this memory, the figure of sovereignty. This chapter, then, addresses Jacques Derrida's deconstructive treatment of sovereignty as the "keystone," "cement," or "weld" of the "onto-theological-political," which he links directly to "cruelty."[28] For Derrida, the concept of sovereignty is inseparable from the two "ages" of cruelty of today's wars: one techno-scientific, from which the *cruor* of blood seems to have been wiped away, including the supposedly "surgical" war conducted with drones, and another, bloodily "archaic," reacting savagely to the first, but as dependent as the former on electronic mediality. Derrida and the French-Tunisian psychoanalyst Fethi Benslama examine the two "ages" of cruelty as closely intertwined, with today's media playing a crucial role for both, as far apart as they may seem in terms of technological sophistication.

For Derrida, the "revolution of psychoanalysis" would consist in addressing cruelty without alibi, without political, moral, theological, or other justifications, while refusing to neutralize ethics and politics, that is, the specific geo-political realm in which psychoanalytic theory and practice intervene. In this spirit, Benslama attempts an analysis and a psychoanalysis of the particular new cruelty with which Middle Eastern and, by extension, Western countries are confronted today. Derrida's explanation of the disturbingly intimate interconnectedness of the two "ages" allows to understand what drives the auto-immune and mediatic production, as well as the endless mediatic reproduction of today's cruelties.

---

27 Mitchell, *Cloning Terror*, 145.
28 Jacques Derrida and Elisabeth Roudinesco, *For What Tomorrow…: A Dialogue*, trans. Jeff Fort (Stanford: Stanford University Press, 2004), 148.

The prolific reproduction of the photograph of the hooded man whose "original" was produced in an endlessly reproducible medium, turning any distinction between "original" and "reproduction" into absurdity, is here again paradigmatic. As Derrida points out in the context of his reflection on the attacks of September 11, 2001, for the perpetrators and those who declared the "War on Terror" alike, the endless "media coverage was, like the good sense of which Descartes speaks, the most widely shared thing in the world."[29] The potential of "cloning" to "accelerate the reproduction of images and to endow them with an almost virus-like vitality" exemplifies the delocalization and expropriation of tele-technoscience and its media.[30] Chapter Five thematizes this delocalization and expropriation and the corresponding attempts at reappropriation especially with regard to the drone war.

Given the hooded man's haunting significance for all the chapters of this book, I pause here for a short digression to address another crucial potential media of endless reproducibility hold: their promise of subversiveness. The abovementioned mural by Sallah Edine Sallat which quotes and reframes the hooded man is a prominent example for Mitchell's observation that from the moment it became public, the infamous photograph took on a "life of its own":

> if ever an image has been cloned in the circuits of the mass media, this one was, both in the sense of indefinite duplication and in the further sense of taking on a "life of its own" that eludes and even reverses the intentions of its producers. [...] As famous as advertizing logos and brand icons like the Nike Swoosh or the Golden Arches, the image rapidly mutated into a global icon. [...] The Man with the Hood appeared throughout the world, on television, over the Internet, in

29 Jacques Derrida, "Autoimmunity: Real and Symbolic Suicides," in Giovanna Borradori, *Philosophy in a Time of Terror: Dialogues with Jürgen Habermas and Jacques Derrida* (Chicago: University of Chicago Press 2003), 108.

30 W.J.T. Mitchell, "Sacred Gestures: Images from Our Holy War," *Afterimage* 34, no. 3 (Nov–Dec 2006): 18-23.

protest posters, and in murals, graffiti, and works of art from Baghdad to Berkeley. Guerilla artists around the world found ways to reframe, mutate, and multiply the figure in an astonishing variety of ways.[31]

A second example of the photograph's treatment, this time in an endlessly reproducible medium, gives it indeed a "life of its own" by enormously amplifying its potential of address. The viewer is at first addressed almost surreptitiously, but the address proves all the more persevering for its initial stealth. In 2004, the anonymous artist collective Forkscrew Graphics undertook a particularly ingenious reframing and cloning of the image of the hooded man from Abu Ghraib prison. Under the title "iRaq," the artists plastered a series of guerrilla posters on billboards, highway walls, and other highly visible public places in Los Angeles, San Francisco, New York, and some European cities.[32] One of the posters featured the hooded man; three others showed armed combatants (figs. 2 and 3).

The "iRaq" posters were offered as free downloads to all visitors of Forkscrew's website. It was possible to print and circulate them materially, but, "designed to blend into Apple Computer's own viral postering efforts," they were also available as iPDFs.[33] Each time a user downloaded one of the posters, the casualty statistics included at the bottom were automatically updated through a link to www.iraqbodycount.org and www.icasualty. org.[34] Mimicking the line of the iPod's ad, "10,000 songs in your pocket. Mac or PC," one version of the iRaq poster read "10,000

---

31 Mitchell, *Cloning Terror,* 104.

32 Selz, *Art of Engagement,* 71. See also Charles Garoian and Yvonne Gaudelius, *Spectacle Pedagogy* (Albany: State University of New York Press, 2008), 81–84.

33 Susanne Lummerding, "Signifying Theory_Politics/Queer?" in *Hegemony and Heteronormativity: Revisiting "The Political" in Queer Politics,* eds. M. do Mar Castro Varela, N. Dhawan, and A. Engel (Farnham: Ashgate, 2012), 160. iPDFs allow for an "interactive combination of PDF documents and the Internet" (Lummerding, "Signifying Theory", 160n17).

34 While as of January 2017, "iraqbodycount" is still in existence, Forkscrew's website and "icasualty.org" no longer exist.

Fig. 2: Forkscrew Graphics, "iRaq," Silkscreen, 2004, interposed between iPod advertisements.

Fig. 3: Forkscrew Graphics, "iRaq," Silkscreen, 2004.

Iraqis killed. 773 US soldiers dead."[35] The version of the graphic with the hooded man read "10,000 volts in your pocket, guilty or innocent."

A number of scholars has analyzed the visual strategies employed by Forkscrew's "iRaq" posters and unpacked the interplay between Apple's advertisements and Forkscrew's work. Mitchell noted that it was the very ubiquity and recognizability of the hooded man that allowed the image to "insinuate itself subtly into commercial advertisements for the iPod [...] where it merged almost subliminally with the figures of 'wired' dancers wearing iPod headphones and the 'iRaqi' with his wired genitals."[36] Abigail Solomon-Godeau explained how in public space,

> the iRaq images seamlessly blend into the urban landscape and, if not really looked at, can pass undetected. But when they are noticed, it is in the split second between the viewer's automatic — i.e. distracted — perception of the poster as poster, and the shocked recognition of the identity of the silhouetted figures, that the possibility of reflection rather than visual consumption is enabled.[37]

---

35 The website *Blood for Oil* claims to still allow for free downloads of the posters, but at the time of this writing, the download was refused: http://archive.thr5.com/bloodforoil.org/iRaq-posters/. The casualty statistics on this website are no longer updated, even though the date shown is always the date of access. For example, between February 2014, and August 2016, the casualty count has not been changed: "Over 77,566 Iraqis killed. And over 4,025 US soldiers dead as of 19 Feb 2014." According to Iraq Body Count, as of January 2017, the number of civilians killed since the US invasion in March 2003 is between 170,171 and 189,627, with an estimated total of 268,000 violent deaths, including combatants. The number of civilian deaths in Iraq in December 2016 alone is at least 1,145, with an estimated total of more than 16,000 for the year 2016.

36 Mitchell, *Cloning Terror,* 105.

37 Abigail Solomon-Godeau, "Torture and Representation: The Art of Détournement," in *Speaking about Torture,* eds. Julie Carlson and Elisabeth Weber (New York: Fordham University Press, 2012), 127.

Solomon-Godeau distinguishes between two kinds of shock mobilized by the iRaq posters, both of which are crucial for the poster's effectiveness:

> First, there is the shock of recognition: the instant when one recognizes the hooded detainee from Abu Ghraib or any of the posters' other icons of resistance as the sources for the silhouettes. Then there is the shock of dissonance — the desirable commodity transformed into confrontational emblems of warfare or torture. In this respect, the use of the iPod — a technology not only of solitary entertainment and distraction, but also a globalized commodity that "everyone" recognizes — is significant. Sequestering the user in his or her hermetic aural world, the iPod is thus likened to the indifference or disregard that has, among other things, prevented any serious consequences for those in the Bush administration who sanctioned and indeed prescribed the use of torture.[38]

Lisa Nakamura contrasts the anonymity of the figure in the Forkscrew image with the way anonymity works in the Apple advertisement:

> the facelessness of the masked figure in [this] image with the electrocution wires replaced by white iPod earbud wires underscores the evacuation of personal identity that is necessary to the act of torture. [...] These shocking images critique consumer culture and the military industrial complex with which consumer culture is imbricated; not just anyone can occupy that desired space of musical free volition, expression and consumption.[39]

This "desired space of musical free volition, expression and consumption" is revealed by Forkscrew's work as one of consciously

---

38 Ibid., 127f.
39 Lisa Nakamura, *Digitizing Race: Visual Cultures of the Internet* (Minneapolis: University of Minnesota Press, 2007), 115.

or unconsciously embraced obliviousness to the pervasive practice of torture perpetuated by American officials at the time, and the subsequent culture of almost total impunity, that is still ongoing, in spite of the December 2014 publication of a 525-page portion of the "Committee Study of the Central Intelligence Agency's Detention and Interrogation Program," also known as the "Senate Torture Report."[40]

The effectiveness of Forkscrew's series and the "shock of dissonance" it administers depend on the iPod's status as globally recognized commodity. The posters took advantage of the Warholian seriality of the original advertisement, designed for the swiping of iPod and iPad screens.[41] In a similar vein, Mitchell suggests that

> perhaps the best way to understand the iPod/iRaq culture jamming is to analyze the relation between the self-pleasuring dancers, narcissistically absorbed in a music only they can hear, and the self-torturing stasis of the Hooded Man, absorbed in a pain and terror only he can feel, accompanied by the menacing anticipation of electrocution to come if he

40 The report, written by the bipartisan United States Senate Select Committee on Intelligence (SSCI), counts 6,700 pages, most of which remain classified. After the SSCI worked for five years to compile the report, its publications was blocked numerous times. The unclassified portion is accessible online: http://www.intelligence.senate.gov/publications/committee-study-central-intelligence-agencys-detention-and-interrogation-program. Already in 2012, Alfred McCoy's book *Torture and Impunity: The U.S. Doctrine of Coercive Interrogation* (Madison: University of Wisconsin Press, 2012) traced the history of public acceptability of torture within the United States, in particular the bipartisan policy of "impunity at home and rendition abroad." McCoy stresses that impunity and forgetfulness in the US does not mean that the world has forgotten or will forget.

41 As Daniel Weidner has observed, swiping is in principle interminable, but is "irritated" in this one moment when the consumer realizes that something doesn't fit. Moreover, given that the "minimalist, but extremely eroticized icons of the Apple advertisement" surround Forkscrew's insertion, the latter heightens the ambivalence between moral compassion and voyeuristic pleasure that always accompanies the viewing of images of torture (Daniel Weidner, oral communication, May 2014).

steps off his box. The intervention of the Bagman icon into the iPod iconography is [...] a provocative to thought on a host of issues — the relation of art and politics, of pleasure and pain, motion and stasis, wired bodies, technologies of the sensorium, torture and sexuality.[42]

The "shock of dissonance" also depends on the fact that the hooded man from Abu Ghraib is no less globally recognized than the iPod. According to Mitchell, Forkscrew's version of the image amplifies its iconicity, because the

> stasis of the image is further reinforced by its symmetry and contrastive color scheme. It makes a simple and singular impression as a black, diamond-shaped form against a light background, a form that can be instantly recognized from a distance, and copied in a schematic silhouette without any need for further details. The hood covering the face renders the figure even more abstract and anonymous. It could be any Iraqi, or, for that matter, any suspected terrorist captured by the U.S. military.[43]

---

42 Mitchell, *Cloning Terror,* 106–7.

43 Ibid., 145–47. Mitchell continues: "The true identity of the Man on the Box was the subject of debate for several years after the first revelation of the Abu Ghraib photographs. He was first identified as Satar Jabar, a carjacking suspect, by a story in *Newsweek,* July 19, 2004. In the winter of 2006, however, several sources, including the *New York Times,* claimed that he was a former Baath Party official named Ali Shalal Qaissi." (ibid., 147–48.) See Julie Scelfo, "Beneath the Hoods", *Newsweek,* July 18, 2004. Qaissi's assertions were put in doubt by the *New York Times* shortly after they had been reported. Mark Benjamin and Michael Scherer write that the man in question was probably named Saad (Mark Benjamin, Michael Scherer, "Electrical Wires," "The Abu Ghraib Files," Chapter 4, *Salon,* March 14, 2006). "Errol Morris has claimed a definitive identity for the man as an innocent bystander swept up in one of the nightly raids of the U.S. Marines, but we would still have to admit that, if the 'Jesus position' was standard operating procedure, there could have been other individuals who played this role at Abu Ghraib and elsewhere" (Mitchell, *Cloning Terror,* 148). Indeed, the US military's official "Taguba Report," written by Major General Antonio Taguba, "cites the sworn testimony of Specialist Sabrina Harman of the 372nd Military Police Company. Harman reports on at least one prisoner whose fingers,

While the question of the hooded man's identity may be contested, the iconic character of the image is seared into people's minds around the globe:

> Like the image of Jesus "proper," it has a life of its own that acquires new dimensions of meaning in every new context that it encounters. Among the many images that emerged from the Abu Ghraib scandal, it stands out as the only one that conforms to Schapiro's concept of the "theme of state."[44]

Anticipating objections to his assertion that the image resembles Christ on the cross, Mitchell cites differences such as Christ's upward- rather than downward-stretched arms, Christ's almost complete nakedness, and the visibility of his face. But these differences don't invalidate Mitchell's thesis of an "iconographic resonance." For Mitchell, another distinction made by Schapiro comes here into play: the "devotional" versus the "narrative" interpretations of sacred images. While a narrative reading would

---

toes and penis were attached to wires. But the widely distributed image of the 'hooded man' only depicts wires attached to the fingers, suggesting that there were other, similar cases. Indeed, US investigators have reported that a number of prisoners have claimed to be the hooded man hooked up to electric wires, men like former prisoner Satar Jabar – yet another indication that several prisoners were tortured in the manner shown in the photos" (Hoppe and Blasberg, "Photos from Abu Ghraib").

44 Mitchell continues: "Although the hood renders him anonymous, he appears as a singular figure elevated on a pedestal, an image of dignity and poise that becomes even more remarkable when one reflects on what we know about the event being captured by this photograph. The most elementary way of doing this is to project yourself into the situation depicted. Imagine yourself balancing precariously atop a cardboard C-ration box, with electrical wires attached to your fingers and genitals, stifled and blinded by a hood. You have been told by your torturers that if you fall off the box, you will be electrocuted. In the context of uncounted days of sleep deprivation, beatings, and cries of pain from your fellow prisoners, it would be something of a miracle to remain balanced on top of this box for even a minute. And yet you do this long enough to be photographed, and thus are transformed into an image that will maintain this pose, this composure, as long as the image continues to exist" (*Cloning Terror,* 149–50).

recapitulate the identity of the man and specify time, location and circumstances, a devotional reading, by contrast,

> is contemplative and empathic, slowing down the time of the image to a kind of stasis that mirrors the bodily state of the figure in the mental state of the beholder. It puts the viewer in the position of the figure, a process that is encouraged by the frontality of the theme of state, in its (paradoxically blind) "face to face" encounter with the beholder.[45]

Moreover, a devotional reading allows the image to directly address the beholder. Such a reading will allow for the question "what it means to live with the image and the world it depicts," and, insisting even more, what the image "wants from us":

> Perhaps the most obvious thing the picture demands from the devoted viewer — particularly a U.S. citizen — is an acknowledgment of responsibility. To put it in the crudest terms, this photograph and what it reveals was paid for by our tax dollars. We "own" it, and must "own up" to what it tells us about ourselves [...]. Even if we opposed the Bush regime and its war in Iraq, as so many did, we are still responsible for this image.[46]

As a society we are still responsible for this image. A "devotional" reading of this image is still waiting to happen on a publicly relevant scale. What was revealed in Abu Ghraib, what continues to happen in Guantánamo Bay, and what happens in places such as Waziristan and Oruzgan, whose names are hardly known by American citizens, is massively paid for by American tax dollars. "We 'own' it, and must 'own up' to what it tells us about ourselves" — we need to own up to such shocks of recognition too. Ulla Haselstein has characterized allegory as a figure that can serve to strategically integrate the culturally "prohibited"

---

45 Ibid., 150–52.
46 Ibid., 152.

or the "politically precarious."[47] In this sense, the photograph of the hooded man can be read as an allegory of the American torture paradigm. The culturally "prohibited" is to be found in the resonance between a Muslim torture victim and/or terrorist suspect with Christ, bringing to mind Talal Asad's analysis of Jesus's crucifixion as an indirect suicide, which in turn brings the "sacrifice" necessary for redemption into resonance with suicide bombing.[48] The "politically precarious" might be found in the fact that the hooded man

> positions the American spectator as caught between two incompatible positions: in a state of empathy with the tortured victim or as accomplice of the leering torturers. The shaming, which was the avowed motive of photographing these scenes in the first place, comes back redoubled to haunt the photographer, the spectator, and the state of the union and the world that he represents. No wonder that George W. Bush, although both shameless and incapable of admitting any guilt, remarked that "nobody wants to see images like this."[49]

In stark contrast to Bush's refusal or willful blindness, an eye-opening and transformational reading of the image and of its tortured body would lead to the realization that it might be a "hermeneutical figure" in the sense explained by Thomas Lentes, who recalls that in the Christian tradition, the "hermeneutical" function of *Ecce Homo* images of the crucified Christ was even more significant than the devotional. If in the Christian tradition of the Middle Ages, only an accurate reading of the body of Christ made it possible to feel compassion, which, in turn, was considered the *conditio sine qua non* for a correct reading of scripture, then nothing less than the correct reading of the

---

47 Ulla Haselstein, "Vorbemerkungen der Herausgeberin," in Ulla Haselstein, *Allegorie: DFB-Symposion 2014* (Berlin: De Gruyter, 2016), xii.

48 Talal Asad, *On Suicide Bombing* (New York: Columbia University Press, 2007).

49 Mitchell, *Cloning Terror,* 159.

Gospel was at stake in the contemplation of the *Ecce Homo* figure.[50] In the photograph of the hooded man, the "scripture" to be read would be what McCoy has called the "the CIA's massive mind-control project," and the multi-layered heritage stored and condensed in it.[51]

Lentes shows how in images of the crucified Christ from the late Middle Ages, the frontality of the Christ figure not only emphasizes the appeal to compassion, but also "pulls the beholder into the position of being an accomplice to and accused of Christ's passion."[52] Arguably, this can also be said of the hooded man.

Testimony quoted by Mitchell from Specialist Sabrina Harman, one of the more prolific photographers at Abu Ghraib prison, compounds this complicity by the production of images through torture. Harman testified that she was "prompted to begin taking pictures" when she saw the prisoner nicknamed "'the taxicab driver' handcuffed backwards to his window naked with his underwear over his head and face. He looked like Jesus Christ. At first I had to laugh so I went and grabbed the camera and took a picture."[53] A number of photos taken at the infamous prison were clearly staged. The unsettling consequence is that the hooded man may have, consciously or unconsciously, been *staged* as *Ecce Homo*, and, at the same time, as an allusion to the Ku Klux Klan. Those who produced these images arranged a picturesque torture, a "becoming-art" of torture by those who inflicted it.[54] Forkscrew's rendering of the hooded man of Abu Ghraib mobilizes this heritage, conscious and unconscious.

---

50 See Thomas Lentes, "Der hermeneutische Schnitt: Die Beschneidung im Christentum," in *Haut ab! Haltungen zur rituellen Beschneidung,* ed. Felicitas Heimann-Jelinek (Göttingen: Wallstein, 2014), 109.

51 McCoy, *A Question of Torture,* 12, see also 51.

52 Thomas Lentes, "Der Blick auf den Durchbohrten," 458–59.

53 Mitchell, *Cloning Terror,* 114, see also 141.

54 For the German art historian Michael Zimmermann, the same applies to Christ's crucifixion when the inscription is taken into account. It too already worked as production of an image through torture. In an oral communication, referring to Otto Karl Werckmeister's book on "political image strategies since September 11, 2001," Zimmermann also recalled that in the

In addition to the hooded man's iconographic resonance with images of Christ, two more layers of "recognition" reveal the intense political precariousness of the photograph and of Forkscrew's image. First, the public outrage over the Abu Ghraib images focused mainly on their pornographic aspects and the supposed "collapse of discipline" in military ranks producing a "few bad apples" (as then-US Secretary of Defense Donald Rumsfeld put it) or "creeps" (according to *New York Times* political columnist William Safire). Yet, as alluded to above, some scholars, in particular McCoy, recognized immediately the hallmark of the CIA:

> If we look closely at those grainy images, we can see the genealogy of CIA torture techniques, from their origins in 1950 to their present-day perfection. Indeed, the photographs from Iraq illustrate standard interrogation practice inside the global gulag of secret CIA prisons that have operated, on executive authority, since the start of the war on terror. These photos, and the later investigations they prompted, offer telltale signs that the CIA was both the lead agency at

---

very moment in which image-producing techniques participate in war, for example, when surveillance cameras and "the all-seeing eye" (P.W. Singer, *Wired for War. The Robotics Revolution and Conflict in the 21st Century* [New York: Penguin, 2009], 308) of unmanned drones are integrated into the "technology of video-electronic warfare," war photography becomes "anachronistic" if not obsolete. Werckmeister shows in the cases of the wars in Iraq and Afghanistan that the "video-electronic capture of reality through war-technology" is part and parcel of the "operative image sphere" which is manipulated and often confined to secrecy by military and governmental power, in stark contrast to the "informative sphere" to which war photography belongs. As a consequence, the war photographer must resort to expedients such as close-ups, aesthetization and dramatization (Otto Karl Werckmeister, *Der Medusa-Effekt: Politische Bildstrategien seit dem 11. September 2001* [Berlin: Form + Zweck, 2005], 27–28). Among the resulting images, those infused with religious allusions are particularly efficient. According to Zimmermann, those "secondary effects" are responsible for the phenomenon of war images being aesthetisized, transformed into art and appearing in art galleries. At the same time, images produced in the "operative image sphere" are withheld from the public in whose name war is fought.

Abu Ghraib and the source of systematic tortures practiced in Guantánamo, Afghanistan, and Iraq.[55]

The following "telltale signs" are immediately recognizable for those who are versed in the CIA's repertoire of stealth torture methods: the hood achieved sensory deprivation and disorientation. The extended arms and forced standing in stillness ensured self-inflicted pain, while the threat of electrocution is a third method in the US array of psychological torture. Forced nudity, forced simulation of sexual acts and the use of dogs added massive humiliation and shame, exploiting cultural sensitivities. The CIA's methods have "evolved into a total assault on all senses and sensibilities — auditory, visual, tactile, temporal, temperature, survival, sexual, and cultural. Refined through years of practice, the method[s] rel[y] on simple, even banal procedures — isolation, standing, heat and cold, light and dark, noise and silence — for a systematic attack on all human senses." None of these "no-touch" or "stealth" torture methods leave perceptible scars, while their "synergy [...] is a hammer-blow to the fundamentals of personal identity." Adding impunity to a crime that should fall under universal jurisdiction, the absence of visible scars makes proof and prosecution of the psychological devastation caused by stealth torture excessively difficult.[56]

Second, the Abu Ghraib photograph's resemblance to christological representations, the "uncanny sense" of recognition, even familiarity, resonated differently in the Middle East. In Rejali's words, "what is necessary proof of modern stealthy violence [...] revives painful colonial memories and ancient humiliations." The cross, the most visible and most recognized religious symbol in the West, stood for the worst and cruelest of public executions in the Ancient World, a practice early Muslim rulers rejected.[57] While no actual crucifixion occurred at Abu

---

55 McCoy, *A Question of Torture*, 5–6.
56 Ibid., 8–9.
57 See Darius Rejali, "The Real Shame of Abu Ghraib", *Time*, May 20, 2004, discussed in Chapter 2.

Ghraib, many of the characteristics that made it particularly abhorred did, including the denial of a proper burial.

The photograph of the hooded man and, in its wake, Forkscrew's graphic are then quintessential treatments of the theme of state: *Ecce Homo*. The image of the hooded man, as forcibly blind as he may be, presents him as an "I," addressing us as "you": I am a man being tortured. And you are watching. The injustice denounced by the hooded man of Abu Ghraib is the injustice of a state, and the injustice as a state, in both senses of that word. Forkscrew's contraband reinforces and allegorizes this denunciation: making everything but the outer contours of the tortured body invisible, it relegates the tortured body to what in graphic design is called "negative space."[58] Thereby, the graphic starkly underlines torture's absence from public space and discourse in the US. A shift of awareness, however, will reveal this absence as overpowering presence.

In the aftermath of the closure of Abu Ghraib and of the disastrous legacy of Guantánamo, capture of suspected combatants has largely been replaced by extrajudicial assassination. The method through which the latter is carried out, a war primarily conducted with unmanned aerial vehicles, is, with a few exceptions, also glaringly absent from public debate in the United States, all the while its impacts in the affected areas, far away from the operational bases on American soil, are wide-ranging, inescapable, and deadly.[59] As Medea Benjamin observes, with

---

58 Lisa Nakamura described what she named the "iPod Ghraib" series as employing the "basic visual template of the iPod ads: solid [...] background colors, the iPod depicted in detail, and the negative space of the alpha channel replaced and filled in by soldiers and torture victims from the infamous Abu Ghraib photographs, as opposed to the iconic dancers in the iPod ads" (*Digitizing Race*, 115).

59 "The irony of President Obama's drone war has been widely noted: an administration that wanted to stop torturing detainees and close down the controversial prison at Guantánamo Bay has wound up with an aerial killing campaign instead. There have been hundreds of drone strikes, killing thousands of people, during Obama's presidency, but details about the drone campaigns, especially in areas outside Iraq and Afghanistan, have been difficult to obtain" (Jeremy Scahill and Glenn Greenwald, "Death by

"drones substituting more and more for boots on the ground, the conflicts become [...] more obscure. The paradox is that while the U.S. military is engaged in more and longer conflicts than ever in our history, fewer people are involved, touched, concerned, or engaged. The public is barely even aware of these conflicts."[60] Jeremy Scahill points out another paradox: "the more people the United States kills with drones and special forces, the longer its target list becomes."[61] Drone operations, in other words, do not quell the insurgency, but seem to feed into it, leading Hugh Gusterson to speak of the "insurgency as a perpetual-motion mechanism."[62]

Metadata," in *The Assassination Complex: Inside the Government's Secret Drone Warfare Program,* ed. Jeremy Scahill [New York: Simon and Schuster, 2016, Kindle Ed.], 1619). See also Lisa Hajjar's insightful analysis in "Drone Warfare and the Superpower's Dilemma," Part 1: "The disgraceful legacy of torture coupled with the multitude of cases to challenge aspects of post-9/11 detentions and the treatment of prisoners (many of which continued to be brought and litigated during the Obama administration in federal and foreign courts) had made capture a *political* liability. This liability was compounded by domestic politics; the Republican Party opposed President Obama's anti-torture reforms and advocated the resurrection of 'enhanced interrogation techniques' (the official euphemism for US torture), and there was substantial bipartisan opposition to the closing of Guantánamo. If terror suspects were to be captured, significant elements in Washington would want them sent to Guantánamo and interrogated violently. Consequently, while kill-or-capture both remained strategic options in principle, the Obama administration rarely authorized the capture of high-level suspects. In 2009, CIA director Leon Panetta made a statement that remains true today: in the fight against al-Qaeda, drones are 'the only game in town.' Under the Obama administration, drone warfare escalated dramatically in terms of the number of strikes per month and the widening geographic scope. By 2011, targeted killing operations were occurring at a rate of 1,000 a month" (*Jadalliyya,* Sept. 21, 2015).

60 Medea Benjamin, *Drone Warfare: Killing by Remote Control* (New York: OR, 2012, Kindle edition), ch. 7, para. 8.

61 Jeremy Scahill quoted in Hugh Gusterson, *Drone: Remote Control Warfare* (Cambridge: MIT Press, 2016), 107.

62 Ibid. Gusterson also quotes the counterinsurgency expert David Kilcullen: "if there is a way to prevail in counterinsurgency, it is by showing cultural sensitivity to occupied populations, creating widespread new economic opportunities, and refraining from the use of violence as much as possible. Instead, the United States has channeled economic aid to a corrupt few;

Chapter Six returns to the issues surrounding drone warfare discussed in Chapter Five via a reading of Franz Kafka's famous short story "The Metamorphosis" (*Die Verwandlung*), whose protagonist Gregor Samsa finds himself one morning transformed into a giant vermin. I show the uncanny premonition, in this story, of what in the vocabulary of the drone war is called a "kill box." A "kill box," in the succinct definition of French philosopher Grégoire Chamayou, is "a temporary autonomous zone of slaughter," meaning that "within a given cube, one may fire at will." In this operational model, Chamayou continues,

> the conflict zone appears as a space fragmented into a provisional multitude of kill boxes that can be activated in a manner both flexible and bureaucratic. As General Richard P. Formica explained, with undisguised enthusiasm, in an email: 'Kill boxes enable us to do what we wanted to do for years [...] rapidly adjust the delineation of battlespace [...]. Now with automation technology and USAF [U.S. Air Force] employment of kill boxes, you really have a very flexible way of delineating battlespace both in time and on the ground.'"[63]

In the mid 1970s, the German philosopher Hans Blumenberg described the trap as the philosophical concept's "prototype" and "first triumph," because it unites in one device the mastery over distance and the mastery over absence, given that during its engineering, the prey is absent, and during the capture or kill, the engineer can be absent or remote. First introduced during "Operation Desert Storm" in 1991, the "kill box" brings the con-

---

burned down the opium crops on which many peasants rely for income, leaving them angry and destitute; used drone attacks to blow people apart from the skies; and trained troops to bash in the doors of family homes in the middle of the night, pointing guns at women and children, while screaming at them in English. If one set out to create an insurgency, it is hard to imagine a set of policies better calculated to do so. And drone attacks are an integral part of the mix on which insurgency thrives" (109).

63 Grégoire Chamayou, *A Theory of the Drone*, trans. Janet Lloyd (New York: The New Press, 2015), 55.

cept truly and literally to new heights.[64] The assertion of mastery and of sovereignty is for Blumenberg *in essence* one that acts *at a distance*. The concept of sovereignty, which is so crucial for the entire Western philosophical tradition, is here closely linked to a radical asymmetry, which Chamayou describes as being "able to kill without being able to be killed; to be able to see without being seen. To become absolutely invulnerable while the other is placed in a state of absolute vulnerability." The concern with "deformities (*Verunstaltungen*) which have not yet penetrated our consciousness," which Kafka is reported to have attributed to Picasso's art, can be detected in "The Metamorphosis" as well.[65] In the end, Gregor is reduced to bug splat. An analysis of this word in Chapter Six yields some of the deformities that have or should by now have entered our consciousness. These deformities are perhaps best identified as defacements, including in the literal sense of the removal of or abstraction from a face. This is what another frontally posed figure and its treatment of the theme of "state" addresses.

In April 2014, challenging the language of drone operators who reportedly refer to killed drone victims as "bug splat," an artist collective installed a huge reproduction of a photograph by the journalist Noor Behram on a field in the "heavily bombed Khyber Pukhtoonkhwa region of Pakistan, where drone attacks regularly occur" (fig. 4).[66]

---

64 Major James E. Mullin III, "The JFA: Redefining the Kill Box," *Fires Bulletin: A Joint Publication for U.S. Artillery Professionals* (March–April 2008): 38. "JFA" stands for "Joint Fires Area" and is another name for "kill box." "The JFCM [Joint Fires Coordination Measures] first sought to align the term 'kill box' doctrinally with other FSCM [Fires Support Coordinating Measures] naming conventions and redefined it as a JFA" (38).

65 Gustav Janouch, *Conversations with Kafka* (New York: Praeger, 1953), 85.

66 Anon., "A Giant Art Installation Targets Predator Drone Operators." Chris Woods notes that the origins of the term "Bugsplat" lay "in data modeling carried out by drone crews and analysts, seeking to mitigate civilian casualties" with the help of modeling software. Woods quotes an interview with a former senior US intelligence official who described the process to him: "'You say something like 'Show me the Bugsplat.' That's what we call the probability of kill estimate when we were doing this final math before the 'Go go go' decision. You would actually get a picture of a compound, and

Fig. 4: #NotABugSplat, based on a photograph by Noor Behram.

The 90 by 60 feet portrait featured an unnamed girl who lost her parents and her seven-year-old brother in a drone attack in the village of Dande Darpa Khel on August 21, 2009.[67] The original photograph, published in *Wired,* shows the girl with two surviving siblings, a younger sister and an older brother. Not yet

there will be something on it that looks like a bugsplat actually with red, yellow, and green: with red being anybody in that spot is dead, yellow stands a chance of being wounded; green we expect no harm to come to individuals where there is green. 'I don't like that bugsplat, we're not going to use it. What direction are you coming in on?' 'I am coming in from the North.' 'No, try from the South. Get me a bugsplat from the South'" (Chris Woods, *Sudden Justice: America's Secret Drone Wars* [Oxford: Oxford University Press, 2015], 150). Even though the term may have been introduced in the context of trying to reduce civilian casualties, Woods's quote clearly shows that in any case, the word replaces the faces of assassinated singular human beings with the amorphous mass of a squashed insect.

67 Noor Behram quoted in Spencer Ackerman, "Rare Photographs Show Ground Zero of the Drone War," *Wired,* Dec. 12, 2011. Behram names two of the family members killed in the blast: Bismullah Kahn and his seven year old son, Syed Wali Shah. His wife, also killed in the explosion, and the surviving three children are not named. According to another source, the organization Reprieve/Foundation for Fundamental Rights, the girl lost "both her parents and two young siblings" (Anon., "A Giant Art Installation Targets Predator Drone Operators").

aware of their parents' and brother's death, the three children hold small pieces of the bombed-out remains of their house, "as if the rubble could comfort them."[68]

Facing directly up from the giant reproduction of the photo, cropped to feature only the girl, her eyes are "squarely trained on the lens of the camera."[69] She frontally addresses, literally con-fronts the drone operator, thousands of miles away, and with him or her all those in whose name the attacks are carried out, with nothing but the vulnerability of her face, thereby, to quote Mitchell's formulation again, "hailing the viewer as the 'you' who is addressed by an 'I'." The result, I would argue, is not so much "empathy," which, "in the context of empire," as Keith Feldman cautions, "has the capacity to exacerbate a liberal divide between the civil enlightenment of Euro-American nations and the objects of former colonial rule."[70] Rather, belying the official discourse replete with words like "the enemy," "collateral damage," "targets of opportunity," a "shadowy foe" to be eliminated in a "signature strike" (in which the killed person's name is actually not known), the girl's face is inescapable, and with it the realization that what occurs in a drone strike cannot be called by any other name than murder. For Emmanuel Levinas, the "alterity that is expressed in the face provides the unique 'matter' possible for total negation." What "resists" in the face is precisely *the face,* "the primordial *expression,* [...] the first word: 'you shall not commit murder.'"[71] Behram's photograph reintroduces a face into a war zone where a death sentence can be executed on the basis of fitting the target demographic alone: all males aged 18 to 65, since the United States deems these men

---

68 Ackerman, "Rare Photographs Show Ground Zero of the Drone War."

69 Keith P. Feldman, "#NotABugSplat. Becoming Human on the Terrain of Visual Culture," in *The Routledge Companion to Literature and Human Rights,* eds. Sophia McClennen and Alexandra Schultheis Moore (London: Routledge, 2016), 224.

70 Feldman, "#NotABugSplat," 228. Feldman recapitulates here Sherene Razack's scepticism.

71 Emmanuel Levinas, *Totality and Infinity,* trans. Alphonso Lingis (Pittsburgh: Duquesne University Press, 1991), 198–99.

to be combatants "unless there is explicit intelligence posthumously proving them innocent" — again: "posthumously."[72] The photograph might puncture what Peggy Kamuf has called in the context of the acceptability of the death penalty in the US the "wholesale anesthetizing of public sensibility."[73] The image contrasts and confronts the fatal "kill boxes," into which suspected combatants and everybody else in their vicinity are trapped for extrajudicial assassination, with the wide-open field of a face.

In their reflection on the "ethics of drone warfare," John Kaag and Sarah Kreps, inspired by and quoting Hannah Arendt, come to the conclusion that the "banality of evil emerges in the tyranny of the thoughtless majority. [...] 'There is a strange interdependence between thoughtlessness and evil.'"[74] They address an exhortation to their readers that is as simple as it is — or should be — heavy of consequences: "let us be shocked."[75] We "own" the photograph of the hooded man from Abu Ghraib and must "own up" to "what it tells us about ourselves." We own the drone war no less, and must own up to what it tells us about ourselves.

---

72 Gusterson, *Drone,* 87, 94. See also Reprieve, "Investigations: Drones."

73 Peggy Kamuf, "Protocol: Death Penalty Addiction," *Southern Journal of Philosophy* 50 (2012): 12–13.

74 John Kaag and Sara Kreps, *Drone Warfare* (Cambridge: Polity, 2014), 124.

75 Ibid., 120.

I.
TORTURE

CHAPTER 1

"Torture Was the Essence of National Socialism": Reading Jean Améry Today[1]

1.

Commenting on "a newspaper page with photos that show members of the South Vietnamese army torturing captured Vietcong rebels," Jean Améry, the Austrian-born essayist and survivor of Nazi torture and death camps, wrote in 1966: "The admission of torture, the boldness — but is it still that? — of coming forward with such photos is explicable only if it is assumed that a revolt of public conscience is no longer to be feared. One could think that this conscience has accustomed itself to the practice of torture."[2]

Alfred McCoy has compellingly argued that TV series like *24* have, more than four decades later, contributed to create a broad consensus on the acceptability of torture.[3] In February 2007, *24*'s executive producer Howard Gordon announced that the show would "have fewer torture scenes in the future," but this decision was not made because of the complaints he had received from several high-level military and FBI officials and interro-

---

1   Originally published in *Speaking about Torture*, eds. Julie Carlson and Elisabeth Weber, 83–98 (New York: Fordham University Press, 2012).

2   Jean Améry, "Jenseits von Schuld und Sühne," in *Werke, vol. 2*, ed. G. Scheit (Stuttgart: Klett-Cotta, 2002), 57–58; Améry, *At the Mind's Limits: Contemplations by a Survivor on Auschwitz and its Realities*, trans. Sidney Rosenfeld and Stella P. Rosenfeld (Bloomington: Indiana University Press, 1980), 22–23.

3   McCoy, *A Question of Torture*, 190–96.

gators, who had expressed their concerns over the effects 24's depictions of torture had on US military personnel in Iraq and elsewhere.[4]

Rather, the reason for the shift was, in Gordon's words, that "torture 'is starting to feel a little trite. [...] The idea of physical coercion or torture is no longer a novelty or surprise."[5] The title of Rosa Brooks's February 23, 2007, editorial in the *Los Angeles Times* aptly summarized this state of affairs: "America Tortures (Yawn)."[6]

The military order issued by the US president in November 2001, which authorized the "indefinite detention" and trial by military commissions of foreign combatants suspected of involvement in "terrorist activities," in fact erased, as Giorgio Agamben put it, "any legal status of the individual, thus producing a legally unnamable and unclassifiable being." The detainees of Guantánamo Bay don't have "the status of POWs as defined by the Geneva Convention, they do not even have the status of persons charged with a crime according to American laws." They are "subject now only to raw power; they have no legal existence."[7] Even after two habeas corpus decisions by the US Supreme Court in 2004 and 2008 and under the Obama administration they fit the paradigm of the "homo sacer," who finds himself, in Agamben's formulation, as "bare life," subjected to

---

4   The group that met with Gordon included the dean of the United States Military Academy at West Point, General Patrick Finnegan, and three of the country's most experienced military and FBI interrogators.

5   Jane Mayer, "Whatever It Takes," *New Yorker*, Feb. 12, 2007. The typical "dilemma" with which the viewer of 24 is presented is well-known: "a resistant suspect can either be accorded due process — allowing a terrorist plot to proceed — or be tortured in pursuit of a lead. [...] With unnerving efficiency, suspects are beaten, suffocated, electrocuted, drugged, assaulted with knives, or more exotically abused: almost without fail, these suspects divulge critical secrets."

6   Rosa Brooks, "America Tortures (Yawn)," *Los Angeles Times*, Feb. 23, 2007.

7   Giorgio Agamben, *State of Exception*, trans. Kevin Attell (Chicago: Chicago University Press 2005), 3; Ulrich Rauff, "Interview with Giorgio Agamben — Life, A Work of Art Without an Author: The State of Exception, the Administration of Disorder and Private Life," *German Law Journal* 5 (May 2004). On the current status of the prison camp, see below, chapters 3 and 4.

the sovereign's state of exception.[8] The fact that many "enemy combatants" in Guantánamo and elsewhere have been tortured seals their extra-legal status, insofar as the CIA sees them, in McCoy's words, as "too dangerous for release, [and] too tainted for trial."[9]

Agamben's book *Homo Sacer* is best known for his analysis of another "legally unnamable and unclassifiable being," the *Muselmann* of the Nazi death camps, to whom Agamben dedicated his important book, *Remnants of Auschwitz.*[10] Given the vast differences between the historical and political contexts, it would be devoid of sense to simply juxtapose or compare the victims of US-endorsed torture and those men and women Primo Levi called the "drowned," the "anonymous mass, continually renewed and always identical, of non-men (*non-uomini*) who march and labour in silence, the divine spark dead within them, already too empty to really suffer."[11] However, one of Améry's assertions creates a link between the two contexts. Torture, Améry writes, was "the essence of National-Socialism." To understand this categorical assertion, it is helpful and even necessary to reflect on the absence of legal existence inflicted on *Muselmänner* of the Nazi death camps and on torture victims. The category of "unlawful enemy combatants" used by the US administration in its so-called war on terror, to designate the prisoners in Guantánamo Bay, for example, reflects the legal void analyzed by Agamben. Such absence of legal existence was even more

---

8 On March 7, 2011, President Obama signed a new executive order, one that stands in stark contrast to the executive orders he signed a day after taking office, to "create a formal system of indefinite detention for those held at the U.S. military prison at Guantanamo Bay, Cuba, who continue to pose a significant threat to national security" (Peter Finn and Anne E. Kornblut, "Obama Creates Indefinite Detention System for Prisoners at Guantanamo Bay," *The Washington Post,* March 8, 2011).

9 McCoy, *A Question of Torture,* 195. McCoy continues: "The ideal solution to this conundrum, from a CIA perspective, is extrajudicial execution."

10 Giorgio Agamben, *Remnants of Auschwitz: The Witness and the Archive,* trans. Daniel Heller-Roazen (New York: Zone Books, 2002).

11 Primo Levi, *Survival in Auschwitz* [*Se questo è un uomo* (If this is a man)], trans. Stuart Woolf (New York: Touchstone, 1996), 90.

flagrant for a smaller group of men whose status can only be properly referred to by using a word created during Argentina's "Dirty War": the disappeared. These detainees were held in so-called "black sites," secret US-run prisons whose locations were unknown to anyone but CIA operatives.[12] The name given to those highly secret prisoners points to an ordeal that forms a certain link between *Muselmänner* and torture victims: the men who had been disappeared into CIA black sites were referred to as "ghost detainees."

In Levi's account, the *Muselmänner* are walking dead, "non-men," ghostlike beings, whose overwhelming majority did not survive the camps.[13] The question of why they were called *Muselmänner* — an antiquated word for "Muslim" in German — has been met with different hypotheses, most of which focus on the widespread assumption in early-twentieth-century Europe that Muslims were people "of unconditional fatalism."[14]

---

12 The prisoners had no registration numbers, no access to lawyers or visits from the International Red Cross, and their families had no knowledge of their whereabouts. The very existence of these prisons was first revealed to a larger audience through an article by Dana Priest: "CIA Holds Terror Suspects in Secret Prisons," *Washington Post*, Nov. 2, 2005, A01. In 2006, Dana Priest won the Pulitzer Prize for this article and others she had written on the CIA and the "War on Terror." In one of his first executive orders, given on Jan. 22, 2009, President Obama ordered all US personnel, including the CIA, to conduct interrogations in compliance with the Army Field Manual. The same day, the president also ordered the secret CIA-run prisons closed; see President Obama's "Executive Order 1349 — Ensuring Lawful Interrogations," Jan. 22, 2009.

13 Levi, *Survival in Auschwitz*, 90: "Their life is short, but their number is endless: they, the *Muselmänner*, the drowned, form the backbone of the camp, an anonymous mass, continually renewed and always identical, of non-men [*non-uomini*] who march and labour in silence, the divine spark dead within them, already too empty to really suffer. One hesitates to call them living: one hesitates to call their death death, in the face of which they have no fear, as they are too tired to understand."

14 Giorgio Agamben, quoting Eugen Kogon in *Remnants of Auschwitz*, 45. Agamben mentions the controversy surrounding the term; see ibid., 44–48. "There is little agreement on the origin of the term Muselmann" (44). Through a study of the history of the word in Occidental thought and literature, Gil Anidjar proposes what he calls a "genealogy of a figure of absolute

In the Nazi camps, not only *Muselmänner* were irrevocably marked by death. Based on his clinical experience, the psychiatrist William Niederland describes the survivors of the death camps as frequently marked by a "deep psychic trace [*psychische Tiefenspur*] that results from the *encounter with death* in the latter's most atrocious forms." Niederland calls this "trace" a "death-engram," using a term from neuropsychology that designates memory traces, which as a result of external stimuli have triggered biophysical or biochemical changes in the brain or other neural tissue.[15] In Geoffrey Hartman's words, the "Nazi machine" tried to ensure that "even in their afterlife, once out of the camps, [the survivors] would not escape the fate of the *Muselmann*."[16] As a consequence, many survivors' appearance and behavior, in Niederland's words, are "shadow-like" and "ghost-like."[17]

On the side of torture victims, it should be noted that "ghost detainee" was an "official term used by the US administration to designate a person held in a detention center, whose identity has been hidden by keeping them unregistered and therefore anonymous."[18] The term was, for example, used, and the practice condemned, in the courageous report written by Major General Antonio Taguba in early 2004, documenting the now infamous abuses of Abu Ghraib prison.[19] Another neologism was formed

---

subjection" (*The Jew, the Arab: A History of the Enemy* [Stanford: Stanford University Press 2003], 119).

15 William G. Niederland, *Folgen der Verfolgung: Das Überlebenden-Syndrom Seelenmord* [Consequences of persecution: the survivor-syndrome soul-murder] (Frankfurt am Main: Suhrkamp, 1980), 232. The term "death-engram" was coined by early twentieth-century German biologist Richard Semon.

16 Geoffrey Hartman, *Scars of the Spirit: The Struggle Against Inauthenticity* (New York: Palgrave Macmillan, 2002), 88.

17 Niederland, *Folgen der Verfolgung*, 232; see also Agamben, *Remnants of Auschwitz*, 47–48, and passim.

18 "Ghost Detainee," *Wikipedia*, http://en.wikipedia.org/wiki/Ghost_detainee; see also McCoy, *A Question of Torture*, 115.

19 See Lisa Hajjar, "Our Heart of Darkness," *Amnesty Now* 30, no. 4 (Summer 2004): 5.

in this context: the act of making someone disappear at a secret site was called "ghosting."[20]

These linguistic creations, intended to refer to the victims' invisibility from public witnessing or scrutiny, contain a proposition about torture that is, of course, unintentional, but for that matter all the more telling, and which is central to Améry's reflection: in Améry's text, as well as in other texts on torture, such as Ariel Dorfman's *Death and the Maiden,* the torture survivor is described as dead while still alive, or alive while already dead. In other words, while there is no doubt that "ghosting" is done in order to torture, torture, in other ways, is also a practice, and determined pursuit, of "ghosting."

2.

Before approaching the issue of torture, Améry reflects on what he suspects is routine in most police stations in most countries: the beating of people in custody. With the first blow received from an agent of the state, a person's "trust in the world breaks down" irreparably.[21] "The expectation of help, the certainty of help, is indeed one of the fundamental experiences of human beings, and probably also of animals [...] with the first blow from a policeman's fist, against which there can be no defense and which no helping hand will ward off, a part of our life ends and it can never again be revived" (67/28–29). Already in this first-degree experience of state-sponsored violence, one that happens daily in countless places around the world, "a part of

---

20 Josh White, "Army, CIA Agreed on 'Ghost' Prisoners," *Washington Post,* March 11, 2005, A16.

21 In the following, Améry's text will be quoted by first indicating the pagination of the German edition (*Werke,* vol. 2), followed by the pagination of the English translation, here 65/28. The lost "trust in the world" (*Weltvertrauen*) has been commented on by a number of scholars. For example Siegbert Wolf, *Von der Verwundbarkeit des Humanismus: Über Jean Améry* (Frankfurt: Dipa Verlag, 1995), 67; Thomas Mavridis, "'Wer der Folter erlag, kann nicht mehr heimisch werden in der Welt': Vom verlorenen Weltvertrauen Jean Amérys," *Fussnoten zur Literatur* 38 (1996): 73.

our life ends and it can never again be revived."[22] Torture, Améry writes, "contains everything" that he "ascertained" in "regard to beating by the police: the border violation of my self by the other, which can be neither neutralized by the expectation of help nor rectified through defending oneself [*Gegenwehr*]. Torture is all that, but in addition very much more" (74/33, trans. slightly modified).

In formulations that have strongly influenced Agamben's, Améry provides a glance into facets of the psychology of "bare life":

> If from the experience of torture any knowledge at all remains that goes beyond the plain nightmarish, it is that of a great amazement [*große Verwunderung*] and a foreignness in the world [*Fremdheit in der Welt*] that cannot be compensated by any sort of subsequent human communication. Amazed [*Staunend*], the tortured person experienced that in this world there can be the other as absolute sovereign, and sovereignty revealed itself as the power to inflict suffering and to destroy [*zu vernichten*; literally: to annihilate]. The dominion of the torturer over his victim has nothing in common with the power exercised on the basis of social contracts, as we know it. It is not the power of the traffic policeman over the pedestrian, of the tax official over the taxpayer, of the first lieutenant over the second lieutenant. It is also not the sacral sovereignty of past absolute chieftains or kings; for even if they stirred fear, they were also objects of trust at the same time. The king could be terrible in his wrath, but also kind in his mercy; his autocracy was an exercise of authority [*seine Gewalt war ein Walten*].[23] But the power of the torturer, under which the tortured moans, is nothing other than the

---

22 It is noteworthy that Darius Rejali starts his monumental *Torture and Democracy* with the account of police brutality, the Rodney King beating; Rejali, *Torture and Democracy*, 1.

23 Améry might be alluding here to Walter Benjamin's "Zur Kritik der Gewalt," in *Gesammelte Schriften*, vol. 2.1, ed. R. Tiedemann (Frankfurt: Suhrkamp, 1980), 203.

triumph of the survivor over the one who is plunged from the world into agony and death. (84/39–40)

The German is here even more emphatic: The "power of the tormentor [*Peiniger*], [...] is the limitless triumph of the survivor over the one who is pushed out of the world into agony and death [*der schrankenlose Triumph des Überlebenden über den, der aus der Welt in Qual und Tod hinausgestossen wird*]" (84/39–40). Améry's qualification of this "triumph" as "limitless" is decisive; omitting it as the English translation does deprives the text of one of its furthest reaching argumentative moves.

In what follows, it will thus be necessary to pay close attention to the formulations chosen by the English translators of Améry's text. The intent is not to criticize an overall excellent translation, but to point out specific word choices that, if not taken literally, or, as in this case, if omitted, substantially alter Améry's argument. In a text on Paul Celan, Jacques Derrida observes that "all responsible witnessing engages in a poetic experience of language."[24] In bearing witness to the torture he underwent, Améry engages in this singular experience of language by creating language. Since this creation of language enacts, in Dori Laub's formulation, the "creation of knowledge *de novo*" that can occur during the process of bearing witness to massive trauma, it is the reader's responsibility to listen to the uniqueness of that language, including its rawness in German, even if this comes at the cost of elegance in the English translation.[25] Améry continues:

Astonishment [*Staunen*] at the existence of the other, as he boundlessly [*grenzenlos*] asserts himself through torture, and astonishment at what one can become oneself: flesh and

24 Jacques Derrida, "Poetics and Politics of Witnessing," in *Sovereignties in Question: The Poetics of Paul Celan,* eds. Thomas Dutoit and Outi Pasanen (New York: Fordham University Press, 2005), 66.

25 Dori Laub, "Bearing Witness, or the Vicissitudes of Listening," in *Testimony: Crises of Witnessing in Literature, Psychoanalysis, and History,* eds. Shoshana Felman and Dori Laub (New York: Routledge, 1992), 57.

death. The tortured person never ceases to be amazed that all those things one may, according to inclination, call his soul, or his mind [*seinen Geist*], or his consciousness, or his identity, are destroyed when there is that cracking and splintering in the shoulder joints. (85/40)

This is a reference to the torture he suffered: at Breendonk, the main interrogation center in Nazi-occupied Belgium, "torturers suspended victims from a hook-and pulley system" while their hands were tied in the back.[26] Améry concludes: "That life is fragile is a truism that he has always known [...]. But only through torture did he learn that a living person can be transformed so thoroughly into flesh [*verfleischlichen*] and by that, while still alive, be partly made into a prey of death" (85/40).[27]

The most famous line of Améry's text summarizes his analysis: "Whoever has succumbed to torture [*Wer der Folter erlag*] can no longer feel at home in the world. The shame of destruction cannot be erased" (85/40). Again, the German is stronger: "*Die Schmach der Vernichtung läßt sich nicht austilgen,*" which translates literally: "The ignominy (or infamy) of annihilation cannot be erased." The one who has "succumbed" to torture has been annihilated, even though he or she is still among the living.[28]

In perhaps one of the best texts on Améry, G.W. Sebald pointed out the necessity of replacing the "abstract discourse about the victims of national-socialism" with Améry's essays "on his personal past and present" because they provide the "content-heaviest insights into the irreparable state of the victims, out of which alone the true nature of terror can be extrapolated with

---

26 Rejali, *Torture and Democracy*, 101.

27 The frequency of the word *Staunen*, astonishment or amazement, in this passage may indicate how philosophy, which is said to have had its beginning in astonishment (Plato, Aristotle, Heidegger) is here unfounded, if not demolished, in a very different "astonishment" or "amazement."

28 See also Siegbert Wolf's commentary: *Von der Verwundbarkeit des Humanismus,* 68.

some precision."[29] I will attempt a patient reading of substantial passages of Améry's text, listening to it as closely as possible, including to the semantic fields of the original German words, in order to amplify the voice of someone who not only underwent torture, but also had the strength to bear witness to it with breathtaking lucidity.

One of the words used by Améry stands out: the word rendered in the English translation as "transformation of the person into flesh." Other than in theological debates about the incarnation of Christ, it is a word used rather rarely in German: *Verfleischlichung* (77/33). In German, the word means, indeed, the utter transformation, through and through, into flesh, and there is, most likely, no alternative to the choice in English. Even though the word is not a neologism, Améry's use of it arguably gives it an entirely new meaning, thereby exemplifying the assertion by Derrida mentioned above, that all responsible witnessing engages in a poetic experience of language.

Among several meanings the German prefix *ver-* can have, one indicates the pursuit of an action to the end, until the fulfillment of a goal (as in *verrichten*, accomplish). Another meaning is the intensification of an action and the pursuit of something beyond a goal, such as *verschlafen* (oversleep) or *versalzen* (oversalt).[30] A third meaning is the negation of the verb that follows the prefix *ver-*, such as in *bieten* (bid/offer) and *ver-*

---

29 G.W. Sebald, "Mit den Augen des Nachtvogels," *Études Germaniques* 42 (July–Sept. 1988): 314. For Sebald, such "content-heaviest insight" is possible "not in the willingness for reconciliation, but only in the unceasing denunciation of injustice [*Unrecht*]" (320). In a similar vein, Améry asserts, for example: "The piles of corpses that lie between them [sc. my torturers] and me cannot be removed in the process of internalization, so it seems to me, but, on the contrary, through actualization, or, more sharply stated, by carrying-out the unresolved conflict in the field of influence [*Wirkungsfeld*] of historical practice" (129/69; trans. modified).

30 Jacob und Wilhelm Grimm, *Deutsches Wörterbuch* (Munich: DTV, 1984), vol. 25, s.v. "ver": "neben der bedeutung des zu ende führens entwickelt sich der begriff 'über das ziel hinaus': verschlafen, versalzen." In the latter sense, it is an intensification of the action, but with the result of turning the intended goal into something negative.

bieten (forbid). *Verfleischlichung* is, in a way, an intensified incarnation — but an incarnation out of which any spirit has been driven. The German *Fleisch* can mean both "flesh" and "meat." Christ's incarnation, for example, is usually referred to in German as *Fleischwerdung*, becoming flesh (of God), or, as John put it in the Gospel, the word become flesh. Grimm's *Deutsches Wörterbuch* has "Verfleischung" for the incarnation of Christ.[31] The "transformation into flesh" of the English translation of Améry's expression would correspond more to such *Fleischwerdung*. By contrast, *Verfleischlichung* through torture drives the word and all spirit out of the flesh. In Améry's redefinition, the expression comes to stand for a boundless intensification of the physical existence of a being, to the extent that the torture victim's "flesh becomes a total reality in self-negation" (74/33, trans. modified).

Améry's German is of exceptional perspicuity and elegance, and he frequently comments on the semantic field of a word or its components.[32] Listening to a word such as *Verfleischlichung*, whose semantic field he actually remapped, is, thus, not only legitimate, but also necessary, because it exemplifies the irreplaceable singularity of testimony. In Améry's usage, *Verfleischlichung*, the "fleshization" — if I may — of the torture victims, their utter reduction to flesh in pain, makes them experience death while still alive.[33] "Whoever is overcome by pain through torture experiences his body as never before. In self-negation, his flesh becomes a total reality. [...] [O]nly in torture does

---

31 Ibid., s.v. "Verfleischung."

32 See for example, Améry's reflections on the etymology of the word "torture" (73/32), the emphasis on the prefix *mit-* (74/33), and the reflections on the hostility of the persecuted person's mother tongue (103–6/51–54); see also Petra S. Fiero, *Schreiben gegen Schweigen: Grenzerfahrungen in Jean Amérys autobiographischem Werk* (Hildesheim: Olms, 1997), 62–63.

33 While many commentators quote this "transformation into flesh" (for example, Marianne Hirsch, "Editor's Column: The First Blow — Torture and Close Reading," *PMLA* 121, no. 2 (March 2006): 361–70, I have not yet found a commentary that listens to Améry's specific use of the word "Verfleischlichung." Two books in German on Améry are no exceptions: Fiero, *Schreiben gegen Schweigen*, esp. 48–54, and Wolf, *Von der Verwundbarkeit des Humanismus*, esp. 69–70.

the transformation of the person into flesh [*Verfleischlichung*] become complete. Frail in the face of violence, howling out in pain, awaiting no help, capable of no resistance [*Notwehr*: legitimate defense], the tortured person is only a body, and nothing else beside that" (74/33).

Verfleischlichung is "fleshization," but can also be "meatization," becoming meat. Even though Améry was a fierce critic of French thinkers of the 1960s and '70s, such as Roland Barthes, Gilles Deleuze, and Michel Foucault,[34] one is here reminded of Deleuze's commentary on Francis Bacon's paintings, where Deleuze observes "such convulsive pain and vulnerability [...]. Bacon does not say 'Pity the beasts,' but rather that every man who suffers is a piece of meat [*de la viande*]. Meat is the common zone of man and the beast, their zone of indiscernibility. [...] The man or woman who suffers is a beast [*une bête*], the beast that suffers is a human being."[35]

---

34 See Jean Améry, "Unmeisterliche Wanderjahre," in *Werke*, vol. 2, ed. G Scheit (Stuttgart: Klett Cotta, 2002), 324, 329; Améry, *Aufsätze zur Philosophie*, in *Werke*, vol. 6, ed. G. Scheit (Stuttgart: Klett Cotta, 2004), passim. Against Foucault, see esp. in vol. 6 of the *Werke* the essays "Michel Foucault's Vision des Kerker-Universums," 205–18, and "Michel Foucault und sein 'Diskurs' der Gegen-Aufklärung," 219–31. The criticism against French thinkers of the 1970s as the "new irrationalists" (6:163) characterizes most of the essays collected in vol. 6; against Deleuze, specifically 6:148–51, 165, 190, 197, 206; against Roland Barthes, ibid., 141–42; see also Hans-Martin Gauger, "Er fehlt uns, er ist da: Über Jean Améry," *Merkur: Deutsche Zeitschrift für Europäisches Denken* 59, no. 671 (March 2005): 254.

35 "[L]'homme qui souffre est une bête, la bête qui souffre est un homme" ("The man who suffers is a beast, the beast that suffers is a man") (Gilles Deleuze, *Francis Bacon: The Logic of Sensation*, trans. Daniel W. Smith [Minneapolis: University of Minnesota Press, 2002], 22; Deleuze, *Francis Bacon: Logique de la sensation* [Paris: Éditions de la Différence, 1981], 1:20–21). Roberto Esposito writes on Bacon's images in the context of the above-quoted commentary by Deleuze: "I don't know if flesh is to be related to the Nazi violence, as Deleuze would have it in his admirable comment (though the horror of that violence always remained with Bacon). The fact is that in no one more than Bacon is the biopolitical practice of the animalization of man carried out to its lethal conclusion, finding a reversed correspondence perfectly in the disfigured figure of butchered flesh. [...] That the painter always saw in animal carcasses hanging in butcher shops the shape of man (but also of himself) signifies that that bloody mount is the condition today

In Améry's text, this "zone of indiscernibility" becomes manifest in the scream. Améry describes "my own howling that is strange and uncanny to me [*mein eigenes, mir fremdes und unheimliches Geheul*]." And he continues: "There is howling-out under torture. Perhaps in this hour, this second" (59/23–24, trans. modified). Améry does not say "someone is crying out under torture," as the English translation reads. Again, the choice in English is appropriate, guided as it is by the requirements of idiomatic word usage and elegance. The reason it needs to be changed is that in German, the grammatical structure enacts what is at stake: the sentence is formulated in the impersonal passive voice: "Es wird aufgeheult unter der Tortur. Vielleicht zu dieser Stunde, in dieser Sekunde" ("There is howling-out under torture. Perhaps in this hour, this second"). There is no longer a *some*body. There is a body that is only flesh, and it howls in the "zone of indiscernibility" of becoming meat.

In his novel *Waiting for the Barbarians*, J.M. Coetzee describes the same torture Améry underwent, and here too, the screams are the howling of an animal: "my arms come up behind my back, and as my feet leave the ground I feel a terrible tearing in my shoulders as though whole sheets of muscle are giving way. From my throat comes the first mournful dry bellow [...]. I bellow again and again, there is nothing I can do to stop it, the noise comes out of a body that knows itself damaged perhaps beyond repair and roars its fright."[36]

"Fleshization" is indiscernible from becoming "meat" while still alive. "Flesh" is here what Roberto Esposito calls "an abject material," because "it is intrinsic to the same body from which it seems to escape (and which therefore expels it)." This "flesh [...] does not coincide with the body; it is that part or zone of the body, the body's membrane, that isn't one with the body, that exceeds its boundaries or is subtracted from the body's

---

of a large section of humanity" (*Bíos: Biopolitics and Philosophy*, trans. Timothy Campbell [Minneapolis: University of Minnesota Press, 2008], 169).

36 J.M. Coetzee, *Waiting for the Barbarians* (New York: Penguin, 1982), 118–19.

enclosing."[37] The flesh in Améry's "fleshization" is truly one that, according to Merleau-Ponty, whom Esposito quotes here, "has no name because no philosophy has known how to reach that undifferentiated layer [...] in which the same notion of body, anything but enclosed, is now turned outside [*estroflessa*] in an irreducible heterogeneity."[38]

The "irreducible heterogeneity" manifests itself as pain of the flesh that breaks the path to an experience of dying that, according to Améry, is, under other circumstances, radically impossible:

> Pain [...] is the most extreme intensification imaginable of our bodily being. But maybe it is even more, that is: death. No road that can be traveled by logic leads us to death, but perhaps the thought is permissible that through pain a path of feeling and premonition [*gefühlsahnender Weg*] can be paved [or carved out: *gebahnt*] to it for us. In the end, we would be faced with the equation: Body = Pain = Death, and in our case this could be reduced to the hypothesis that torture, through which we are turned into body by the other, blots out the contradiction of death and allows us to experience our own death. (75/33–34, trans. slightly modified)[39]

This is why Améry calls torture "indelible": once this "path" has been carved, it cannot be undone. For Améry, there is no path back from having experienced death while alive. Torture dissolves the limit between life and death. The tortured one, "while still alive," has been "partly made into a prey of death." Part alive, part dead, neither dead, nor alive, the torture victim occupies a zone in-between in which torture never ends. Three times, Améry returns to the indelible character of torture: "Whoever was tortured, stays tortured. Torture is ineradicably [*unaus-*

---

37 Roberto Esposito, *Bíos,* 159. A close reading of Améry informed by Esposito's path-breaking analyses of Nazi "biopolitics" and "thanatopolitics" cannot be undertaken in this context. I hope to do it elsewhere.

38 Ibid., 159.

39 See also 49/18.

löschlich] burned into him, even when no clinically objective traces can be detected" (75/34).[40] And: "It was over for a while. It still is not over. Twenty-two years later I am still dangling over the ground by dislocated arms, panting, and accusing myself" (79/36).

The torture victim is branded, even if the mark is invisible. He or she is suspended in the arrested time of unending torture in which he or she is forever "a defenseless prisoner of fear. It is *fear* that henceforth brandishes its sceptre above his head [*waffenlos der Angst ausgeliefert. Sie ist es, die fürderhin über ihm das Szepter schwingt*]" (85/40).[41]

The *Verfleischlichung* that, as Améry repeatedly underlines, brutally expels any spirit, is at the same time an expulsion into death. And because this happens to the living body, it can also be called, albeit now in a different sense, a "ghosting."

In his chapter on Auschwitz, Améry writes that the fear of death is really fear of dying, and that the inmates in Auschwitz did not fear death, but were tormented by the fear of certain ways of dying (49/18). While these ways of dying are dreaded, death is actually wished for. In the torture scene Améry describes, death is wished for at the time of what is self-accusingly referred to as a "betrayal":

[T]hey continued asking me questions, constantly the same ones: accomplices, addresses, meeting places. To come right out with it: I had nothing but luck, because especially in regard to the extorting of information our group was rather well organized. What they wanted to hear from me in Breendonk, I simply did not know myself. If instead of the aliases I had been able to name the real names, perhaps, or probably,

---

40 "Wer gefoltert wurde, bleibt gefoltert. Unauslöschlich ist die Folter in ihn eingebrannt, auch dann, wenn keine klinisch objektiven Spuren nachzuweisen sind" (75). In the passage about the specific torture method he was subjected to, Améry describes "a crackling and splintering in my shoulders that my body has not forgotten until this hour" (73/32).

41 The English translation, again softening Améry's word choice, reads: "It is fear that henceforth reigns over him."

a calamity would have occurred, and I would be standing here now as the weakling I most likely am, and as the traitor I potentially already was. Yet it was not at all that I opposed them with the heroically maintained silence that befits a real man in such a situation and about which one may read (almost always, incidentally, in reports by people who were not there themselves). I talked. I accused myself of invented absurd political crimes [*Staatsverbrechen*], and even now I don't know at all how they could have occurred [*einfallen*] to me, dangling bundle that I was. Apparently I had the hope that, after such incriminating disclosures, a well-aimed blow to the head would put an end to my misery and quickly bring on my death, or at least unconsciousness. (78–79/36)

Elaine Scarry's book *The Body in Pain* could be described as a long meditation on Améry's above-mentioned assertion that "whoever has succumbed to torture can no longer be at home in the world. The ignominy of annihilation cannot be erased." Without ever mentioning Améry, Scarry describes how intense pain is world-destroying. This destruction engulfs the entire space of the victim's existence: body, shelter, objects, language. The torture victim's body is turned into a weapon against her or himself. The rooms in which the torture takes place "are often given names that acknowledge [...] the generous, civilizing impulse normally present in the human shelter," such as "'guest rooms' in Greece and 'safe houses' in the Philippines." What has the welcoming name of shelter is "converted into another weapon, into an agent of pain. All aspects of the basic structure — walls, ceiling, windows, doors — undergo this conversion." Equally, "the contents of the room, its furnishings [bathtubs, chairs, beds, etc.], are converted into weapons." Thus, "the objects themselves, and with them the fact of civilization, are annihilated."[42]

---

42 Elaine Scarry, *The Body in Pain: The Making and Unmaking of the World* (New York and Oxford: Oxford University Press, 1985), 40–41. Fiero dedicates several pages on the proximity between Scarry's and Améry's text in

Even though Idelber Avelar's criticism of Scarry's approach is justified when he "take[s] distance" from "her understanding of terms such as 'world,' 'language,' 'representation,' and 'body' as contents already constituted in advance and only subsequently threatened and destroyed by torture," when he objects to the assumption that "civilization exists precisely because it is *the opposite* of torture," and when he underlines that, rather, the histories of concepts such as "civilization," "truth," and "democracy" are "quite indebted to the development of technologies of pain," Scarry's text is a powerful account of the devastating effects of torture on the fundamental trust that characterizes the "pre-ontological" understanding of "being-in-the-world."[43]

One of the perversities of torture is that this "shredding" or "collapse" of the torture victim's world "earns the person in pain not compassion but contempt."[44] This "contempt" becomes obvious in the word choice that calls the so-called confession obtained under torture "betrayal." The implication, that "confessing" torture victims are "traitors," perpetuates their expulsion from the world of the living. Calling the words obtained under torture "confession" and "betrayal" is thus nothing short of becoming complicit with the torturer.[45] That the victims, too, espouse these terms confirms how not only their bodies but also their minds and language have been converted into weapons against them.

The perverted names, including the widespread practice of naming torture methods after everyday objects or practices,

---

Schreiben gegen Schweigen, 55–56, as well as in her essay "The Body in Pain: Jean Améry's Reflections on Torture," *Publications of the Missouri Philological Association* 18 (1993): 26–32.

43   Idelber Avelar, *The Letter of Violence: Essays on Narrative, Ethics, and Politics* (New York: Palgrave MacMillan, 2004), 32. The "pre-ontological" understanding of "being-in-the-world" is here understood in the sense Heidegger gives these notions; see, for example, *Being and Time,* trans. Joan Stambaugh (Albany: State University of New York Press, 1996), 12, 15, passim. We have seen above that it is this trust that, for Améry, is the first irretrievable victim of state violence.

44   Scarry, *The Body in Pain,* 37.

45   See Fiero, *Schreiben gegen Schweigen,* 55–56.

such as the "telephone" or the "frequent flyer program," indicate that torture not only "contains" and uses language, but that "it is itself a language." In Scarry's words, interrogation is "internal to the structure of torture, exists there because of its intimate connections to and interactions with the physical pain."[46] This is why in French (just as in Latin), as Voltaire noted, torture is sometimes simply called *la question*, just as in German, *peinliche Frage* is synonymous with *Folter*.

Améry's verdict that "[w]hoever has succumbed to torture can no longer feel at home in the world. The ignominy (or infamy) of annihilation cannot be erased" (84/40, trans. modified), shows that for him, torture is an irreparable assault on what Heidegger called "being-in-the-world." Following Scarry's analyses, it is also an irreparable assault on the "house of being" that is language.[47]

3.

About halfway through his essay on torture, Améry sets out to "substantiate why, according to my firm conviction, torture was the essence of National Socialism — more accurately stated, why it was precisely in torture that the Third Reich materialized in all the density of its being [*Bestandsdichte*]." After listing names of other countries where torture was and is practiced, he continues: "Torture was no invention of National Socialism. But it was its apotheosis. The Hitler vassal did not yet achieve his full identity if he was merely as quick as a weasel, tough as leather, hard as Krupp steel. [...] He had to *torture*, destroy" (70/30).[48] Again, in German, the word is *vernichten*: annihilate.

---

46 Scarry, *The Body in Pain*, 27, 29.

47 Martin Heidegger, "Letter on Humanism," in *Basic Writings*, ed. David Farrell Krell, trans. Frank Capuzzi, 2nd ed. (New York: Harper and Collins, 1993), 213.

48 The quote continues: "He had to be capable of handling torture instruments, so that Himmler would assure him his Certificate of Maturity in History; later generations would admire him for having obliterated his feelings

The difference between the English "destroy" and the German *vernichten* is decisive. One can destroy without annihilating. What Améry explores here is not the connection between torture and destruction, but between torture and a heightened form of destruction: annihilation. Just as in *Verfleischlichung,* the German prefix *ver-* in *vernichten* indicates an intensification that pursues an action beyond the goal. After addressing several possible objections, especially the depiction of communism as prime torturer, Améry writes:

> As a hint, allow me to repeat here in my own name and at the risk of being denounced what Thomas Mann once said in a much attacked interview: namely that no matter how terrible Communism may at times appear, it still symbolizes an idea of man, whereas Hitler-Fascism was not an idea at all, but depravity [*Schlechtigkeit*]. [...] National Socialism [...] was the only political system of this century that up to this point had not only practiced the rule of the antiman [*die Herrschaft des Gegenmenschen*; literally: the regime/sovereignty of the antiman], as had other Red and White terror regimes also, but had expressly established it *as a principle.* [...] The Nazis tortured, as did others, because by means of torture they wanted to obtain information important for national policy. But in addition, they tortured with the good conscience of depravity. They martyred [*marterten*] their prisoners for definite purposes, which in each instance were exactly specified. Above all, however, they tortured because they were torturers [*Folterknechte*]. They placed torture in their service. But even more fervently they were its servants. (70–71/31, my emphasis)

Again, it is useful to listen to the German. The word for "torturers" Améry chooses here is *Folterknechte,* literally "torture-servants" or "torture-slaves." The word indicates that being a *Folter-*

---

of mercy [*um seiner Austilgung der eigenen Barmherzigkeit willen*]," literally, for his "obliteration" or "extermination of his own mercy."

knecht was considered a lowly profession, but Améry's point lies elsewhere: as he puts it, the torturers are torture's "fervent servants" — *Inbrünstiger aber noch dienten sie ihr:* "Even more burningly they served it." How is this "fervent" or "burning" "service" to be understood? Nazi torture, Améry writes, has to be understood as sadism, not in terms of sexual pathology, but in the terms of the philosophy of the Marquis de Sade, as read by Georges Bataille (76–77/34–35). In other words, Nazi torture has to be understood as sadism in terms of an "existential psychology," as "the radical negation of the other" (77/35).

This is where the difference between destruction and annihilation comes to bear. The Nazi torturer wants to "nullify this world, and by negating his fellow man [...] he wants to realize his own total sovereignty. The fellow man is transformed into flesh [again, literally: fleshisized], and in this fleshization he is already brought to the edge of death; but in the end he is driven *beyond* the border of death into nothingness [*das Nichts*]." The torturer, with his "control over the other's scream of pain and death" becomes "master over flesh and spirit, life and death" (77/34–35, my emphasis). The true purpose of such "fleshization" is to drive the victim "*beyond* the border of death into nothingness." Death is not enough.

Agamben quotes Wolfgang Sofsky on the *Muselmann*: "Power abrogates itself in the act of killing. The death of the other puts an end to the social relationship. But by starving the other, it gains time. It erects a third realm, a limbo between life and death."[49] We can add: in torture, power prolongs itself indefinitely, if not infinitely. The torture victim too is suspended between life and death, and that suspension is not over with the torture's ending. Annihilation goes "beyond" death, and it is the limitless power and anticipation of annihilation that transforms a man or a woman into a fervent servant of torture.

The faces of the torturers Améry encountered were not swollen "with sexual-sadistic delight, but concentrated in murderous self-realization. With heart and soul they went about their

---

49 Wolfgang Sofsky, quoted in Agamben, *Remnants of Auschwitz*, 47–48.

business, and the name of it was power, dominion over spirit and flesh, orgy of unchecked self-expansion. I also have not forgotten that there were moments when I felt a kind of wretched admiration for the agonizing sovereignty [literally: torturing sovereignty] they exercised over me. For is not the one who can reduce a person so entirely to a body and a whimpering prey of death a god or, at least, a demigod?" (78/36).

What the torturer is pursuing is not just destruction, but annihilation, not just the other's "death," but the other's "nothingness." The difference, again, is decisive: the power to drive another human being into nothingness goes further than destruction. This is what the torturer's passion or "fervor" has become, and this is why the figure of a god or demigod is invoked. Destruction is not enough; in the Marquis de Sade's texts, a destruction that would undo creation is the goal. It is worth noting that some fictional representations of torture also invoke the torturer's godlike powers, such as S. Yizchar's "The Prisoner," Ariel Dorfman's *Death and the Maiden,* and J. M. Coetzee's *Waiting for the Barbarians.*[50]

Thus Améry defines National Socialism as a *system* based on sadism: the sadist wants to "nullify this world, and by negating his fellow man, who also in an entirely specific sense is 'hell' for him, he wants to realize his own total sovereignty" (77/35). But for that, he has to "obliterate/exterminate his feelings of mercy" (70/30).

---

50 Ariel Dorfman, *Death and the Maiden* (New York: Penguin, 1994), 59–60; Coetzee, *Waiting for the Barbarians,* 113–19. In S. Yizhar's story "The Prisoner," the witness of the prisoner's entirely unjustified mistreatment, who accompanies the prisoner in a jeep to an interrogation center and who could "stop the jeep" and "let the poor devil go," is described as having the powers of a "lesser demigod": "The fellow here at your feet, his life, his well-being, his home, three souls, the whole thread of his existence with all that was involved, were in your grip somehow or other as though you were some lesser demigod here in the Jeep. The man carried along, the collective flock of sheep and several souls in the mountain village, these variegated threads of life were twined together to be cut or grow inextricably involved, all because you were suddenly their master" ("The Prisoner," trans. I. M. Lask, in *Midnight Convoy and Other Stories* [New Milford: Toby Press 2007], 82–83).

In another text, "Zur Psychologie des deutschen Volkes" (1945), Améry describes how such "negation" is achieved: namely through the "*Selbsterziehung* [...] *zur Grausamkeit*" (self-education to cruelty), that can be successful only at the condition of the complete eradication of "human emotion" (*menschliche Regung*), such as pity, mercy, and goodness, an eradication that is then cast as "heroism": for example, in the German writer Rudolf Binding's assertion of 1933, quoted by Améry, "We Germans are heroic in bearing the suffering of others."[51]

This trait is also a crucial part of Bataille's analysis of Sade: "crimes committed in cold blood are greater than crimes carried out in the ardor of feelings; but the crime 'committed when the sensitive part has been hardened,' that dark and secret crime is the most important of all because it is the act of a soul which having destroyed everything within itself has accumulated immense strength, which identifies itself completely with the movement of total destruction that it is preparing."[52]

---

51 Améry, *Werke*, 2:506–7.

52 Georges Bataille, *L'érotisme, Oeuvres complètes,* vol. 10 (Paris: Gallimard, 1987), 172; Bataille, *Eroticism: Death and Sensuality,* trans. Mary Dalwood (San Francisco: City Lights Books, 1986), 173 (trans. modified). This is perhaps how the torturers in Améry can have breakfast after the torture session (78/35). Compare the questions the Magistrate asks the torturer in Coetzee's *Waiting for the Barbarians*: "'Forgive me if the question seems impudent, but I would like to ask: How do you find it possible to eat afterwards, after you have been [...] working with people? That is a question I have always asked myself about executioners and other such people. Wait! Listen to me a moment longer, I am sincere, it has cost me a great deal to come out with this, since I am terrified of you, I need not tell you that, I am sure you are aware of it. Do you find it easy to take food afterwards? I have imagined that one would want to wash one's hands. But no ordinary washing would be enough, one would require priestly intervention, a ceremonial of cleansing, don't you think? Some kind of purging of one's soul too — that is how I have imagined it. Otherwise how would it be possible to return to everyday life — to sit down at table, for instance, and break bread with one's family or one's comrades?'" The torturer's reaction shows that the Magistrate's questions have hit a nerve: "He [sc. the torturer] wrenches himself free and hits me so hard in the chest that I gasp and stumble backwards. 'You bastard!' he shouts. 'You fucking old lunatic! Get out! Go and die somewhere!'" (*Waiting for the Barbarians,* 123–24).

Jacques Lacan was one of the French thinkers criticized by Améry.[53] However, Lacan's analysis of Sade is helpful in this context. Lacan describes a "border" or "limit" (*limite*) that leads "to the point of apocalypse or of revelation of something called transgression."[54] According to Lacan, the transgression pursued in Sade is *structurally* limitless. The "limitless triumph" that for Améry characterizes Nazi torture in principle and thus structurally is (especially when taking into account Améry's own mention of the torturer's godlike expansion) structurally apocalyptic.

Again, George Bataille: "Transgression is not the negation of the interdiction, but goes beyond it and completes it [*La transgression n'est pas la négation de l'interdit, mais elle le dépasse et le complète*]." As a consequence, Bataille asserts that "organized transgression forms together with interdiction a whole [*un ensemble*] that defines social life."[55] While Bataille proposes this analysis in the context of his reflection on war and certain religious rituals, it is equally valid for National Socialism as the apotheosis of torture: organized, generalized torture.

Ariel Dorfman's play *Death and the Maiden* gives a precise account of the intensifying dynamics of transgression in the mind and actions of a torturer. The play stages Doctor Roberto Miranda's forced confession of his involvement in torture during a military dictatorship that could be Chile's. The reader or spectator never learns for sure whether Miranda was, indeed, Paulina Salas's torturer, but she asserts she recognizes enough of him, his voice, "the way he laughs, certain phrases he uses," to subject him to forms of torture in return, a forced confession

---

53 Améry, "Unmeisterliche Wanderjahre," *Werke*, 2:324; see also Améry, "Ein neuer Verrat der Intellektuellen" (1977), and Améry, "Neue Philosophie oder alter Nihilismus" (1978), *Werke*, 6:164, 240.

54 Jacques Lacan, *Le Séminaire Livre VII : L'Éthique de la psychanalyse 1959–1960*, ed. J.-A. Miller (Paris: Éditions du Seuil, 1986), 245; Lacan, *The Seminar of Jacques Lacan, Book VII : The Ethics of Psychoanalysis 1959–1960*, ed. J.-A. Miller, trans. Dennis Porter (New York: Norton, 1992), 207.

55 Bataille, *L'érotisme*, 66, 68; Bataille, *Eroticism*, 63, 65 (trans. modified).

among others.[56] Without engaging in the debate over whether Miranda is, in fact, Paulina Salas's torturer, his "confession" illuminates Bataille's theses. Miranda starts his "confession" with an attempt at an exculpating explanation: he was first called to monitor the torture with electricity, and he told himself that his participation "was a way of saving people's lives." But then,

> bit by bit, the virtue I was feeling turned into excitement — the mask of virtue fell off and it, the excitement, it hid, it hid, it hid from me what I was doing, the swamp of what — By the time Paulina Salas was brought in it was already too late. Too late. …too late. A kind of — brutalization took over my life, I began to really truly like what I was doing. It became a game. My curiosity was partly morbid, partly scientific. How much can this woman take? More than the other one? How's her sex? Does her sex dry up when you put the current through her? Can she have an orgasm under those circumstances? She is entirely in your power, you can carry out all your fantasies, you can do what you want with her.[57]

In the next sentence Miranda makes it clear that, to quote Bataille's sentence again, "transgression is not the negation of the interdiction, but goes beyond it and completes it": "She is entirely in your power, you can carry out all your fantasies, you can do what you want with her. […] Everything they have forbidden you since ever, whatever your mother ever urgently whispered you were never to do."[58]

---

56 Dorfman, *Death and the Maiden,* 23. Cathy Caruth has analyzed the not-ending "disappearance" of the torture victim, as exemplified in the "disappearance" of Paulina's words behind Roberto's voice, which mirrors the reader's inability to hear them. Moreover, "Paulina's experience of not being saved [by the doctor] is […] bound up with the very perpetuation of her life," thus a "betrayal into life." Cathy Caruth, "Disappearing History: Scenes of Trauma in the Theater of Human Rights," in *Literature in the Ashes of History* (Baltimore: Johns Hopkins University Press, 2013), 54–74.

57 Dorfman, *Death and the Maiden,* 59.

58 Ibid., 59–60. The reference to the mother is telling, since it insinuates that in the doctor's mind, it is the mother who is at the origin of the fantasies and

If one wants to exclude the possibility that the mother actually verbalized, in her whispering, the concrete possibilities of transgression and thus insinuated them, one is left with the option that what this sentence suggests is an original prohibition, a prohibition at the origin, akin to the one described by Jacques Lacan in his discussion of the ten commandments. For Lacan, the ten commandments, notwithstanding that they are violated every day, have an "indestructible character," because they are "the very laws of speech" (*les lois mêmes de la parole*), insofar as they spell out (*explicitent*) "that without which there is no speech" (*parole*), not discourse, but speech.[59] Lacan's reading of the ten commandments enacts a series of "disruptions." To quote Carol Jacobs from a different context: "disruptions" that are "not the failure of the ethical but rather the beginnings of a redefinition of it as responsibility [...] a nontyrannical ethical no longer irrevocably bound by a must."[60] In another context, Lacan described speech as "a symbolic gift [...] ripe with a secret pact."[61] Speech, *la parole*, is in this context the given word, in

their transgression. It would invite an analysis based on the Lacanian definition of "desire" and what Lacan calls "La chose," but this would go beyond the scope of this chapter. Bianka Ballina has shown how the intimate bond between Paulina Salas and her torturer marks her language through the use of informal Chilean Spanish, particularly the Chilean *voseo*, "which is formed by combining the pronoun 'tú' with a modified version of the conjugations used for the alternative second person pronoun 'vos.' While Paulina uses the 'tú' and the more formal pronoun 'usted' in her interactions with her husband Gerardo and Miranda respectively, the voseo appears during those instances in which Paulina takes on and performs the voice of her torturer. The use of the voseo implies considerable familiarity and intimacy with the addressee [...]. This intimacy is all the more striking in contrast to the palpable [...] distance that characterizes Paulina and Gerardo's marriage." Bianka Ballina, "Violent Intimacy and Gendered Betrayal: Sexualized Torture and State Power in *La muerte y la doncella*," 2016, unpublished manuscript.

59 Lacan, *L'Éthique de la psychanalyse*, 205, 84; Lacan, *The Ethics of Psychoanalysis*, 174, 68–69; English trans. slightly modified.

60 Carol Jacobs, *Skirting the Ethical* (Stanford: Stanford University Press, 2008), xvi.

61 Lacan, *Écrits* (Paris: Éditions du Seuil, 1966), 291; Lacan, *Écrits: A Selection*, trans. Bruce Fink (New York: Norton, 2002), 77.

the sense of whenever I address myself to you, whenever I speak to you, I already, even prior to any spoken word, give my word, that "I give you my word." This promise, this promise of keeping a promise, as Derrida has shown so eloquently, is the condition of possibility of any contract, any community, any society. It is the surplus beyond any contract that makes every contract possible.[62] It is thus the most delicate fabric of society.

In this perspective, the torturer's perversion of language confirms and underscores the apocalyptic totality of annihilation: the laws without which there is no speech are obliterated in torture.

Torture, to quote another text by Dorfman, "corrupts the whole social fabric."[63] As Jane Kramer, Alfred McCoy, Darius Rejali, and others have noted (including some of the interrogators interviewed for Rory Kennedy's film *Ghosts of Abu Ghraib*), whenever torture is used, it is impossible to control its ever-widening reach or the ever-intensifying torture methods used. Furthermore, as Britta Jenkins has observed in her work with trauma survivors, "the ramifications of torture are like the ever-widening circles made by tossing a stone into water."[64]

Torture is the "essence" of National Socialism. Améry specifies while using Aristotelian concepts that torture is not just an "accidental quality" (*Akzidens*) — an unnecessary, secondary trait of National Socialism — but its "essence" (*Essenz*), its core. Other regimes — many other regimes — torture. For Améry, the uniqueness of National Socialism is the apotheosis of torture as the *principle* of a state. Torture as the "essence" of National Socialism is the totalization of the transgression onto the other's physical and mental boundaries. The floodgates of transgression

---

62 For example, Jacques Derrida, "Nombre de oui," in *Psyché: Inventions de l'autre* (Paris: Galilée, 1987), 646–48.

63 Ariel Dorfman, "Foreword: The Tyranny of Terror," in *Torture: A Collection,* ed. Sanford Levinson (Oxford: Oxford University Press, 2004), 9.

64 Britta Jenkins, "There, Where Words Fail, Tears Are the Bridge," in *At the Side of Torture Survivors,* eds. S. Graessner, N. Gurris, and C. Pross, trans. J.M. Riemer (Baltimore: Johns Hopkins University Press, 2001), 143.

were opened, in plain sight, deliberately, systematically, and as a principle.

This does not mean that the effects of torture are less severe on victims when used by governments that have not systematized, generalized, the rule of torture. Améry's famous sentence is categorical: "Whoever has succumbed to torture can no longer feel at home in the world. The infamy of annihilation cannot be erased." As such, even if used on an individual, and not generalized, basis, torture as transgression is *structurally* limitless, and structurally it pursues not destruction, but annihilation.[65]

This may be one of the reasons that, at least since the Geneva Conventions, the prohibition against torture is stronger than the prohibition against killing; while it is possible to legally kill, it is never possible to legally torture — except in a society in which, to quote Améry once again, the social world has been "totally turned inside out" (*totalen Umstülpung der Sozialwelt*) (77/35, trans. modified).[66]

---

65 Améry's categorical assertion may be problematic insofar as it is itself a totalization, a totalization that made it impossible for him to engage, for example, with Hannah Arendt (62/25). This totalization may be read as a testimony to the all-encompassing destructivity Améry experienced in flesh and spirit, and as a symptom of a repetition compulsion. In his book *The Belated Witness*, Michael Levine proposes a highly original reinterpretation of "repetition" and "compulsion," revealing a new, rich potential of these concepts that can be made productive for Améry. Levine seeks "to view repetition as a movement that is never one with itself, as a compulsion that is not only internally divided but doubly driven, impelled by *competing impulses* at work within it. Indeed, what comes together and insists in the mode of repetition [...] are both a drive to return obsessively to the same place and a driving, desperate search for some place different — for an uncanny difference that might emerge in the place of the same" (*The Belated Witness: Literature, Testimony, and the Question of Holocaust Survival* [Stanford: Stanford University Press, 2006], 12). In this context, one may add that Améry's insistence on "astonishment" (see note 27, above) may indicate moments where the overwhelming totality of the trauma is broken. I thank Rainer Nägele, Rüdiger Campe, Dori Laub, and Michael Levine for the insights they shared.

66 "Torture is universally condemned, and whatever its actual practice, no country publicly supports torture or opposes its eradication. The prohibition against torture is well-established under customary international law as *jus cogens*; that is, it has the highest standing in customary law and is so

---

fundamental as to supersede all other treaties and customary laws (except laws that are also *jus cogens*). Criminal acts that are *jus cogens* are subject to universal jurisdiction, meaning that any state can exercise its jurisdiction, regardless of where the crime took place, the nationality of the perpetrator or the nationality of the victim" (Human Rights Watch News, "The Legal Prohibition Against Torture," June 1, 2004.)

CHAPTER 2

Living-with-Torture-Together[1]

In the introduction to his massive *Torture and Democracy,* Darius Rejali relates the story of Mordehy Petcho, a member of the Jewish guerrilla group Irgun, who, in 1939, lay in a cell after being tortured by the British CID.

> [Petcho] describes how an old Arab brought food. As he could not eat, the Arab fed him, and when Petcho felt sharp pains, the old man asked to lift the blanket. Then he saw the bruises and "cursed the English as the worst of savages." One can scarcely imagine a stranger scene in which a Palestinian Arab and an Irgun supporter bind themselves in common recognition of each other's humanity. Sixty years later, Palestinians had a hard time appreciating the suffering Israeli positional torture effected on their own relatives, and the Israelis denied torture had happened at all, since it left no marks. It took hard work for people to learn how to read the bodies that were subjected to *shabeh* technique, to question state power and accord respect to its victims.[2]

This account of the interaction of a member of a militant Zionist group and an Arab man in what was then the British Mandate of Palestine exemplifies in a striking way what Derrida calls "a

---

1 Originally published in *Living Together: Jacques Derrida's Communities of Violence and Peace,* ed. Elisabeth Weber (New York: Fordham University Press, 2013).
2 Rejali, *Torture and Democracy,* 30.

fundamental mode [...] of 'living together'": compassion.[3] More precisely, it offers a glimpse into the moving power of compassion (in the sense of "moving to action") that is not limited to members of a defined "community," of a constituted "ensemble."[4]

As Derrida emphasizes in his "lesson," "Avowing — The Impossible: 'Returns,' Repentance, and Reconciliation,"

> The adverb, in the expression "living together" [*vivre ensemble*], appears to find its sense and dignity only there where it exceeds, dislocates, contests the authority of the noun "ensemble," to wit, the closure of an ensemble, be it the whole of something "living" [*d'un "vivant"*], of a system, a totality, a cohesiveness without fault and identical with itself, of an indivisible element containing itself in its immanence and simply larger, like the whole [*tout*], than its parts. The authority of the whole [*ensemble*] will always be the first threat for all "living together." And inversely, all "living together"

---

3   Derrida, "Avowing — The Impossible," 30. Henceforth, A. Further references will be made parenthetically in the text. Irgun (also known as "Etzel") was formed in 1931 and existed until the foundation of the State of Israel in 1948, when it was absorbed into the Israeli military. The group's goal was to defend the right of every Jew to enter Palestine and to carry out armed retaliation against Arabs who attacked Jews. Several authors described the militant group as a "terrorist" organization, for example, in 1946 the *New York Times* reporter Julian Louis Meltzer ("Zionists Condemn Palestine Terror," *New York Times*, December 24, 1946, 1). The Israeli historian Tom Segev describes Irgun as an "anti-British terrorist group" in *The Seventh Million: The Israelis and the Holocaust,* trans. Haim Watzman (New York: Hill and Wang, 1993), 33. Segev quotes the German writer Arnold Zweig, who had fled the Nazis and emigrated to Palestine, and wrote to Sigmund Freud a day after Irgun had detonated a bomb in a busy Arab marketplace in Jerusalem: "A terrible vengeance will descend upon us all. [...] The Jews, who came to this country against the will of the Arab majority and who since 1919 have been incapable of winning the goodwill of the Arabs, had only one thing in their favor: their moral position, their passive endurance. Their aggression as immigrants and the aggression of the Arab terrorists cancelled each other out. But if they now throw bombs, I see a dark future ahead for us all" (39).

4   This idea is at the heart of Julie Carlson's work. See, for example, her *England's First Family of Writers: Mary Wollstonecraft, William Godwin, Mary Shelley* (Baltimore: Johns Hopkins University Press, 2007).

will be the first protestation or contestation, the first testimony against the whole [*ensemble*]. (A, 21)[5]

Rejali's description of the scene between the Jewish guerrilla fighter and the Arab man offers a glimpse into a mode of "vivre ensemble," "living together," which, indeed, offers a "protestation or contestation [...] against the whole," a mode of "living together" in which the "together" is one not between allies, but between enemies sworn to the other's death. Moreover, this "together" makes "living," in the most concrete and basic sense, possible for one of them.

Rejali introduces his account by stating that "communities treat victims that have marks of violence upon their bodies entirely differently from those who have no marks to show." The visibility of wounds thus kindles this "fundamental mode [...] of 'living together'" that is compassion. The absence of such visibility, caused by the use of what Rejali has termed "stealth torture," is the result of a deliberate calculation to avoid the radar and publicity of human rights monitors, as well as compassion's power to cause public outcry and activism, by stifling this "fundamental mode" of "living 'together'" with the torture victim, *both* in the community of the perpetrator *and* in the torture victim's own community.[6] Some stealth methods have been scientifically developed or refined at prestigious North American

---

5   See also "Avowing," 37–38: "Those whom I call, in this undeniable but unjustifiable hierarchy, *my own*, are not those who belong to me; it is the ensemble of those with whom, precisely, it is *given to me,* prior to any choice, to 'live together,' in all the dimensions of what one calls so easily a community: my family, my congeners, countrymen, coreligionists, my neighbors [*mes voisins*], my close ones, those who speak my language."

6   As Darius Rejali shows, besides applying the old, and still-prevailing techniques of inflicting severe physical pain (beating, kicking, slamming detainees against walls, etc.), modern democracies have developed so-called clean or stealth techniques, that make use of electricity, water, temperature control, noise, music, drugs, stress positions, and, as was evident in Abu Ghraib, sexual humiliation — all techniques that leave no visible scars (*Torture and Democracy,* passim).

universities.[7] They are often belittled as "torture lite" but are as brutal as they are, in the words of the CIA Inspector General's Torture Report, "precise, quiet and almost clinical."[8]

This chapter proposes to read Derrida's reflections about "living 'together'" in the context of the use of torture by the most powerful country in the world.[9] Its title does not refer to what it might mean to live "with" torture after having suffered it. It would not dare to. Rather, it refers to the fact that since the Bush administration's official espousal of torture (under the euphemism of "enhanced interrogation") in the summer of 2002, every person living in the United States has been living knowingly or unwittingly with the legacy of this fateful policy decision.[10] "In any case [*de toute façon*]," Derrida writes in his "lesson," "in any fashion [*de toutes les façons*], 'live together' one must, and one must do so well, one might as well do so [*et il le faut bien*]. [...] one has no choice" (A, 23).

Is torture, however, not the limit of the "we must live together"? If "forgiveness, if there is such, must forgive the unforgivable," must then "living together," if there is such, live the unlivable (A, 19)? Would Derrida's thinking lead us to this conclusion?

1.

Right from the start of Derrida's text, the question of how to live together "makes us tremble":

---

7 McCoy, *A Question of Torture*, 32–51.

8 This report was written in 2004. The release of 525 unclassified pages (less than 8% of the report) was delayed three times before being finally obtained on August 24, 2009; Greg Miller, "CIA's Black Sites, Illuminated," *Los Angeles Times,* August 31, 2009, 1. See also Shayana Kadidal, "The CIA Inspector General's Torture Report: First Reactions from CCR Senior Managing Attorney Shayana Kadidal."

9 For Derrida's work on torture perpetrated in South America, see Chapter 5. He mentions torture also in the context of other forms of violence, for example, Jacques Derrida, "Faith and Knowledge," in *Acts of Religion,* ed. Gil Anidjar (New York: Routledge, 2002), 88–89.

10 See McCoy, *A Question of Torture,* 121–23.

Wisdom teaches us: Given that living is always "living together," and that it must be so, let us only learn "how to live
together," let us determine rules, norms, maxims, precepts,
even an ethical, juridical, and political jurisprudence. But
despair protests and replies: "But *how*? How to live together?
I will not, you will not, he/she will not, we will not, you will
not, they will not, achieve it, ever" — and the variation of
these persons speaks also a deeper paradox as to the same
concern: Who addresses whom in asking "how to live together?" or still: Does not "living together" take place from
the instant that the concern over this question makes us
tremble in our solitude and avow, yes, declare our despair
and share it? (A, 19–20)

In the present context, the "despair" that must first be declared
and shared, avowed, is over what appears to be a bolstered public acceptability of torture, and, especially in the aftermath of the
attacks of September 11, 2001, the despair over a massive campaign to relegitimize torture undertaken by American officials
up to the highest levels. In the foreword to a collection titled
Torture, published in 2004, Ariel Dorfman observes that

we live in a world where torture is practiced on a regular
basis in more countries than ever — 132 at the latest count,
but who knows if there are not more — and where torture is
being contemplated as inevitable and even beneficial in nations that call themselves democratic and respectful of the
rights of their citizens. [...] I live in a country — the United
States — where a leading civil rights lawyer has suggested
that the courts might issue "torture warrants" as a way of
fighting terrorism. We live in times where people, in this land
and in so many other supposedly "civilized" nations, are so
filled with primal fear that they look on with apparent indifference at the possibility of extreme maltreatment of their

presumable enemies — indifference, indeed, at the evidence and televised images of this sort of maltreatment.[11]

The increased presence of the issue of torture in the public debate in the United States after the revelations of Abu Ghraib should not blind us, however, to the fact that US endorsement of torture did not start with the infamous "torture memos" or the signing into law of the Military Commissions Act in October 2006.[12] As Alfred McCoy has shown, when in December 1984, "after years of global grass-roots agitation," the UN General Assembly adopted the Convention Against Torture, it took the United States ten years to ratify it. McCoy sees the reason for this long delay in the "CIA's clandestine maneuvering," through the State and Justice Departments, to protect the "torture paradigm" it had developed over at least three decades from international sanction. To this effect, the US administration proposed "a record nineteen reservations that stalled the convention's ratification in the Senate." Among those, the Reagan administration "focused, above all, on the issue of psychological torture." The result was a redefinition of "mental harm" and the exclusion, from the US ratification, of "sensory deprivation (hooding), self-inflicted pain (stress positions), and disorientation (isolation and sleep denial) — the very techniques the CIA had refined at

11 Ariel Dorfman, "Foreword," 5. In his criticism of "torture warrants," Dorfman alludes to Alan Dershowitz, whose essay "Tortured Reasoning" is also included in Levinson's collection; see, in particular, 257. For another critique of "torture warrants," see McCoy, *A Question of Torture,* 111. During his campaign to win the Republican nomination, the new President of the United States vowed not only to leave the Guantánamo Prison Camp open, but to expand its operations and to bring back techniques such as waterboarding, because "only a stupid person would say it doesn't work." "If it doesn't work," the then-candidate said, "they deserve it anyway, for what they're doing." His "call for waterboarding and more extreme measures is always met with warm applause and cheers at his rallies" (Jenna Johnson, "Trump Says 'Torture Works,' Backs Waterboarding and 'Much Worse,'" *Washington Post,* Feb. 17, 2016). In his first nationally televised interview as president, Trump claimed again that torture "absolutely works" (Interview with David Muir, *ABC News,* Jan. 25, 2017).

12 See McCoy, *A Question of Torture,* 121–23.

such great cost over several decades. [...] Through this process, the United States, in effect, accepted just half the UN Convention Against Torture — affirming only the ban on physical methods. This decision, unnoticed when Congress finally ratified the convention in 1994, would effectively exempt the CIA's interrogation methods from international law."[13]

The publication, in April 2004, of the infamous Abu Ghraib photos, following Major General Antonio Taguba's 2004 report, and the passing into law of the Military Commissions Act in October 2006, which was tantamount to the official adoption of torture (without mention, of course, of the word "torture") by the US government, can be understood as two answers to the question of "living 'together,'" two answers that deny the possibility of any "together." To the question how one can live with the presumed "enemy," when this enemy is suspected of plotting the deaths of thousands of people and massive destruction, these answers reply that one cannot, ever, live together. These two answers also betray a fundamental refusal to be answerable to the question how those targeted as enemies might answer the question of "living together," considering that they have had to "live together" with *their* enemy ever since he colonized, bombed, exploited them. Those two answers' radical refusal and denial notwithstanding, even if "the enemy" is locked away in faraway offshore detention camps such as Guantánamo, and in overseas prisons such as Abu Ghraib and Bagram, in order to deny him, or rather the many men and women lumped together in this demagogic singular, to be heard in American courts, "'live together,' one must," as Derrida emphasizes.[14] Moreover,

one must well "live together" [*il faut bien "vivre ensemble"*]. In any case [*de toute façon*], in any fashion [*de toutes les façons*],

---

13 McCoy, *A Question of Torture*, 100–101.
14 The use of the singular ("the enemy") is an absurdity that seeks to establish an identifiable "whole" ("ensemble") where there is none. The use of the singular was one of the hallmarks of the Bush administration's statements about detainees in Guantánamo and other American-run prisons overseas. On the Guantánamo Bay prison camp, see Chapters 3 and 4.

"live together" one must, and one must do so well, one might as well do so [*et il le faut bien*]. [...] [O]ne has no choice. It is, indeed, always a matter of a necessity, and therefore of a law: One cannot not "live together" even if one does not know how or with whom, with God, with gods, men, animals, with one's own, with one's close ones, neighbors, family, or friends, with one's fellow citizens or countrymen, but also with the most distant strangers, with one's enemies, with oneself, with one's contemporaries, with those who are no longer so or will never be so, so many names that I draw from daily language and of which I do not yet presume that we know what they designate. (A, 23–24)

Living together "one must," and, as Derrida underlines, one must even "live together" with the dead. The "nightmare" of Eric Fair, a former interrogator in Iraq, who is haunted frequently during his sleep by the memory of the man he tortured, starkly illustrates this, and his plea to the American public demonstrates that he is not the only one living with the dead: "The scars of guilt are no longer mine alone. They are carried now by this entire nation, its people, its institutions, and its leaders. The failure of men like me to prevent these egregious acts is now eclipsed by the failure of the nation to bring 'enhanced interrogations' to an immediate end," and those responsible to trial.[15] Fair's testimony confirms, to quote Derrida's text again, that "'living together,' with the dead, is not an accident, a miracle, or an extraordinary story [*histoire*]. It is rather an essential possibility of existence. It reminds us that in 'living together' the idea of life is neither simple nor dominant even if it remains irreducible" (A, 20). Although films such as Rory Kennedy's *Ghosts of Abu Ghraib* and Alex Gibney's *Taxi to the Dark Side* suggest that shame and guilt haunt some of the torturers, the impunity of those who devised and ordered the torture at the highest level of

---

15 Eric Fair, "An Iraq Interrogator's Nightmare," *Washington Post,* Feb. 9, 2007; Fair, in "No More: No Torture, No Exceptions," *Washington Monthly,* Jan.–March 2008.

government evince that we seem to have learned all too easily to live with torture and torturers.

While politicians, pundits, and scholars discuss in editorials, in academia, and at the highest levels of the US administration whether torture under the Bush administration should be prosecuted, and whether the use of torture may be justified in some cases, the prohibition of torture has a distinctive status in the pantheon of international rights: It is absolute.[16] It cannot be derogated under any circumstances, as the 1984 UN *Convention on Torture and Other Cruel, Inhuman or Degrading Treatment or Punishment* states in unequivocal terms: "No exceptional circumstances whatsoever, whether a state of war or a threat of war, internal political instability or any other public emergency, may be invoked as a justification of torture."[17] The use of torture thus flagrantly violates international law. For Derrida, international law (whose importance he underlines repeatedly and consistently) or any other "law" is not sufficient to "live together well," not only because they often are not respected or because "radical changes in international law are necessary."[18] Rather, the incommensurability of any "law" with "justice" pits the generality of the rule against the irreplaceable singularity of the event. When Derrida calls compassion a "fundamental mode of living together," he clearly does not consider it a derivative. While compassion may be kindled most easily by the witnessing of the other's suffering (as in the scene of recognition between the old Arab man and Mordehy Petcho), it is not exhaustible in a reaction. Rather, for Derrida, who follows Emmanuel Levinas here, it suspends the economy of "being," in Levinas's terms, the economy of the "third," to plunge the witness into the exorbitant call of the other, the "face to face" in which it is impossible not to respond. Again, in Levinas's concepts, compassion could be

---

16 The by-now famous "ticking time-bomb" scenario has been discredited as entirely fictitious. See, for example, McCoy, *A Question of Torture*, 190–95.

17 UN *Convention on Torture and Other Cruel, Inhuman or Degrading Treatment or Punishment*, Article 2.

18 See Derrida, "Autoimmunity," 106; see also 114.

described as an-archic living-with, where I have been called before being able to say "I."

Torture destroys this most fundamental "with" or "together" between the perpetrator and the victim.[19] "Clean," "democratic torture" is designed to undermine the future of any "together" as well. In the words of Veena Das, whom Rejali quotes, "denial of the other's pain is not about the failings of intellect, but the failings of spirit. In the register of the imaginary, the pain of the other not only asks for a home in language, but also seeks a home in the body."[20] Stealth torture "denies precisely this home in the body, tangling the victims and their communities in doubts, uncertainties, and illusions."[21] Rejali distinguishes between "different kinds of inexpressibility that follow from torture" and focuses on the "inexpressibility that matters politically," which is "not the gap between the brain and the tongue, but between victims and their communities, a gap that is cynically calculated, a gap that shelters a state's legitimacy."

What does it take then, for a community to respond, for "citizens [to] learn to hear torture victims and read their bodies"? According to Rejali,

What enables us to reconstitute our ability to speak with each other about pain is an activity different from capturing pain in works of art, stories, statues, and other objects of worldly

---

19   I need to leave aside the huge question of the torturer's compassion, or rather the necessity to make himself or herself impervious to it. Françoise Sironi's work is here of great importance, for example her *Bourreaux et victimes: Psychologie de la torture* (Paris: Odile Jacob, 1999). "L'étude de la torture en tant que système m'a permis de mettre en évidence le fait suivant: on ne naît pas tortionnaire, on le devient; soit par une violente expérience de déculturation, soit par une initiation spécifique qui utilise des techniques traumatiques [The study of torture as a system has allowed me to clearly reveal the following fact: one isn't born a torturer, one becomes one, either through a violent experience of de-culturation, or through a specific initiation that uses traumatizing techniques]" (129).

20   Veena Das, "Language and Body," quoted in Rejali, *Torture and Democracy*, 31.

21   Rejali, *Torture and Democracy*, 31.

making. What it takes is something fundamentally more powerful and fragile, the ability to create a common political space. When the old Arab reached across that prison cell, lifted the blanket, and read Petcho's body, for a brief moment he and Petcho occupied such a space. Such reading has become much harder in modern times, and, consequently, the spaces in which we can appear before each other in our pain have become more scarce.[22]

The "fragile" together of a "common political space" is created in Rejali's account through the surge of compassion. Using Derrida's language one could say that the occurrence of compassion bridges the aporia between the singular and the general, between the radical singularity of pain and the potential generality of a common political space. Stealth torture is designed to quell the surge of compassion in the victim's and the perpetrator's communities where it is most easily stirred: in the possibility of witnessing the other's pain, not just intellectually, but in the flesh. Compassion, far from being reducible to an emotional response, is critical in serving as powerful motivation for the creation of a "common political space," however fragile it may be, of protest, opposition, and activism. The purpose of stealth torture inflicted by democracies is to thwart this critical activism by undermining this incalculable source.

2.

The "fundamental mode" of compassion is a nodal point in Derrida's "lesson," because just as in Rejali's example, it has the capacity of bridging aporetic incompatibilities. Compassion is the tangible affect or emotion, at least in a young boy's experience, that taught him to "name justice and what in justice at once exceeds and demands law." In other words, it is in compassion where the child first encounters what the philosopher will later gauge as aporetic impossibilities of "living 'together.'"

---

22 Ibid.

After depicting the hardship he suffered as a "little black and very Arab Jew" in his native Algeria, for his audience consisting mostly of "intellectuals said to be French-speaking Jews," Derrida concludes:

> If I let a Jewish child speak, it is neither to move you cheaply, nor to shelter provocations behind an alibi. Rather it is to convince you that my questions, my reticences, my impatiences, my indignation sometimes (for example, when faced with the politics of almost all the Israeli governments and the forces that support them, from within and from without) are not inspired by hostility or by the indifference of distance. On the contrary, shared with so many Israelis who are exposed and concerned otherwise than I am, and together with so many Jews in the world, this innocent concern for compassion (a fundamental mode, in my view, of "living together"), of this compassion of justice and equity (*rahamim,* perhaps), I will claim it, if not as the essence of Judaism, at least as what remains in me inseparable from the suffering and disarmed memory of the Jewish child, there where he has learned to name justice and what in justice at once exceeds and demands law [*le droit*]. Everything comes to me, no doubt, from this source, in what I am about to say, under the title "avowing — the impossible" (A, 22).[23]

"Compassion [...] (*rahamim*, perhaps)" is the "source," then, for thinking the adverbial "*ensemble*/together" that fractures the substantive "*ensemble*/whole" and thereby makes "living together" possible. As always in Derrida's texts, the parenthesis is not to be taken lightly. Derrida has written extensively on the modality of the "perhaps," which does not, as he specifies, belong "to a regime of opinion," nor does it signify "haziness and

---

23 Derrida gave the address in 1998 at the occasion of an annual conference held in Paris, the Colloque des intellectuels juifs de langue française. See "Avowing," 20. The self-description as a "little black and very Arab Jew" is found in Geoffrey Bennington and Jacques Derrida, *Jacques Derrida,* trans. Geoffrey Bennington (Chicago: University of Chicago Press, 1993), 58.

mobility, the confusion preceding knowledge or renouncing all truth." If the "perhaps" is "undecidable and without truth in its own moment (but it is, as a matter of fact, difficult to assign a proper moment to it), this is in order that it might be a condition of decision, interruption, revolution, responsibility and truth."²⁴ In Derrida's *Politics of Friendship,* "perhaps" indicates the interruption of a politics and a justice reduced to rationality, calculability, predictability. "Perhaps" introduces the chance of an event that for once deserves its name: a radical arrival, which Derrida, in the creation of the neologism "arrivance," invites to enter into resonance with another term of invention of the future: *aimance* ("lovence").²⁵ The difficulty to think such an event becomes apparent in the words themselves. The French word for "perhaps," *peut-être,* is, as Derrida points out, "perhaps, too rich in its two verbs (the *pouvoir* [literally: to have the power to do…] and the *être* [to be])," whereas the English *perhaps* and the German *vielleicht* still resonate with the chance of an unforeseeable happening.²⁶

The first word of the parenthesis, *rachamim,* is no less decisive. It is the Hebrew word for "compassion," deriving from רחם, *rechem,* womb. In the Bible, God is recognized as the "Compassionate" (רחמן); one of the Jewish memorial prayers invokes the Father of Compassion (אב הרחמים).²⁷ The plural of *rechem, rachamim* means both "entrails" and "compassion," the entrails as the seat of compassion. *Rachamim* inspired Emmanuel Levinas's description of the "subject" as immemorially "persecuted," as "maternity, gestation of the other in the same" and as

24 Jacques Derrida, *Politiques de l'amitié* (Paris: Galilée, 1994), 63; *Politics of Friendship,* trans. G. Collins (London: Verso, 1997), 43. The "Perhaps" was first introduced into philosophy as an unheard-of dimension by Nietzsche, to whom *Politics of Friendship* dedicates a long section, especially chapters 2 and 3.

25 Derrida, *Politics of Friendship,* 7 [23].

26 Ibid., 39 [59], trans. modified. "Le pouvoir et l'être": Derrida adds the definite article to both verbs, because they can serve, in French, as substantives as well, in which case they are translated as "power" and "being."

27 On these words in Hebrew and their relatives in Arabic, see Chapter 4.

"the groaning of the wounded entrails."[28] The metaphor of the "wounded entrails" that stands for maternity in Levinas's later work, however, does not necessarily give preference to one's "own," one's own children in particular. According to Levinas, the subject's infinite responsibility is *first* an entirely involuntary being-held-hostage by the compassion toward the orphan and the stranger. In Levinas's thinking, this is a "fundamental mode" of the very constitution of the subject, even if, in the concrete "living together," counting and calculability, that is, the imposition of an "economy" on such infinite compassion becomes unavoidable. However, as Levinas's own metaphor of "maternity" and the origin of *rachamim* in *rechem* suggest, *rachamim* points to a difficulty that Levinas does not directly address, and that Derrida's essay confronts by describing it as the site of one of the "aporias" of "living 'together.'"

"I will never be able to renounce and to say no to a preference for 'my own' [*les 'miens'*], nor, inversely, to justify it, to have it approved as the law of a universal justice." My "preference for all the forms of the proximate, of this proximity that, at the limit, in situations of mortal danger, would carry me to the rescue of my children rather than of those of another, rather than to the rescue of all these others who are not only my others, to the rescue of a man rather than an animal, and even of my cat rather than a cat unknown to me and dying in Asia," is as undeniable as it is unjustifiable. Derrida continues: "In the eyes of justice or of universal equality, how to justify a preference for one's own children, a preference for one's own, parents and friends, even a preference among one's own, as far as death and ultimate sacrifice, the privilege of Isaac, for example, rather than Ishmael? My own do not belong to me, nor does my 'home [*chez moi*]'" (A, 37–38).

In Derrida's text, "*rachamim*, perhaps" is the "source" of his meditation on "living together," because, as mentioned above, it is here that the aporias of "justice," and thus the aporias of

---

28 Emmanuel Levinas, *Otherwise than Being, or Beyond Essence,* trans. Alphonso Lingis (Pittsburgh: Dusquesne University Press, 1998), 75.

"living 'together,'" are acutely lived, viscerally and in the flesh. By the same token it is here that the binaries defining a thinking that is de facto still all too metaphysical ("nature"/"culture," "human"/"animal," "friend"/"enemy," etc.) are vividly questioned. Derrida forcefully states that there will not be any "living together" if those binaries are left standing.

> One will never think the "living together" and the "living" of the "living together" and the "how together" unless one transports oneself *beyond everything* that is founded on this opposition of nature and culture. That is to say, beyond everything, more or less everything. This excess with regard to the laws of nature, as well as to the laws of culture, is always an excess with regard to the whole [*ensemble*], and I do not take the difficulty lightly. It is almost unthinkable, very close to impossible, precisely. (A, 27)

One of the "impossibles" that through *rachamim* might take place, for example, is a profound rethinking of "what one names stupidly and confusedly the animal" (A, 38). The aporia of the preference for the "proximate" would logically need to lead to a rethinking of the "cardinal criteria of the anthropological difference," from Aristotle to Heidegger (and certainly beyond) that consolidate the "abyss" (in Heidegger's formulation) between the human being and the animal.[29] Derrida does not deny this "abyss," but asserts that it needs to be fundamentally, that is, radically rethought. Its destructive potential is conjured when human beings are identified with animals in order to justify their exploitation, persecution, torture, and murder. Well-known historical examples would include the justification of slavery in the United States before the Civil War and the ideology of

---

29 See Elisabeth de Fontenay, *Le Silence des Bêtes: La philosophie à l'épreuve de l'animalité* (Paris: Fayard, 1998), 703. These "cardinal criteria" mutually imply each other: "world, hand, death, vertical posture, logos, glance, questioning" (703). See also Jacques Derrida, *The Animal That Therefore I Am,* ed. Marie-Louise Mallet, trans. David Wills (New York: Fordham University Press, 2008), 30–31.

National Socialism, but the practices of American military personnel and CIA operatives who dehumanized their victims in prisons such as Abu Ghraib, Bagram, and Guantánamo must also be listed. In spite of the many and deep differences between the two huge issues of human torture and animal mistreatment (that according to Derrida has known an unprecedented acceleration over, roughly, the last two hundred years[30]), they overlap on at least three points that are constitutive of both: the "indubitable" knowledge that the victims suffer, an undeniability that "*precedes* any other question"; the doubtless possibility "within us," of a "surge of compassion, even if it is then misunderstood, repressed, or denied"; and an ongoing "war" that is "waged over the matter of pity."[31] In his great lesson on animals, which focused on "the immense question of pathos and the pathological, [...] of suffering, pity, and compassion; and the place that has to be accorded to the interpretation of this compassion, to the sharing of this suffering among the living, to the law, ethics, and politics that must be brought to bear upon this experience of compassion," Derrida writes that this "war" is "passing through a critical phase. We are passing through that phase, and it passes through us. To think this war we find ourselves waging is not only a duty, a responsibility, an obligation, it is also a necessity, a constraint that, like it nor not, directly or indirectly, no one can escape."[32]

Without conflating the two enormous issues, then, "*rachamim,* perhaps" is the nodal point from which Derrida's appeal regarding the necessity and urgency to rethink the suffering of animals can be transposed verbatim on the issue of torture.

---

30 Derrida, *The Animal That Therefore I Am,* 24.

31 Ibid., 28–29, trans. slightly altered.

32 Ibid., 26, 29. On the question of compassion, see also Frans de Waal's book *The Age of Empathy.* I am indebted to Aaron Gross for sharing his work on animals and animal rights with me. See Aaron Gross, *The Question of the Animal and Religion: Theoretical Stakes, Practical Implications* (New York: Columbia University Press, 2015); Aaron Gross and Anne Vallely (eds.), *Animals and the Human Imagination: A Companion to Animal Studies* (New York: Columbia University Press, 2012).

3.

The rupture of an established "whole" or "totality" in *rachamim,* in the compassion for the other, does not concern only a collective. It concerns oneself, one's "self" or "one"'s self as well: "The alterity of past and future, the irreducible experience of memory and of the promise, of mourning and of hope, all suppose some *rupture,* the interruption of this identity or of this totality, this accomplishment of a presence to self — a fracturing openness in what one calls *un ensemble* [whole, gathering, ensemble], with the noun *ensemble,* which I will distinguish here from the adverb *ensemble* in the expression '*vivre ensemble*'" (A, 21). For Derrida, there will be no "living together" without the recognition and acknowledgment of "this division, this tearing, this rift, this dissociation from oneself, this difficulty of living together with oneself." He continues, "[t]he first step of a 'living together' will always remain rebellious to totalization," including the "totalization" of one's "own" "self" (A, 35). This "fracturing openness," this "dissociation from oneself" implies that one is a "stranger" to oneself, in a "strangeness" inseparable from an "inviolable separation" between "oneself" and others. For Derrida, "any 'living together' supposes and guards, as its very condition, the possibility of this singular, secret, inviolable separation, from which alone a stranger accords himself to a stranger, in hospitality. To recognize that one lives together, well then, only with and as a stranger, a stranger 'at home [*chez soi*],' in all the figures of the 'at home'" is the "very condition" of a living together in "the justice of a law above laws" (A, 28).

Torture is the *achieved* destruction of compassion, the moving and groaning of the "entrails" that, to quote Levinas, have always already, immemorially contested the sovereign assurance of "self-identity." In a perverse twist, torture also assaults this immemorial "fracturing openness" or "strangeness" to oneself (that *is* the "self") by forcing the victim to betray what could be called *rachamim,* compassion, for oneself. This is where Derrida's argument resonates with one of the most powerful voices against torture of the early Enlightenment, Christian Thomasius, who identifies such self-betrayal as *constitutive* of torture.[33]

In 1705, almost sixty years before Cesare Beccaria's famous *Crimes and Punishments,* Thomasius published a short treatise in Latin, *On the Torture That Needs to Be Banned from Christian Courts.*[34] Of course, Thomasius's treatise is separated from today's torture practice by what Michel Foucault has described as the redistribution of "the entire economy of punishment" in the eighteenth and nineteenth centuries, and the resulting disappearance, as Foucault puts it, of "the body as the major target of penal repression," otherwise described as the "humanization" of penal justice, an expression Foucault lists as an example of the proliferation of "inflated rhetoric."[35] What Foucault describes as the "disappearance of torture as a public spectacle" has, on the one hand, been completed with the invention of the so-called "no touch" or stealth torture by democratic societies, but, on the other hand, it has also been thoroughly refuted with the publication of the infamous photos of Abu Ghraib, and the increasing

33 As Ernst Bloch notes, Thomasius, a scholar of natural law and "anti-wig in epitome," had "caused a sensation [*machte Furore*]," when he dared, in 1687, to announce at the University of Leipzig a lecture in German, rather than Latin. His fearless and methodical book against the prosecution of witches caused the King of Prussia, Friedrich Wilhelm I, to make the prosecution of witches illegal in 1714. Cf. Ernst Bloch, *Christian Thomasius, ein deutscher Gelehrter ohne Misere* (Frankfurt: Suhrkamp, 1967 [1953]), 8, 13. Influenced by Thomasius, the Elector Friedrich I insisted in 1721 that "torture could only be applied after the monarch had consented to each particular case. [...] In 1754, all torture was abolished in Prussia, the earliest date of complete abolition in European history" (Edward Peters, *Torture* [New York: Basil Blackwell, 1985], 90). See also 76 for Peters's brief mention of Thomasius.

34 *De tortura ex foris Christianorum proscribenda, Über die Folter, die aus den Gerichten der Christen verbannt werden muss.* Even though Thomasius contributed significantly to the abolition of torture in Prussia, a German translation of his treatise was published only in 1960: Christian Thomasius, *Über die Folter: Untersuchungen zur Geschichte der Folter,* ed. and trans. Rolf Lieberwirth (Weimar: Hermann Böhlaus Nachfolger, 1960). See also Uwe Wesel, "Das Fiasko des Strafrechts," *Die Zeit* 49, Dec. 1, 2005.

35 Michel Foucault, *Discipline and Punish: The Birth of the Prison,* trans. Alan Sheridan (New York: Vintage, 1979), 7.

popularity of torture as manifested by TV series such as *24* and a number of recent movies.[36] Foucault writes that "physical pain, the pain of the body itself, is no longer the constituent element of the penalty. From being an art of unbearable sensations punishment has become an economy of suspended rights." This may accurately describe most of modernity's penal practices, but it is doubtful that it can be said of the practice of torture. On the contrary, torture could be described as the "art of unbearable sensations" that is *inseparable* from an "economy of suspended rights."[37]

At the outset of his text, Thomasius reiterates Cicero's condemnation: The "goal" of the *quæstio,* the "question," or, as the German expression specifies, the "painful question [*peinliche*

---

36 One might see here evidence of a return to the old "spectacle" regime. Kathryn Bigelow's 2012 thriller *Zero Dark Thirty* was criticized by then-acting CIA director Michael Morell for creating "the strong impression that the enhanced interrogation techniques that were part of our former detention and interrogation program were the key to finding Bin Laden. That impression is false" (Scott Shane, "Acting C.I.A. Chief Critical of Film 'Zero Dark Thirty,'" *New York Times,* Dec. 22, 2012). For a list of TV shows and movies glorifying torture, see Maura Moynihan, "Torture Chic: Why Is the Media Glorifying Inhumane, Sadistic Behavior?," *AlterNet,* Feb. 2, 2009: "From 2002 through 2005, the Parents Television Council counted 624 torture scenes in prime time, a six-fold increase. UCLA's Television Violence Monitoring Project reports 'torture on TV shows is significantly higher than it was five years ago and the characters who torture have changed. It used to be that only villains on television tortured. Today, 'good guy' and heroic American characters torture — and this torture is depicted as necessary, effective and even patriotic.'"

37 In Greek and Roman antiquity and in European countries inspired by Roman law, the standard procedure in criminal cases stipulated that the state had the right to punish only once the accused had confessed. In absence of a confession, the "queen of proof [*Confessio regina probationis*]" and in absence of two eyewitnesses of guilt or innocence, torture was applied. Thomasius denounces torture that targets the victim *before* any conviction of guilt, which Foucault comments on briefly under the name of judicial torture (Foucault, *Discipline and Punish,* 40–42). But the implications of Thomasius's critique also reach the practice of punitive torture as described in detail by Foucault, by which the convicted person was made to suffer a "thousand deaths" before his or her execution (12).

Frage]," does not seem to be to investigate the truth, but to force the tortured person to give "false statements."[38]

Thomasius observes that "because of torture, the poorest of the poor of all accused, whose guilt has not been proven yet, receive punishments that surpass hugely the punishments they would receive if proven guilty." That proves the "godless perversity [*perversitas*] in punishing" and there is nothing "more unjust" (F, 118–19). But Thomasius's decisive argument against torture, not mentioned by the opponents of torture before him, is the following: "The miserable defendants are pushed towards their demise under the torments of torture, in order to supplement what, due to the absence of witnesses or proofs, is missing in the judge's certitude to condemn them. They are forced to fight against themselves through their own confession, and thus, become traitors of themselves [*sui ipsius proditores torti constituuntur*]" (F, 170–71).[39]

---

38   Thomasius, *Über die Folter*, 122–23. Henceforth, F. In this edition, the Latin text (even-numbered pages) faces the German translation (uneven-numbered pages). In the following, pages from this text will be given in parentheses. As Thomasius specifies, Ludovicus Vives had made the same point. With Cicero and Ulpian (who nonetheless did not categorically oppose the use of torture) Thomasius notes that people who are tortured will end up confessing to anything the torturer wants to hear, and that this is precisely why one should not believe a testimony given under torture (122–23). On Cicero and Ulpian, see Werner Riess, "Die historische Entwicklung der römischen Folter- und Hinrichtungspraxis in kulturvergleichender Perspektive," 208. See also Peters, *Torture*, 54–55.

39   Commenting on examples from the twentieth century, Elaine Scarry points out that calling the confession obtained under torture "betrayal" is nothing short of becoming complicit with the torturer: the implication that confessing torture victims are "traitors" perpetuates the destruction of their world that torture has caused. The "contempt" with which the collapse of the world of the victim is met becomes obvious in this word choice. Scarry also uses the concept of self-betrayal: "There is a second equally crucial and equally cruel bond between physical pain and interrogation that further explains their inevitable appearance together. Just as the interrogation, like the pain, is a way of wounding, so the pain, like the interrogation, is a vehicle of self-betrayal. Torture systematically prevents the prisoner from being an agent of anything and simultaneously pretends that he is the agent of some things." The "unseen sense of self-betrayal in pain" is "objectified in forced confession" and in "forced exercises that make the prisoner's body an

This argument of "self-betrayal" needs to be considered in the context of Thomasius's "demand for a fundamental equality in rights," which sharply contradicted the prevalent notion of "rights" of his time. [40] As a consequence, Thomasius emphasizes one of the principles of his understanding of natural law: nobody should be prevented from defending himself (F, 168–71). This principle is "entirely exterminated" with state-sponsored torture that forces human beings — Thomasius calls them sometimes "mortals" — "to prepare their own demise [*exitium/Untergang*]" (F, 168–71), by incriminating themselves (F, 170–71), and thus hasten their condemnation to capital punishment. [41] With the abolition of the abovementioned principle of natural law, torture victims are instead pushed (*adiguntur*) to their own ruin/destruction (*sui perniciem/Verderben*) by supplementing what the judge is lacking for their condemnation. Through their confession, they are "forced to conduct battle against themselves," to, "as it were, cut their own throat with a sword (or knife) [*quasi gladium ad illud iugulandum, exigere/so dass er sich gleichsam selber das Messer an die Kehle setzen muss*]" (F, 170–71). And: "Can it be reconciled with natural reason to force human beings [*homines*] to their own slaying/slaughter/carnage [*caedem*]?" (F, 174–75). [42]

Torture victims are forced into becoming traitors of themselves (*sui ipsius proditores*): They are coerced into the betrayal not only of their existence, but of their very "nature."

As Werner Riess recalls, in the early modern period in certain Northern German cities, someone who had undergone torture had lost his or her honor forever, even if he/she was able to

---

active agent, an actual cause of his pain." (*The Body in Pain*, 29–30, 47). See also Chapter 1 in this volume.

40 Peter Schröder, *Christian Thomasius zur Einführung* (Hamburg: Junius, 1999), 68.

41 For example, Thomasius, *Über die Folter*, 160: "mortals."

42 The German translation of the last quote reads "Is it compatible with natural reason to force people to their own death?" [*zu ihrem eigenen Tod zu zwingen*]" (F, 174–75), but this translation is not precise enough, as the Latin *caedes* should be rendered by a noun such as *Gemetzel, Blutbad, Ermordung*.

prove his/her innocence.[43] The mere suspicion of being guilty of an infamy so great that it warranted torture in the eyes of the juridical system was thus sufficient for the expulsion from civil society.[44]

Thomasius presents the flip side, and perhaps even the unspoken motivation of this expulsion: one cannot be tortured without being forced to betray oneself. I would claim here that this is the case even if no confession is made. Thomasius asserts that torture was a pagan practice, initially applied by the Romans only to slaves who were "treated as equal with four-legged creatures (animals) [*quadrupedibus/Vierfüsslern (Tiere)*]" (F, 176–77).[45] The betrayal of oneself is, one the one hand, the hastening of one's own slaughter through false statements, but on the other, even if this is only intimated in Thomasius's text, a forced crossing over into bestiality.[46] It is, one could say, the betrayal of the human community.

Let me recall that in Abu Ghraib, humiliation, including the leashing of victims as if they were four-legged creatures, was

---

43 Riess, "Die historische Entwicklung der römischen Folter- und Hinrichtungspraxis," 215n50. Riess sees here a parallel to the Roman "infamy" that followed certain punishments.

44 This is, of course, a counterargument to "living together we must," or, in any case, a modality of it which cannot be simply placed on a continuum and which calls for an investigation of its own.

45 In her seminal study *Torture and Truth*, Page duBois shows how already in Greek antiquity, the separation between slaves who could be "tortured" and "free men and women" who in principle could not, was constantly threatened and could not be sustained. (*Torture and Truth* [New York: Routledge, 1991], 40–45, 62). See also Peters, *Torture*: "From the second half of the thirteenth century to the end of the eighteenth, torture was part of the ordinary criminal procedure of the Latin Church and of most of the states of Europe" (54). "By the end of the fifteenth century every man might be tortured, as the groundwork of early modern criminal law was firmly and professionally laid out" (62). McCoy convincingly traces the "slippery slope" from the hypothesis of "selective, surgical" use of torture of the few to "torture in general"; see, for example, *A Question of Torture*, 190–95.

46 See also Foucault quoting Damhoudère's description of the executioner's cruelty towards the condemned man, exercising "every cruelty with regard to the evil-doing patients, treating them buffeting and killing them as if they had a beast in their hands" (*Discipline and Punish*, 51).

part and parcel of the use of torture: the intent to shame the victims to such a degree as to virtually exclude them from their own communities.[47] In our days, then, more than three hundred years after Thomasius's treatise, one of the arguments that branded torture for him as an unconscionable, godless perversity, has returned as one of the principal goals of "enhanced interrogation" methods.

Even if the confession obtained under torture is no longer automatically followed by capital punishment as was still the case in Thomasius's time, the latter's argument also holds for victims of torture of later centuries, and for victims of the least admitted form of torture, that inflicted by Western democracies. The "stealth" techniques do not only undermine the power of activism that compassion is susceptible to kindle, but also threaten to lock up victims in unavowable shame. "Physical scars can be shown without shame; they win sympathy and recognition from families and communities. But the photographs at Abu Ghraib put the survivors in a vicious bind."[48] In revealing their ordeal, they would repeat the utter humiliation that not only shamed them to the cores of their beings, but was also purposefully designed never to be revealable. The victim who would publicly expose what was done to him would be treated as if he had betrayed his extended self, his community, but also his very humanity. In other words, he cannot hope for the compassion of others, nor for compassion for himself. "'Shoot me here,' said an Abu Ghraib prisoner pointing to the space between his eyes, 'but don't do this to us.'"[49]

Marc Nichanian's analysis of the aporias of "testimony" to genocide is perspicacious for the present context as well: "There is no testimony of shame. It might even be the only thing for which there cannot be testimony. Shame itself is its own testimony." There is no testimony, because giving testimony means

47 See McCoy, *A Question of Torture,* 157–60, and Rejali, "The Real Shame of Abu Ghraib."

48 Rejali, "The Real Shame of Abu Ghraib."

49 Ibid.

to become a "living proof of one's own death [...]. That is the moment of shame. Testimony is shame."[50] The shame of the torturer, if it occurs as in Eric Fair's statement, is thus of a different nature.

Given that the victims of US-sponsored torture are almost exclusively Muslim men, it is necessary to follow Rejali even further.[51] In a piece entitled "The Real Shame of Abu Ghraib,"

---

50 Marc Nichanian, *The Historiographic Perversion*, trans. Gil Anidjar (New York: Columbia University Press, 2009), 118, 120–21.

51 Whereas in the US "War on Terror" the victims of torture have been almost exclusively Muslim men, it should be noted that the treatment of inmates of the US prison system frequently also amounts to torture. The title of a 2011 "position paper" by the Center for Constitutional Rights on the "Death Row Experience from a Human Rights Perspective" bluntly summarizes the analyses presented in the document by asserting "The United States Tortures before It Kills"; see below, Chapter 4. However, conditions of torture are not limited to death row. In May 2011, the US Supreme Court upheld a ruling by a panel of three federal judges holding that conditions in California's prisons amount to a violation of the Eighth Amendment ban on cruel and unusual punishment. The fifty-two-page court opinion, authored by Justice Kennedy, described among others the dismal conditions for mentally or physically ill inmates: "Prisoners in California with serious mental illness do not receive minimal, adequate care. Because of a shortage of treatment beds, suicidal inmates may be held for prolonged periods in telephone-booth-sized cages without toilets. A psychiatric expert reported observing an inmate who had been held in such a cage for nearly 24 hours, standing in a pool of his own urine, unresponsive and nearly catatonic. Prison officials explained they had 'no place to put him.' Other inmates awaiting care may be held for months in administrative segregation, where they endure harsh and isolated conditions and receive only limited mental health services. Wait times for mental health care range as high as 12 months. In 2006, the suicide rate in California's prisons was nearly 80% higher than the national average for prison populations; and a court-appointed Special Master found that 72.1% of suicides involved 'some measure of inadequate assessment, treatment, or intervention, and were therefore most probably foreseeable and/or preventable.' Prisoners suffering from physical illness also receive severely deficient care. California's prisons were designed to meet the medical needs of a population at 100% of design capacity and so have only half the clinical space needed to treat the current population. A correctional officer testified that, in one prison, up to 50 sick inmates may be held together in a 12- by 20-foot cage for up to five hours awaiting treatment. The number of staff is inadequate, and prisoners face significant delays in access to care. A prisoner with severe abdominal pain died after a 5-week delay in referral

Rejali notes that "in the beginning, Muslim states did not carry forward many of the worst tortures (including crucifixion) of the Persian and Roman empires they replaced. They did introduce tortures of their own, from the amputation of limbs to the common beating of the soles of the feet, the *falaka,* that are cruel by our standards. But Muslim societies were guided by ideals and values that Westerners can recognize and which still animate penal reform today."[52] Rejali moves on to focus on the most abhorred of ancient torture practices, crucifixion. Ancient societies regarded it as "the worst of executions" for the following reasons: "Crucifixions displayed victims naked in public without honor. They subjected victims to the vengeful feelings of a crowd," transforming the onlookers into a jeering mob and allowing them "to take pleasure in pain and breach the bonds of civility. They extended suffering for days. They left victims as food for wild beasts and birds, denying them a proper burial." In short, Muslim societies rejected crucifixion, because it was "the practice of savages and tyrants who did not respect the law."[53] In the Roman empire, this punishment, which subjected "the victim to the utmost indignity," was usually reserved for criminals considered nonhuman (slaves and pirates) or for citizens convicted of high treason who, by their acts, were considered to have excluded themselves from the political and by extension the human community.[54] Rejali's analysis shows that the

---

to a specialist; a prisoner with 'constant and extreme' chest pain died after an 8-hour delay in evaluation by a doctor; and a prisoner died of testicular cancer after a 'failure of MDs to work up for cancer in a young man with 17 months of testicular pain.' [...] Many prisoners, suffering from severe but not life-threatening conditions, experience prolonged illness and unnecessary pain" (Syllabus to *Brown v. Plata,* 563 U.S. 09–1233 (2011), 5–7). The opinion also quotes Doyle W. Scott, the former head of Texas prisons, who described "conditions in California's prisons as 'appalling,' 'inhumane,' and 'unacceptable' and stated that 'in more than 35 years of prison work experience, I have never seen anything like it'" (5).

52 Rejali, "The Real Shame of Abu Ghraib."

53 Ibid.

54 Martin Hengel, "Crucifixion," in *The Cross of the Son of God,* trans. Jon Bowden (London: SCM Press, 1986), 116, 138. Hengel writes that only the

"real shame of Abu Ghraib" and of other American detention facilities lies in what those methods, discussed and approved by the highest ranking government officials and their advisors, stir up in the collective cultural memory of Muslim countries. All of the characteristics of crucifixion were explicitly or implicitly present in the infamous techniques used in Abu Ghraib prison. The hooded man standing on a box with wires attached to his fingers whose photograph became the icon for American brutality in Abu Ghraib, was, according to Rejali, subjected to an "old" technique

> dubbed the "crucifixion" by British solders during World War I. The CIA had hired experts to study it who had reported that the technique caused enormous swelling in the feet, intense pain in the hips, shortness of breath, and after three days, kidney failure. Forced standing on an elevated object is known only in three countries in the late twentieth century, Venezuela, South Africa and Brazil. And only Brazilian torturers used electricity as means of forcing the prisoner to maintain an erect position voluntarily, a technique dubbed "the Vietnam."[55]

Torture techniques like those used in Abu Ghraib that perpetrate an assault on "cultural identity" with their use of intense shame revive the cultural memory of that "'barbaric' form of execution of the utmost cruelty," that already for the people of the ancient world was "an utterly offensive affair, 'obscene' in the original sense of the word."[56]

Carthaginians "tended to crucify especially generals and admirals who had either been defeated or who proved too willful."

55 Darius Rejali, "Speak Frankly about Torture: Exercising International Citizenship," Lecture at Harvard Law School, March 12, 2009.

56 Alfred McCoy, "The U.S. Has a History of Using Torture," *History News Network,* Dec. 6, 2006; see also McCoy, *A Question of Torture,* 129–30; Hengel, "Crucifixion," 114. Hengel quotes sources that show that crucifixion was practiced among the Persians, Indians, Assyrians, Scythians, and later by the Greeks and Romans, whose historians were, however, "fond of stress-

It can be assumed that what happened at Abu Ghraib would be considered intensely shameful for any victim from any cultural background, and for many so shameful that it would threaten to destroy not only their community's compassion, but also their compassion for themselves. At the same time, it is essential not to belittle the fact that the approved techniques were designed to target specific cultural sensibilities, or, bluntly speaking, to humiliate Muslim men. According to McCoy, "The war on terror would develop a conscious strategy of sexual humiliation as an adjunct to the CIA's [torture] paradigm."[57]

Moreover, the fact that the technique known in intelligence circles as "crucifixion," a technique intensely studied by the CIA, has become the "icon" of American torture all over the world, and particularly in Muslim countries, may indicate the necessity to research what Avital Ronell has termed the "phantasmatic history" of the United States, especially when considering that the Brazilian version of this technique, adopted in Abu Ghraib, is known as "the Vietnam." What Ronell wrote about the first war in Iraq, Operation Desert Storm, might be said of Operation "Infinite Justice," rebaptized on September 25, 2001, as "Operation Enduring Freedom": "The war was less a matter of truth than of rhetorical maneuvers that were dominated by unconscious transmission systems and symbolic displacements but which nonetheless have produced material effects."[58] The torture techniques used in Abu Ghraib might be understood as "material effects" of such "unconscious transmission systems and symbolic displacements." They fit Thomasius's formulation: even without confessions, and without the certainty of a death penalty following the confession, they push victims to strive for their own annihilation. "'Shoot me here,' said an Abu Ghraib prisoner pointing to the space between his eyes, 'but don't do this to us.'" The sworn statement of another Abu Ghraib pris-

---

ing *barbarian* crucifixions, and playing down their own use of this form of execution" (115).

57 See for example McCoy, *A Question of Torture*, 130.

58 Avital Ronell, "Support Our Tropes," in *Finitude's Score: Essays for the End of the Millennium* (Lincoln: University of Nebraska Press, 1994), 269, 272.

oner, Ameen Saeed Al-Sheik, read: "They said we will make you wish to die and it will not happen."[59]

4.

"Living together" supposes, as Derrida insists, an "interrupting excess […] with regard to *symbiosis,* to a symbiotic, gregarious, or fusional living together." It also supposes an "interrupting excess […] with regard to statutory convention, to law" (A, 26–27). One of Thomasius's arguments speaks to this "interrupting excess," as I hope to show in concluding.

As I have mentioned, Thomasius recalls that torture was a pagan practice, initially applied by the Romans only to slaves who were "treated as equal with four-legged creatures (animals) [*quadrupedibus/Vierfüsslern (Tiere)*]" (F, 176–77). He insists that torture is "dangerous and irreligious" (F, 134–35, 146–47), that the Holy Scriptures "curse" and "abhor" it (F, 162–63), and that it "should have been banned from the courts of the Christians a long time ago" (F, 176–77, 186–87). But, he observes, even though torture cannot be reconciled with the scriptures, "the Christian people nonetheless persist in holding on to so many pagan things [*tam multa gentilia*] with all their strength [*mordicus*: literally, with their teeth; doggedly], as if they [those pagan things] were the most religious" (or "the holiest" [*religiossima*]) (F, 176–77), and this in spite of the Christian teaching that obliges the believers to "always" hold "a meekness" or "gentleness corresponding to the Gospels" in or "near their heart [*cordi esse debet mansuetudo/Sanftmut am Herzen liegen muss*]." Thomasius calls on gentleness as a matter of the heart in the same paragraph in which he brandishes the Roman doctrine that slaves cannot be subjected to injustice (*iniuria/Unrecht*) because they are the equals of animals, and they can be "killed without punishment" (F, 176–77).

---

59 Scott Higham and Joe Stephens, "New Details of Prison Abuse Emerge: Abu Ghraib Detainees' Statements Describe Sexual Humiliation and Savage Beatings," *Washington Post,* May 21, 2004, A01.

Torture, then, was an accepted practice by Christian states in Thomasius's time, even though the Holy Scriptures "curse" and "abhor" it, and even though forgiveness and compassion are portrayed in the Gospels as specifically Christian. In our time, torture has been and for many still is a practice accepted by citizens of democratic states, even though their constitutions "curse" and "abhor" it.[60] And this may, in Derridean terms, not be so surprising. Derrida has argued that Western democracies are haunted by their unquestioned, repressed foundation in the blood ties that link brothers of noble birth and exclude everybody else.[61] In the context of the adoption of torture as official US policy under the Bush administration, and of the growing acceptability of torture (as evidenced in the dramatic increase of torture scenes in TV shows and movies),[62] one may wonder whether an aspect of the foundation of secular states in Christianity remains as of yet unthought: the mostly forgotten second meaning of the symbol that stands erect at its center as "the most religious" or "the holiest." As unthought, this second meaning of the cross may be "haunting" what, in Derrida's words, "*in fact* governs not the principles but the predominant reality of American political culture," which displays, "despite the separation in principle between church and state, a fundamental biblical (primarily Christian) reference in its official political discourse and the discourse of its political leaders."[63] The second

---

60 See for example, Brooks, "America Tortures (Yawn)," and Chapter 1 in this volume. See also Moynihan, "Torture Chic."

61 This idea is developed in Derrida's *Rogues* and *Politics of Friendship.* See Jacques Derrida, *Rogues: Two Essays on Reason,* trans. Pascale-Anne Brault and Michael Naas (Stanford: Stanford University Press 2005), 92; *Politics of Friendship,* 1–24, 99–106.

62 According to Human Rights First, the number of scenes of torture on TV shows increased significantly increased between 1995 and 2005 (with a peak in 2003). A retired military leader deplored "that the portrayal of torture in popular culture is having an undeniable impact on how interrogations are conducted in the field." U.S. soldiers are "imitating the techniques they have seen on television — because they think such tactics work," in stark contrast to trained interrogators' experience (Moynihan, "Torture Chic").

63 Derrida, "Autoimmunity," 117.

meaning of the cross is synonymous with the most despised and abhorred ancient form of torture and capital punishment. The torture technique dubbed "crucifixion" might be the most visible "material effect" of the "symbolic displacements" in which the "phantasmatic history" of the United States is acted out.[64]

In his study on suicide bombings, Talal Asad pursues a related argument. In the "indirect suicide" of Jesus's crucifixion, "the violent breaking of the body is not an occasion for horror" (such as suicide bombings are in our days), but "becomes the source of a transcendent truth." Most significantly, "it also constitutes, in and through violence, the universal category of 'the human' to whom the gift is offered." In other words, "in Christian civilization, the gift of life for humanity is possible only through a suicidal death."[65] Asad shows how the "Crucifixion represents the truth of violence" even in the "popular visual narratives" of our "secular" age, where the lonely male hero suffers "severe physical punishment or torture," and his excruciating pain comes to pass as "the very vindication of truth."[66]

Following Derrida's logic, the forgotten or repressed "foundation" of a state is not within reach of the "law" nor of "statutory convention" (such as the Holy Scriptures for Thomasius, and the Constitution for US citizens), because it is its "origin." The fact that the Hebrew Bible, or in Christian parlance the Old Testament, "abhors" torture doesn't solve the problem that the New Testament finds its foundational origin in a practice abhorred as the quintessence of torture. Crucifixion figures itself among those "pagan things" defended doggedly as the holiest.

In a believer's perspective, the central symbol of Christianity declares Jesus's radical and revolutionary solidarity with the least of the least (one might say *rachamim*), and declares those

---

64 See Ronell, "Support Our Tropes," 269, 272.

65 Talal Asad, "Horror at Suicide Terrorism," in *On Suicide Bombing*, 84, 86.

66 Ibid., 86. Regarding our "secular age," see Gil Anidjar's analysis, summarized in this succinct formulation: "Secularism is a name Christianity gave itself when it invented 'religion,' named its other or others as 'religions'" (Gil Anidjar, *Semites: Race, Religion, Literature* [Stanford: Stanford University Press, 2008], 48).

expulsed from the human community as being not only human, but belonging to God's kingdom (at the condition, though, of their repentance). Allowing for the forgotten or repressed memory of this symbol to be addressed might come to signify a "mutation" in a sense similar to that evoked by Derrida with regard to the "globalization of avowal." In his lesson, Derrida argues that the scenes of public avowals and repentance he analyzes might

> signify a mutation in process, a fragile one, to be sure, fleeting and difficult to interpret, but, like the moment of an undeniable rupture in the history of the political, of the juridical, of the relations among community, civil society, and the state, among sovereign states, international law, and NGOs, among the ethical, the juridical, and the political, between the public and the private, between national citizenship and an international citizenship, even a metacitizenship, in a word, concerning a social bond that crosses [*passe*] the borders of these ensembles called family, nation, or state. (A, 31)

The scenes of public avowal bear thus the promise of an opening of these "borders" and thus the promise, perhaps, of rethinking what "ensemble" might signify. A few pages later, Derrida evokes the concept of "mutation" again, this time with even greater insistence. He notes that the discourse of institutions like the Truth and Reconciliation Commission in South Africa "forces us to ask ourselves whether the globalization of avowal is a planetarization of the Abrahamic concept, or more specifically Christian concept, of forgiveness, or, on the contrary, a new mutation that brings about [*qui fait arriver*] something unexpected, something even threatening to this tradition — I cannot engage here this necessary but immense question" (A, 36).

This question may become pressing with regard to the present and future legacy of the use of torture by the United States against Muslim detainees in Iraq, Afghanistan, Guantánamo, and elsewhere, most of whom were or are innocent of any crime. Facing the "real shame" of Abu Ghraib and other torture chambers might bring about a mutation, "something unexpec-ted, something even threatening" to the dominant understan-ding of the central symbol of Christianity and the concept of forgiveness that is inseparable from it.

II.
INDEFINITE
DETENTION

CHAPTER 3

Literary Justice?
Poems from Guantánamo Bay Prison Camp[1]

In the introduction to her ground-breaking book, *The Juridical Unconscious: Trials and Traumas in the Twentieth Century,* Shoshana Felman writes that "as a pattern inherited from the great catastrophes and the collective traumas of the twentieth century, the promised exercise of *legal* justice — of justice by trial and by law — has become civilization's most appropriate and most essential, most ultimately meaningful response to the violence that wounds it."[2] To these lines, Felman adds an explanatory note:

These pages were written in the immediate aftermath of the events of September 11; the United States had just entered into a military war on terrorism whose ultimate historical developments and *judicial consequences* cannot be predicted or foreseen with total certainty or with a total clarity of moral vision. My point here is not political but analytical. Whatever the political and moral consequences, it is significant that the idea of justice by trial and by law was immediately envisioned and articulated as America's promised reply, and as Western civilization's most significant and most meaningful response

---

1 Originally published in *Comparative Literature Studies* 48, no. 3, special issue "Trials of Trauma: Comparative and Global Perspectives," eds. Michael G. Levine and Bella Brodzki (2011): 417–34.
2 Felman, *The Juridical Unconscious,* 3.

precisely to the loss of meaning and the disempowerment occasioned by the trauma.[3]

The "promised exercise of legal justice" is thus, as a "pattern,"
Western civilization's "most ultimately meaningful response" to
trauma.

However, within the actualizations of this promise, Felman
asserts, something arises that calls for a different kind of testimony, a call to which literature responds. How does literature,
Felman asks, do "justice to the trauma in a way the law does not,
or cannot?" In her most sweeping answer to this question, she
writes:

> Literature is a dimension of concrete embodiment and a lan-
> guage of infinitude that, in contrast to the language of the
> law, encapsulates not closure but precisely what in a given
> legal case refuses to be closed and cannot be closed. It is to
> this refusal of the trauma to be closed that literature does jus-
> tice. The literary writers in this book thus stand beyond or in
> the margin of the legal closure, on the brink of the abyss that
> underlies the law, on whose profundity they fix their vision
> and through whose bottomlessness they reopen the closed
> legal case.[4]

Literary justice, then, addresses what is in irrecuperable excess to
whatever the language of law can (and must) articulate. As Elizabeth Rottenberg notes, Felman's "exceptionally daring" analyses
break new ground insofar as they show how "an unassimilated
traumatic history, a history that insidiously intrudes upon the
proceedings, literally prevents the law from translating the cases
before the court into 'legal-conscious terminology.'"[5] Furthermore, Felman's close readings provide particularly persuasive

---

3   Ibid., 182n7.
4   Ibid., 8.
5   Elizabeth Rottenberg, "Review of Shoshana Felman, The Juridical Uncon-
    scious: Trials and Traumas in the Twentieth Century," MLN 199, no. 5 (2004):
    1098–99.

arguments in favor of a "hypothesis" Jacques Derrida formulated in the context of the preeminent poet of the Shoah, Paul Celan: the hypothesis that "all responsible witnessing engages in a poetic experience of language."[6] It is the poetic experience of language, the invention of language for what previously lacked language, that encircles the "black hole", the "abyss, the gap that the law tries, but cannot succeed in closing."[7] In their refusal or failure to welcome a discourse that, in Toni Morrison's formulation, "shape[s] a silence while breaking it," the "trials of the century" are condemned, according to Felman, to unintentionally reenact trauma in their very attempts to provide closure.[8]

This chapter critically assesses the concept of a "pattern" of "legal" responses in the context of events postdating the publication of *The Juridical Unconscious*. In a second step, it demonstrates the rich productivity of the concept of "literary justice" in light of the censored production of poetry in Guantánamo Bay Prison Camp.

The Pattern of Legal Justice in Western Civilization

Felman's illuminating analyses show that because of the inherent constraints of legal proceedings, the "trials of the century" reenact the very traumas in which they originated. This powerful thesis, far from diminishing the importance of legal proceedings, opens the possibility to detect precisely those moments in which, *within* the trial, "literary justice" is voiced, be it in moments of silence, moments in which the breakdown of witnesses let the "other scene" of the drama of trial become perceptible. However, the concept of a "pattern inherited from the great catastrophes and the collective traumas of the twentieth century" imperils the compass of this thesis, since it risks, in its turn, the reenactment of trauma. A glance at the history of Western coun-

---

6 Derrida, "Poetics and Politics of Witnessing," 66.

7 Harriet Murav, "The Juridical Unconscious: Trials and Traumas in the Twentieth Century (Review)," *Comparative Literature Studies* 42, no. 3 (2005): 235.

8 Toni Morrison, *Foreword to The Bluest Eye* (New York: Vintage, 2007), xiii.

tries in the twentieth and twenty-first centuries indeed forces us to ask whether the "exercise of *legal* justice" has been "Western civilization's most significant and most meaningful response" in the twentieth century as a "pattern." To what extent has *the promise* of this exercise actually been kept?

While focusing her attention on two "trials of the century," both of which put "on trial" a "whole history," Felman notes that "these two paradigmatic legal examples" figure "among the many other trials (civil as well as criminal) that *judge history as such*," and cites, among others, "the *Brown v. Board of Education* case in the United States [...] the French Klaus Barbie trial; the trials of the officers and torturers of the 'Dirty War' in Argentina; the Turkish trial of those accused of having committed genocide against the Armenians in 1921; the international ad hoc war crimes tribunals for Rwanda and for the former Yugoslavia."[9] One of Felman's goals is to re-evaluate Nietzsche's concept of "monumental history" in displacing it from a historiography "of the great" to a "writing of the dead" and she invokes "the prosecutor's monumentalizing opening address" in the Eichmann trial as evidence for this "displacement."[10]

However, the notion of a "pattern" and the idea of judging "history as such" run the risk of a re-monumentalization of "Western civilization" insofar as they make it difficult to consider and expose the roles countries of that very "civilization" have played in abetting the "great catastrophes and collective traumas" of the twentieth century: the Argentinian "Dirty War," the Rwandan genocide, and the ethnic cleansing in Yugoslavia would not have been possible without Western complicity. In the case of the Armenian genocide, the failed "postwar investigations into the Ottoman crimes committed during World War I, especially the Armenian genocide" testify to the *failure* of "Western civilization's [...] response." Due to what one Foreign Office member called a "complete capitulation to Turkish blackmail," Britain had abandoned the idea of war crimes trials

---

9 Felman, *The Juridical Unconscious,* 12 (emph. added).
10 Ibid., 114.

in Turkey by 1921.[11] As Taner Akçam describes the legal proceedings, "the mountain labored and brought forth a mouse."[12] In this case, the only element that supports Felman's thesis of "judging history as such" is the fact that these proceedings yielded the first use of the concept "crimes against humanity," which was, as Akçam notes, "a significant contribution to international case law." Nevertheless, "the failure of the three different attempts to prosecute the suspects meant that the concept of 'crimes against humanity' was set aside, reemerging on the international stage only at Nuremberg after World War II."[13]

The theses of a "pattern" and of judging "history as such" are further complicated by the very long list of catastrophes abetted by "Western civilization" that have not been addressed by any "exercise of *legal* justice" or even its promise, an unjustly abbreviated version of which would include the genocidal pursuit against Native Americans through their children's forced displacement to boarding "schools" in the US and Canada in which they were criminally neglected, molested, exploited and often left to die, a systematic "rape of the soul," that continued well into the 1980s; the nuclear bombing of Hiroshima and Nagasaki that would have been tried as a war crime had the US not won

---

11 Peter Balakian, *The Burning Tigris: The Armenian Genocide and America's Response* (New York: HarperCollins, 2003), 344. According to Balakian, "This change in British policy came at great cost to international justice. In August 1921, the British released forty-three Turkish prisoners who were accused of perpetrating the Armenian massacres. The abandonment of the Constantinople war trials was a major failure, and it helped to accelerate the amnesia in the West about the Armenian Genocide in the ensuing decades. Nevertheless the trials produced more evidence about the organized plan to exterminate the Armenians. That evidence came from Turkish officials who had themselves organized and participated in the massacres and deportations, and from a body of official government documents. Although there were three hangings and many prison convictions, none of the convicted served out their prison sentences, and the majority of the perpetrators escaped punishment after the British–Turkish prisoner exchange deal" (344–45)

12 Taner Akçam, *A Shameful Act: The Armenian Genocide and the Question of Turkish Responsibility* (New York: Metropolitan Books, 2006), 368.

13 Ibid.

World War II; the overthrow of the thriving Iranian democracy by the British secret service and the CIA in 1953 resulting in a twenty-six-year-long ferocious dictatorship by the US-supported Mohammad-Reza Shah Pahlavi; the ongoing, and possibly continuously amplifying traumatic consequences of the expulsion of Palestinians from their homes and lands that made the foundation of the state of Israel possible; and the atrocities committed by military juntas trained and supported by the US all over South America against their own populations.[14]

Many more instances of blatant impunity in the wake of massive state-inflicted trauma could be cited. In none of these cases has "Western civilization's [...] response" been a promise of *legal* (or of any other) justice. According to John Dower's wide-ranging analysis, the United States has been dominated by "cultures of war" throughout the twentieth century, and, as Scott Martelle's review puts it, "regardless of self-perceptions of righteousness, nations with a culture of war will, indeed, wage war."[15]

---

14 George Tinker, "Preface. Tracing a Contour of Colonialism: American Indians and the Trajectory of Educational Imperialism," in Ward Churchill, *Kill the Indian, Save the Man: The Genocidal Impact of American Indian Residential Schools* (San Francisco: City Lights Books, 2004), xx; Ward Churchill, *Kill the Indian, Save the Man*, 43, 68. The effects of Indian boarding schools however continue to this day: "The ravages of a virulent cluster of psychological dysfunctions that has come to be known in Canada as "Residential School Syndrome" (RSS) — there is no corresponding term in the United States, although the symptomatologies involved are just as clearly present there — not only remains undiminished but may in some respects have intensified during the decades since the last survivors were released from the facilities in which the initial damage was done. Given the proportion of the native population caught up in the residential school system during [the] last two generations of its operation, and the fact that the syndrome is demonstrably transmissible to children and others closely associated with/dependent upon survivors, the magnitude of its ongoing impact upon Native North America is easily discernible" (68). On human rights in the occupied territories, see Richard Falk, "Report of the Special Rapporteur on the Situation of Human Rights in the Palestinian Territories Cccupied since 1967," United Nations, General Assembly, Human Rights Council, 16th session, Agenda item 7, A/HRC/16/72, Jan. 10, 2011.

15 Scott Martelle, "When Nations Live by the Sword," review of John W. Dower, *Cultures of War: Pearl Harbor, Hiroshima, 9–11, Iraq* (New York: W.W.

The assertion that we have "inherited" a "pattern" of promised justice from this history does not only abet a remonumentalization of Western civilization, but also risks inadvertently repeating the trauma, reinflicting it in the refusal to acknowledge acts of terror committed by Western states. Thus, the assertion of a pattern threatens to undermine the analyses conducted in its shadow.

The "culture of war" has clearly also had the upper hand in the response to 9/11. The significance of the "idea of justice by trial and by law" that was "immediately envisioned and articulated as America's promised reply" has proven to be mostly symbolic, falling within the "self-perceptions of righteousness," with devastating "political and moral consequences." In other words, one may suspect that it is precisely the "idea of justice," rooted in the self-perception of righteousness, that caused an abandonment of the *practices* of justice.

Asserting a pattern in response to the events of September 11, 2001, proves particularly thorny. Felman writes that the "idea of justice by trial and by law" was the "most significant and most meaningful response [...] to the loss of meaning" inflicted by the trauma of September 11, 2001, no doubt hoping to see in this idea "immediately envisioned and articulated as America's promised reply" a confirmation of the "pattern" of "Western civilization's" response to collective trauma.[16] At the same time, she notes the beginning of a "military war on terrorism" in the "immediate aftermath of September 11." However, all too soon after the publication of Felman's book, it became abundantly clear that if there was the attempt at a legal response, it was (and to this day continues to be) dwarfed by the military response. In addition to the war in Afghanistan, mentioned by Felman, another was started in Iraq. While a "limited war" against the Taliban regime and Al-Qaeda in Afghanistan was initially understood and widely supported as a "reasonable extension of the right of self-defense in the context of a megaterrorist attack,"

Norton, 2010), *Los Angeles Times,* Oct. 24, 2010, E10.
16 Felman, *The Juridical Unconscious,* 182n7.

arguably related to the perceived threat of future attacks, and "accepted by the Security Council, although less specifically and circumspectly than seems desirable," its continuation more than a decade later lacked its initial — however problematic — justifications.[17] After the official end, in December 2014, of US and NATO combat missions and the departure of most foreign military forces, Taliban attacks rose dramatically, leading President Obama in July 2016 to slow down the withdrawal of the remaining US forces from Afghanistan, ordering 8,400 of them to stay through the end of his presidency.[18]

The Iraqi war, on the other hand, was in Richard Falk's words, "undertaken in violation of international law and the United Nations Charter, in defiance of world public opinion, and without a proper mandate as required by the U.S. Constitution." It deserves to be noted in this context that, to quote Falk again, "it was precisely recourse to aggressive war of this character that was punished at the Nuremberg Judgment after World War II, and declared the supreme crime in international law," whose prevention constitutes "the core commitment of the UN Charter."[19]

---

17 Richard Falk, *The Great Terror War* (New York: Olive Branch Press, 2003), 9. As Carlotta Gall reported in 2006 in *The New York Times,* Afghanistan's opium harvest that year "reached the highest levels ever recorded, showing an increase of almost 50 percent" from the previous year. This record opium production was directly proportional to increased Taliban-led insurgent activity, with participation by Northern Alliance drug lords in the Karzai regime. See Carlotta Gall, "Opium Harvest at Record Level in Afghanistan," *New York Times,* Sep. 3, 2006. According to BBC reporter Alastair Leithead, Afghanistan accounted in 2007 for more than 93% of the world's opiates ("Afghanistan Opium at Record High," *BBC News,* Aug. 27, 2007).

18 Paul Shinkman, "Obama to Leave 8,400 U.S. Troops in Afghanistan Through to 2017," *U.S. News and World Report,* July 6, 2016: "The fledgling [Afghan] military still lacks critical components it needs to function, like aviation, intelligence and logistics. It has also suffered from record numbers of deaths and injuries since taking over the combat role from the U.S., with a 75 percent rise in casualties last year, averaging 330 per week."

19 Richard Falk, *The Costs of War: International Law, the UN, and World Order after Iraq* (New York: Routledge, 2008), 2.

In connection with both of these wars, in addition to the "supreme crime in international law" that the war in Iraq represents, an array of massively *extra*-legal responses was undertaken: the creation of secret detention centers, the so-called black sites, the infamous Guantánamo Prison camp that was created explicitly to deny its detainees access to US courts; the increasing and by now massive deployment of drones whose mission is the extrajudicial assassination of terror suspects, including of American citizens.[20] The state-employed "legal" response con-

---

20 The first US citizen targeted in this way was the US-born cleric Anwar Al-Awlaki, "the one American citizen whom U.S. intelligence agencies [were] authorized to kill on sight", that is, without any constitutionally guaranteed due process. See Kari Huus, "Yemen's Rising Radical Star," *MSNBC*, Oct. 29, 2010. A law suit filed in August 2010 by the American Civil Liberties Union and the Center for Constitutional Rights on behalf of Awlaqi's father, Nasser al-Awlaqi came to an "unsettling" conclusion: "'This Court recognizes the somewhat unsettling nature of its conclusion — that there are circumstances in which the Executive's unilateral decision to kill a U.S. citizen overseas is [...] judicially unreviewable. But this case squarely presents such a circumstance,' judge Bates wrote. 'The serious issues regarding the merits of the alleged authorization of the targeted killing of a U.S. citizen overseas must await another day or another [nonjudicial] forum,' such as before Congress, the judge said." See Spencer S. Hsu, "Judge in D.C. Tosses Suit Challenging Placement of Yemeni Cleric on Terrorist List," *Washington Post*, Dec. 7, 2010. Al-Awlaki was assassinated on September 30, 2011, in an American drone strike in Yemen. However, "four years after the United States assassinated the radical cleric in a drone strike, his influence on jihadists is greater than ever." Scott Shane, "The Lessons of Anwar al-Awlaki," *New York Times Magazine*, Aug. 27, 2015. Not only did "the drone strike that killed [Awlaki] [...] not silence him," but after his death, Awlaki's Internet publications appear to have inspired "the perpetrators of the Fort Hood shooting, the Boston Marathon bombings and the Charlie Hebdo killings in Paris. 'It's very clear that his status as a martyr has given his message — including his message that it's the obligation of every Muslim to attack America — even greater authority,' Shane says. 'Some of the biggest and most devastating terrorist plots in the West since Awlaki was killed very much were a reflection of his influence'" (Anon., "Drone Strike That Killed Awlaki 'Did Not Silence Him,' Journalist Says," *NPR*, Sept. 14, 2015). On October 14, 2011, an American drone strike killed Al-Awlaki's 16-year-old-son Abdulrahman, an American citizen, his teenage cousin, and five other civilians, while they were having dinner at a restaurant. Abdulrahman was not on any "kill list," nor was he a member of Al-Qaeda. Other than Attorney General Eric Hold-

sisted in curtailing civil rights in the United States through, for example, the expansion of the secret networks of surveillance of US citizens, and in a number of cases suspending them.

Only weeks after the collective trauma of September 11, 2001, and the initial promise of "justice," infamously the "gloves came off," resulting already at that early stage in treatment akin to torture not only of "enemy combatants," but of US citizens as well.[21] Far from following a "pattern" of promised justice, the institutions that are supposed to guarantee legal justice were, on the contrary, damaged from the highest levels down. The abuses made infamous in 2004 through the publication of the photos taken by American service men and women in Iraq's Abu Ghraib prison provided chilling confirmations of the observations Freud made during World War I: "When the community no longer raises objections, there is an end, too, to the suppression of evil passions, and men perpetrate deeds of cruelty, fraud, treachery and barbarity so incompatible with their level of civilization that one would have thought them impossible."[22]

---

er's statement that the strike "did not 'specifically' target the young man," the Obama administration has never issued an explanation of Abdulrahman's assassination. Nick Baumann, "The American Teen Whose Death-by-Drone Obama Won't Explain," *Mother Jones*, April 23, 2015. See also the op-ed piece by the teen's grandfather, Nasser al-Awlaki, "The Drone That Killed My Grandson," *New York Times*, July 17, 2013.

21 See for example: Richard A. Serrano, "Prison Interrogators' Gloves Came Off Before Abu Ghraib," *Los Angeles Times*, June 9, 2004: "At the time, just weeks after the Sept. 11 terrorist attacks, the U.S. was desperate to find terrorist leader Osama bin Laden. After Lindh asked for a lawyer rather than talk to interrogators, he was not granted one nor was he advised of his Miranda rights against self-incrimination. Instead, the Pentagon ordered intelligence officers to get tough with him. The documents, read to *The Times* by two sources critical of how the government handled the Lindh case, show that after an Army intelligence officer began to question Lindh, a Navy admiral told the intelligence officer that 'the secretary of Defense's counsel has authorized him to "take the gloves off" and ask whatever he wanted.'" The US citizen John Walker Lindh was captured as an enemy combatant in Afghanistan six weeks after the beginning of the American-led invasion on November 25, 2001.

22 The preceding paragraphs deserve to be quoted as well: "A belligerent state permits itself every such misdeed, every such act of violence, as would dis-

In the case of September 11, the concept of an inherited "pattern" proves to be insufficient also in other respects. For one, it cannot take into account the vastly changed media-technological environment that was a precondition for the attacks and that has rendered obsolete oppositions such as Western vs. non-Western civilization. It also cannot account for a new dimension of what Felman calls the "loss of meaning."

In his reflection on the attacks of September 11, 2001, Jacques Derrida proposed far-reaching and highly productive concepts to address this new "loss of meaning." According to Derrida, 9/11's characterization as a "major event" lies not only in the nature of the attacks, their presumed unpredictability, the number of victims, the destruction of symbols of political, military, or

---

grace the individual. It makes use against the enemy not only of the accepted *ruses de guerre,* but of deliberate lying and deception as well — and to a degree which seems to exceed the usage of former wars. The state exacts the utmost degree of obedience and sacrifice from its citizens, but at the same time it treats them like children by an excess of secrecy and a censorship upon news and expressions of opinion which leaves the spirits of those whose intellects it thus suppresses defenceless against every unfavourable turn of events and every sinister rumour. It absolves itself from the guarantees and treatises by which it was bound to other states, and confesses shamelessly to its own rapacity and lust for power, which the private individual has then to sanction in the name of patriotism. It should not be objected that the state cannot refrain from wrong-doing, since that would place it at a disadvantage. It is no less disadvantageous, as a general rule, for the individual man to conform to the standards of morality and refrain from brutal and arbitrary conduct; and the state seldom proves able to indemnify him for the sacrifices it exacts. Nor should it be a matter for surprise that this relaxation of all the moral ties between the collective individuals of mankind should have had repercussions on the morality of individuals; for our conscience is not the inflexible judge that ethical teachers declare it, but in its origin is 'social anxiety' and nothing else. When the community no longer raises objections, there is an end, too, to the suppression of evil passions, and men perpetrate deeds of cruelty, fraud, treachery and barbarity so incompatible with their level of civilization that one would have thought them impossible" (Sigmund Freud, "Thoughts on War and Death," in *On the History of the Psychoanalytic Movement, Papers on Metapsychology and Other Works,* vol. 14 of *The Standard Edition of the Complete Psychological Works of Sigmund Freud,* trans. James Strachey [London: Hogarth, 1957], 279–80).

capitalist power, but also, and "perhaps especially," in the fact that they threatened the very "system of interpretation, the axiomatic, logic, rhetoric, concepts and evaluations that are supposed to allow one to *comprehend* and to explain precisely something like 'September 11.'"[23] In addition to people, buildings and symbols, what was attacked was

> the discourse that comes to be, in a pervasive and over-whelming, hegemonic fashion, *accredited* in the world's public space. What is legitimated by the prevailing system (a combination of public opinion, the media, the rhetoric of politicians and the presumed authority of all those who, through various mechanisms, speak or are allowed to speak in the public space) are thus the norms inscribed in every apparently meaningful phrase that can be constructed with the lexicon of violence, aggression, crime, war, and terror-ism, with the supposed differences between war and terror-ism, national and international terrorism, state and nonstate terrorism, with the respect for sovereignty, national territory, and so on.[24]

In other words, whatever "pattern inherited from the great ca-tastrophes [...] of the twentieth century" the "promised exercise of *legal* justice" was, in Felman's view, supposed to constitute has been disrupted by the US response to September 11. Indeed, the very notion of such a pattern is, as I have argued, questionable to begin with. I would further argue that what was attacked and exposed in its double standard in the aftermath of 9/11 was pre-cisely the Western self-representation of justice following a "pat-tern." As Derrida reminds us, "[o]ne does not count the dead in the same way from one corner of the globe to the other."[25]

Far from following the assumed Western pattern of legal re-sponses, the response to 11 September has been caught in the

---

23 Derrida, "Autoimmunity," 91–93. The quote is on 93.
24 Ibid., 93.
25 Ibid., 92.

"vicious circle of repression" whose characteristic is, as Derrida writes, that "defenses and all the forms of what is called, with two equally problematic words, the 'war on terrorism,' work to regenerate, in the short or long term, the causes of the evil they claim to eradicate."[26] If there is a pattern, it would be that of an "autoimmunitary" dynamics that Derrida sees at work both in the attacks *and* the aftermath of September 11. What "terrorizes most" is that the aggression actually "comes, *as from the inside* [...] through ruse and the implementation of *high-tech* knowledge": "One will remain forever defenseless in the face of a suicidal, autoimmunitary aggression." Within this autoimmunitary dynamics "repression in both its psychoanalytical sense and its political sense — whether it be through the police, the military, or the economy — ends up producing, reproducing, and regenerating the very thing it seeks to disarm."[27]

One manifestation of this repression happens to be directed against the articulation of "literary justice" in a place that in itself can be considered a glaring symptom of this repression: Guantánamo Bay Prison Camp.

Articulating Literary Justice

Felman's analyses of the Eichmann and the O.J. Simpson trials — and of the ways in which legal justice and literary justice diverge from each other in both cases — are gripping and powerfully illuminating. In these two cases, "literary justice" takes on two very different forms.

In the Eichmann trial in Jerusalem in 1961, it is the testimony of the writer Ka-Zetnik or, more precisely, his collapse following the interruption of his trancelike testimony by both the prosecutor and the presiding judge exhorting the witness to listen to them, that compellingly corroborates Felman's thesis of the

---

26 Ibid., 100.
27 Ibid., 95, 99.

"discrepancy between what culture can articulate as legal justice and what it articulates as literary justice"[28]:

> The call to order by the judge urging the witness to obey — strictly to answer questions and to follow legal rules — impacts the witness *physically* as an invasive call to order by an ss officer. Once more, the imposition of a heartless and unbending rule of order violently robs him of his words and, in reducing him to silence, once more threatens to annihilate him, to erase his essence as a *human* witness. [...] The writer's collapse can be read as a parable of the collapse of language in the encounter between law and trauma. It reveals the literary as a dimension of silence in the courtroom, a dimension of speechless embodiment, which brings to the fore through the very failure of words the importance of the witness's body in the courtroom.[29]

By contrast, the "literary justice" enacted in Tolstoy's "Kreutzer Sonata," "precocious[ly]" in anticipation of the "trial of the century" of O.J. Simpson, is a confession "outside the law" that could not only "not be transformed into evidence in court," but had to be "excluded from the trial" by the Russian law.[30]

In both cases, Felman argues, "the law is, so to speak, professionally blind to its constitutive and structural relation to (both private and collective, cultural) trauma, and [...] its 'forms of judicial blindness' take shape wherever the structure of the trauma unwittingly takes over the structure of a trial and wherever the legal institution, unawares, triggers a legal repetition of the trauma that it puts on trial or attempts to cure."[31]

---

28 Felman, *The Juridical Unconscious*, 8.

29 Ibid., 146, 9. One of the most insightful readings of Felman's discussion of the Eichmann Trial is offered by Michael G. Levine, in his essay "The Day the Sun Stood Still: Benjamin's Theses, Trauma, and the Eichmann Trial," *MLN* 126 (2011): 534–60.

30 Felman, *The Juridical Unconscious*, 97.

31 Ibid., 146.

The aftermath of September 11 has led to a set of cases in which legal justice and literary justice are intertwined in ways that differ fundamentally from the two trials analyzed by Felman but that testify to the relevance of her distinction in this context as well.

In 2007, a slim book was published that, in spite of (literally) prohibitive obstacles, tries to testify to cases in which in the name of the American people, both the articulation of legal justice and the articulation of literary justice were (and in some of them continue to be) denied, silence being imposed on both. Further complicating the matter is the fact that in these cases, the hypothetical pursuit of "legal" justice and that of "literary" justice don't share the same language, nor, as a consequence, the same silence.

The title of the volume *Poems from Guantánamo: The Detainees Speak,* portrays the facts only partially and conditionally. As the introduction to the volume makes clear, the detainees "speak" here only through the translation of "linguists" with "secret-level security clearances."[32] Marc Falkoff, one of the lawyers who represent pro bono detainees of the camp, describes in his introduction the main reason why the collection does not offer a "complete portrait of the poetry composed at Guantánamo":

> Many of the detainees' poems were destroyed or confiscated before they could be shared with the authors' lawyers. The military, for instance, confiscated nearly all twenty-five thousand lines of poetry composed by Shaikh Abdurraheem Muslim Dost, returning to him only a handful upon his release from Guantánamo. [...] In addition, the Pentagon refuses to allow most of the detainees' poems to be made public, arguing that poetry "presents a special risk" to national security because of its "content and format." The fear appears to be that the detainees will try to smuggle coded messages out of

---

32 Marc Falkoff, "Notes on Guantánamo," in *Poems from Guantánamo: The Detainees Speak,* ed. Marc Falkoff (Iowa City: University of Iowa Press, 2007), 4–5. Further references will be made parenthetically in the text.

the prison camp. Hundreds of poems therefore remain suppressed by the military and will likely never be seen by the public. In addition, most of the poems that *have* been cleared are in English translation only, because the Pentagon believes that their original Arabic or Pashto versions represent an enhanced security risk. (5)

In addition, then, to the denial of legal justice (to which end the facility, operated by the Joint Task Force Guantánamo of the United States government since January 2002 in the Guantánamo Bay Naval Base, was after all created), the denial of "literary justice" is attested by the Pentagon's refusal to allow the publication of most of the existing detainees' poems on the grounds that poetry "presents a special risk" to national security because of its "content and format." What is more, the confiscation of thousands of lines of poetry from the inmates evinces that even the private possession of one's own poetic, literary writing is considered an intolerable threat. The silencing of legal justice goes hand in hand here with the silencing of literary justice.[33]

The poet-authors are considered highly suspect, and have therefore been robbed of many of their fundamental legal rights. As many commentators have noted, and as Giorgio Agamben elaborates in his book *State of Exception,* the military order issued by the us President in November 2001, "which authorized the 'indefinite detention' and trial by 'military commissions' [...] of noncitizens suspected of involvement in terrorist activities," in fact "erase[d] any legal status of the individual, thus producing a legally unnamable and unclassifiable being," fitting the paradigm of the "homo sacer."[34]

---

33 The following pages are greatly indebted to the work my colleague and friend Julie Carlson and I have undertaken for our jointly authored introduction to the book we have co-edited: Julie Carlson and Elisabeth Weber, "For the Humanities," in *Speaking about Torture,* eds. Julie Carlson and Elisabeth Weber, 1–9 (New York: Fordham University Press, 2012).

34 Agamben, *State of Exception,* 3. Even though on June 12, 2008, the New York-based Center for Constitutional Rights won a Supreme Court victory in *Boumediene v. Bush,* and secured the right for Guantánamo prisoners

"Legal justice" is, thus, out of reach. But so, too, is "literary justice," the latter being doubly suppressed, both as manifest literature ("manifest" like Tolstoy's "Kreutzer Sonata" that, according to Felman, anticipates the legal proceedings of the O.J. Simpson case), and as latent trauma, trauma that might burst open in any legal proceeding, a likelihood all the greater as the majority of prisoners were tortured after their capture by US and allied forces.[35] Like their "legally unnameable and unclassifiable" authors, the poems are considered "too dangerous for release." The methods of silencing used by the American authorities include "censorship that ranges from the destruction of texts to heavily redacted versions to framing devices that orient the reader in certain ways and translations whose primary task is eradication of the language and culture of origin as well as claims to the originality, autonomy, and value of its speakers."[36]

Assuming that media of transmission are not external to history and its representations, assuming that specific media open up specific spaces of representation of singular events and historical processes and offer varying logics of the ways in which such events and processes are interconnected, the suppression and selective "clearance" of poems from the Guantánamo prison camp censor precisely those media that open up *specific* spaces of representation and offer *singular* logics of connection. As implied in the American decision to keep the original versions of the poems locked up, the poems offer, especially in their original languages, different logics of the interconnectedness of events and processes. By "disappearing" those original languag-

---

and other noncitizens to challenge the legality of their detention through habeas proceedings in federal courts, the Obama administration still sought the power to hold men indefinitely without charge or trial, as the CCR documents for many cases. See for example CCR, Active Cases, "Barhoumi v. Obama."

35 They are thus considered "too dangerous for release, [and] too tainted for trial." McCoy, *A Question of Torture*, 195. "The ideal solution to this conundrum, from a CIA perspective," McCoy adds, "is extrajudicial execution. […] In effect, the logical corollary to state-sanctioned torture is state-sponsored murder" (195–96).

36 Carlson and Weber, "For the Humanities," 2.

es even from their authors, by classifying them as "enhanced security risk" and making accessible a handful of poems only in translations by linguists with security clearance, the American authorities actually confirm one of Jacques Derrida's theses on witnessing: the fundamental possibility that the idiom remains untranslatable, is one of the structural conditions of witnessing.[37] Regardless of content, the materiality of the signifier is here rightly understood to be in itself a witness: insofar as it is "linked to a singularity and to the experience of an idiomatic mark — for example, that of a language — testimony resists the test of translation." "As always," Derrida notes, "the idiom remains irreducible. This invincible singularity of the verbal body already introduces us into the enigma of testimony," where the "possibility of the secret always remains open, and this reserve inexhaustible."[38] But far from being reserved to foreign languages, the censoring activities by the American authorities in Guantánamo Bay reveal that the "singularity of the verbal body" is "invincible" in the seemingly most well-known, the most familiar, idiom too. The following incident reported in Falkoff's collection shows that the feared potential of the "verbal body" is, indeed, fundamental and *structural,* and that the "inexhaustible reserve" of the code and of the secret announces itself, as a consequence, equally in the best known verses of one's mother tongue.[39]

The British citizen Moazzam Begg, who was "arrested in Pakistan and detained for three years in Guantánamo," during which time he was repeatedly tortured, received one day a "heavily censored letter from his seven-year-old daughter," in which "the only legible line was 'I love you, Dad.'" Never charged with a crime, Begg was released in 2005.

Upon his release, his daughter told him that the censored lines were a poem she had copied for him:

---

37 Derrida, "Poetics and Politics of Witnessing," 67–69.

38 Ibid., 69, 67.

39 See also Carlson and Weber, "For the Humanities," 6–7.

One, two, three, four, five,
Once I caught a fish alive.
Six, seven eight, nine, ten,
Then I let it go again. (29)

A nursery rhyme became here an intolerable security risk for the jailors. The counting poem continues as follows:

Why did you let it go?
Because it bit my finger so.
Which finger did it bite?
The little one upon the right.

Through the medium *nursery rhyme* infants learn language and experience their body to be their own. This medium captures *in nuce* the mediation of community and of language necessary for the organization of the fragmented body into a fictive integrity. The assessment of this medium as intolerable security risk is thus highly significant. Most, if not all, censored poets have been tortured. This concurrence of torture and censorship is not a coincidence; on the contrary, the torture is intimately bound up with the suppression of the victims' language. Together, they indicate which fundamental level of community torture attacks. The medium *nursery rhyme* is

exemplary for the medium *language* in the sense of medium defined by Wolf Kittler as a "space to which there is no outside." In this medium the other's face, glance and encouragement are all integral to the process of learning how to recognize, name and tell apart what already "belongs" to one's own body; integral, then, to the infant's subject formation. At the same time, belonging is constituted in this medium as "be-longing," as an integration into the community that is constitutively *open* towards the other. It is in this medium of constitutive openness that a fundamental trust in "the world" originates.[40]

As countless witness accounts from victims show, torture "undoes the formation of the subject as well as of the community, neither of which comes into being without the other — an entangled formation for which the medium *nursery rhyme* is emblematic. Torture is the cruel undoing of the subject and, simultaneously, of his or her be-longing to different communities (family, culture, nation, humanity)."[41]

It is, thus, only logical that the nursery rhyme sent to Begg by his daughter could not be tolerated on two accounts: the practice it invites (learning to count with someone who already knows how to count, while discovering one's fingers with someone who has already discovered his or hers) celebrates belonging to a community, and the relationship between the sender and the addressee is an affirmation of that very constitution of community through the enmeshment of language, body, and belonging. On the most fundamental level, as Felman asserts, "literary justice," as differentiated from "legal justice," concerns the "dimension of speechless embodiment."[42] "Art is the language of infinity

---

40 Carlson and Weber, "For the Humanities," 7. See Wolf Kittler, *The Middle Voice: Steady and Discrete Manifolds in Walter Benjamin,* Center for German and European Studies Working Paper 3.25 (Berkeley: University of California, 1996), 4, and Aimee Carrillo Rowe, "Be Longing: Toward a Feminist Politics of Relation," *NWSA Journal* 17, no. 2 (2005): 15–46. In her reading of some of the poems, inspired by the terminology of Emmanuel Levinas, Judith Butler emphasizes the longing expressed in them as one of the emotions testifying to the body's existence in "exposure and proximity to others," a vulnerability that "can be reduced to injurability." However, "if this precarious status can become the condition of suffering, it also serves the condition of responsiveness, of a formulation of affect, understood as a radical act of interpretation in the face of unwilled subjugation." Judith Butler, *Frames of War: When is Life Grievable?* (London: Verso, 2009), 55–62. For an in-depth exploration of Levinas's introduction of previously unheard-of concepts such as "vulnerability," "trauma," "persecution" into Occidental philosophy, see my *Verfolgung und Trauma.*

41 Carlson and Weber, "For the Humanities," 7–8.

42 Felman, *The Juridical Unconscious,* 9. See also 147–51.

and of the irreducibility of fragments, a language of embodiment, of incarnation, and of embodied incantation or endless
rhythmic *repetition*."[43] Nowhere is this as evident as in nursery
rhymes. Begg's torture and its inherently intended undoing of
belonging, as well as its corresponding refusal of legal justice
is mirrored by the censorship of a poem that through "endless
rhythmic repetition" precisely calls forth, incants, and performs
the subject's "embodiment" and his or her very inscription into
community.

Jean Améry has described in vivid detail how torture pursues
the undoing of a subject endowed with language through his or
her reduction to howling flesh, in which one's "belonging" to
one's own body is experienced as utter calamity and betrayal.[44]
Such undoing of the subject and his or her community is alluded to in another poem from Guantánamo, Jumah Al Dossari's "Death Poem." Al Dossari was released in 2007 to Saudi
Arabia after having been held in detention for five years, three
and a half of which were spent in solitary confinement, without
a formal charge ever brought against him.

Death Poem

Take my blood.
Take my death shroud and
The remnants of my body.
Take photographs of my corpse at the grave, lonely.
Send them to the world,
To the judges and
To the people of conscience,
Send them to the principled men and the fair-minded.
And let them bear the guilty burden, before the world,
Of this innocent soul.
Let them bear the burden, before their children and before
    history,

---

43 Ibid., 153.
44 Améry, *At the Mind's Limits*, 59, 74, 77, 85. See Chapter 1 in this volume.

Of this wasted, sinless soul,
Of this soul which has suffered at the hands of the
"protectors of peace." (32)

The fictive integrity of the body is here reversed: all that is left
are "remnants" and "blood" and the death shroud that may hold
them together. The subject that came into being only within
a community and language has been reduced to a "lonely"
"corpse." "Whether the photographs that the poem commissions to be sent 'to the world' refer to those sent via the internet
and other electronic media from Abu Ghraib cannot be established for certain. But for us readers, the connection cannot not
be established either."[45] The poem turns the media that are integral to the torturer's and executioner's community against their
users: "The burden of the executioner's guilt and the burden of
the innocence of this 'wasted soul' are together entrusted to or
imposed on these photographs of infamy. [...] Unreconciled, a
voice speaks here [...] from *before* the grave: from a place in
which a proper burial, epitome of a person's be-longing to a
community, has not even yet been possible, if not made all but
impossible ('take my death shroud')."[46] Together with their media of transmission, these photographs thus starkly illustrate, in
Susan Sontag's words, a "culture of shamelessness" and of "una-
pologetic brutality."[47]

By contrast, on the other side of the camera, what survives
is shame. As Marc Nichanian explains, the voice that gives testimony becomes a "living proof of [it's] own death [...]. That is
the moment of shame. Testimony is shame."[48] Commenting on
the "thousands upon thousands of testimonies left by Armenian
survivors" of the genocide committed by the Turks during the
first two decades of the twentieth century, Nichanian notes that

---

45 Carlson and Weber, "For the Humanities," 8.
46 Ibid., 8–9. See also Michael Richardson's reading in *Gestures of Testimony:
    Torture, Trauma, and Affect in Literature* (New York: Bloomsbury, 2016), 69.
47 Susan Sontag, "Regarding the Torture of Others," *New York Times Maga-
    zine,* May 23, 2004.
48 Nichanian, *The Historiographic Perversion,* 118, 120–21.

"shame" is hardly ever mentioned. The only "cases of shame" in this vast corpus are "always linked to suicides. He who survives never expresses his shame. There is here a radical impossibility. There is no survival with shame. Only shame survives, would say Agamben. And it can testify to nothing, except to itself."[49] The word "shame" may not be uttered by Al Dossari, but it suffuses the poem. As the collection's editor notes, Al Dossari "tried to kill himself twelve times while in the prison" (31).

There is a different shame that also survives. Any legal actions to hold those responsible for the US torture policies have been thwarted. Former president George W. Bush can boast with impunity in his memoir that his authorization of torture (a crime that according to the UN Convention Against Torture of 1984, article 2, cannot be justified by any "exceptional circumstances whatsoever," including a state of war or a threat of war) was the right "decision." Contrary to President Obama's pledge in January 2009, Guantánamo remains open. According to a *Report on Guantánamo Detainees* published by the Seton Hall University School of Law, 86% of the detainees captured by Pakistan or the Northern Alliance were sold to the United States "during a time in which the United States offered large bounties for capture of suspected enemies," commonly, $5,000 per man, a sum that corresponds to "several years' income" in the tribal areas of Pakistan and Afghanistan.[50]

The numbers provided by the Center for Constitutional Rights speak for themselves: as of January 27, 2017,

739 men have been transferred (including 9 deaths). 41 men remain detained. [...] 5 have been cleared for release but remain imprisoned. [...] 22 or more were children when taken

---

49 Ibid., 120. "It was, as if the shame should outlive him," Kafka has K. say before his death at the end of *The Trial* (trans. Willa and Edwin Muir [New York: Schocken, 1995], 229, trans. modified).

50 Mark Denbeaux, *Report on Guantánamo Detainees,* Seton Hall University School of Law, 2006; former State Department official Lawrence Wilkerson quoted in Gusterson, *Drone,* 102. See also Center for Constitutional Rights, "Guantánamo by the Numbers."

to the detention camp. More men (9) have died at Guantánamo than have been convicted (8) by the military commissions. o senior government officials have been held accountable for the wrongful detention and torture at Guantánamo.
It now costs approximately $454 million per year to keep
Guantánamo open. The Pentagon will have spent $5.242 bil-
lion on the prison by the end of 2014.[51]

As the *New York Times'* Editorial Board pointed out in a text
denouncing the "broken promise of closing Guantánamo," the
United Nations special rapporteur on torture has "sought access
to the detainees for years, seeking to document their treatment
while in custody. The government has refused repeated requests
since 2004, with no good reason."[52]

---

51   Center for Constitutional Rights, "Guantánamo by the Numbers." See also
     The New York Times, "The Guantánamo Docket: A History of the Detainee
     Population." Andy Worthington's book *The Guantánamo Files: The Stories
     of the 774 Detainees in America's Illegal Prison* provides background infor-
     mation of many of the prisoners (London: Pluto Press, 2007). In the last
     months before the presidential election in November 2016, the Obama ad-
     ministration has sped up the pace of transferring detainees, in the hope of
     closing the prison altogether. On February 23, 2016, President Obama sent a
     plan to close down Guantánamo to Congress. Visibly irritated, he presented
     the main points at a press conference. He argued that Guantánamo "does
     not advance our national security, it undermines it," that it is "counterpro-
     ductive" in the fight against terrorism, because terrorist groups use it as a
     "propaganda" tool in their "efforts to recruit," that keeping it open is "con-
     trary to our values," and that the prison is "a stain on our broader record
     of upholding the highest standards of rule of law." "I am absolutely com-
     mitted to closing the detention facilty at Guantánamo." See Charlie Savage
     and Julie Hirschfeld Davis, "Obama Sends Plan to Close Guantánamo to
     Congress," *New York Times,* Feb. 23, 2016. For the reaction of some congres-
     sional Republicans, see Austin Wright and Nick Gass, "Obama Announces
     Plan for Closing Guantanamo Bay Prison," *Politico,* Feb. 23, 2016.
52   *The New York Times* Editorial Board, "The Broken Promise of Closing
     Guantánamo," *New York Times,* June 20, 2016. See also the Editorial on Abu
     Zubaydah's appearance before a panel of government officials, the first time
     since his capture 14 years ago that "a small group of human rights advocates
     and journalists got a fleeting glimpse" of him. After providing valuable in-
     formation to the FBI, he was turned over to the CIA whose interrogators
     waterboarded him at least 83 times and subjected him to other forms of bru-

In his "Report with Respect to Guantanamo," President Obama, in his last communication addressed to Congress, reiterated on January 19, 2017, that "[r]ather than keeping us safer, the detention facility at Guantánamo undermines American national security." His letter included an updated plan for closing the infamous facility.[53]

"A victim," Felman writes following Thomas Szasz and Jean-François Lyotard, "is by definition not only one who is oppressed but also one who has no language of his own, one who, quite precisely, is *robbed of a language* with which to articulate his or her victimization."[54] The confiscation of thousands of verses of poetry by US authorities makes this abundantly clear. What is "available" to the prisoners in Guantánamo "as language" in the few poems released in translation, is, to quote Felman again, "only the oppressor's language. But in the oppressor's language, the abused will sound crazy, even to himself, if he describes himself as abused."[55] Readers of these poems in the English of linguists with security clearance need to keep this quandary in mind. But that does not mean that they are addressed any less. Al Dossari's poem addresses its hypothetical readers, the "judges" and "people of conscience," the "principled men and the fair-minded" in a way that resonates with a question articulated by Felman in the context of her discussion of the trials of domestic violence: "How can we recognize, how can we expiate a violence that is inscribed in culture as invisible, and that cannot be rendered visible in court?"[56]

---

tal treatments that yielded no additional information. "Never charged and never tried, Abu Zubaydah has also never been allowed to speak publicly about his ordeal. His American abusers have never been held to account." *The New York Times Editorial Board,* "A Stark Reminder of Guantánamo's Sins," *New York Times,* Aug. 25, 2016.

53 Barack Obama, "Letter from the President — Report with Respect to Guantanamo."
54 Felman, *Juridical Unconscious,* 125.
55 Ibid.
56 Ibid., 99.

CHAPTER 4

Guantánamo Poems[1]

In a case of massive censorship exercised by the American administration, hundreds, possibly thousands of poems written in the Guantánamo Bay prison camp have been suppressed over the last decade and a half. The poems' authors have been denied some of the most basic human rights, and in most, if not all cases have been subjected to torture. The original Arabic and Pashto versions of the few published poems, along with all the untranslated ones, remain under lock and key in a "'secure facility' in Virginia."[2]

As explained in the previous chapter, English translations of twenty-two poems were declassified and published in an edition prepared by one of the prisoners' pro bono lawyer, Marc Falkoff, at the condition of being done by "linguists with security clearance" who, as Falkoff explains, had to work "without access to the usual dictionaries and other tools of the trade."[3]

As then-senior military correspondent Yochi J. Dreazen wrote in a front-page article of the *Wall Street Journal* of June 21, 2007, shortly before the publication of the anthology,

---

1   Originally published in *Journal of Literature and Trauma Studies* 2, no. 1–2, "Suffering in Literature," eds. David Miller and Lucia Aiello (Spring/Fall 2013): 159–82.

2   Marc Falkoff, "Acknowledgments," in *Poems from Guantánamo*, x; Falkoff, "Notes on Guantánamo," in ibid., 1–5. Judith Butler writes on the collection in her *Frames of War*, 55–62. For a close reading of two excerpts of Falkoff's collection see Chapter 3 in this volume.

3   Falkoff, *Poems from Guantánamo*, x.

U.S. authorities explained why the military has been slow to declassify the poems in a June 2006 letter to one of Mr. Falkoff's colleagues. "Poetry [...] presents a special risk, and DOD standards are not to approve the release of any poetry in its original form or language," it said. The military says poetry is harder to vet than conventional letters because allusions and imagery in poetry that seem innocent can be used to convey coded messages to other militants. The letter told defense lawyers to translate any works they wanted to release publicly into English and then submit the translations to the government for review. The strict security arrangements governing anything written by Guantanamo Bay inmates meant that Mr. Falkoff had to use linguists with secret-level security clearances rather than translators who specialize in poetry. The resulting translations, Mr. Falkoff writes in the book, "cannot do justice to the subtlety and cadences of the originals." For the military, even some of the translations appeared to go too far. Mr. Falkoff says it rejected three of the five translated poems he submitted, along with a dozen others submitted by his colleagues. Cmdr. Gordon says he doesn't know how many poems were rejected but adds that the military "absolutely" remains concerned that poetry could be used to pass coded messages to other militants.[4]

Reading the twenty-two published poems means, thus, to read them torn out of their cultural and especially linguistic and poetological context. It means reading them in the language of the jailor, not just in terms of translation into English, but in terms of translation into the English of "linguists with secret-level security clearances." It also means reading them in the language of a universe created to circumvent the constitutional rights citizens and foreigners alike have on US soil. In short, reading

---

4   Yochi J. Dreazen, "The Prison Poets of Guantanamo Find a Publisher," *Wall Street Journal*, June 21, 2007, 1.

those poems in translation means reading them in a context as
forcibly US-American as the prison camp itself.[5]

---

5 Part of this context is also the fact that the policies governing internment
in Guantánamo need to be understood not as exceptional, developed exclusively for those whom George W. Bush called "the worst of the worst."
Rather, as Colin Dayan has shown based on work done by an array of authors, including Angela Davis, Avery Gordon, and others, "the now-famous
'torture memos'" which "redefined the meaning of torture and extended
the limits of permissible pain" actually "rely upon the last 30 years of court
decisions, which have gradually eviscerated the Eighth Amendment's prohibition of 'cruel and unusual punishments'" (Colin Dayan, *The Story of
Cruel and Unusual* [Cambridge: MIT Press, 2007], 5). The "realm of constitutional minimums — situated between mere need and bare survival,"
Dayan explains, "set the stage for Guantánamo Bay and Abu Ghraib. I recall
the words of Marine Brigadier General Michael R. Lehnert at Guantánamo
Bay in 2002: 'There is no torture, no whips, no bright lights, no drugging.
We are a nation of laws.' But what kind of laws? Laws that permit indefinite
solitary confinement in state-of-the-art units, with cell doors, unit doors,
and shower doors operated remotely from a control center and physical
contact limited to touching through a security door by a correctional officer while being placed in restraints. Inmates have described life in the
massive, windowless super-maximum prison as akin to 'living in a tomb'"
(53–54). The title of a 2011 "position paper" by the Center for Constitutional
Rights on the "Death Row Experience from a Human Rights Perspective"
bluntly summarizes the analyses presented in the document by asserting in
the paper's title that "'The United States Tortures before It Kills." However,
conditions of torture are not limited to death row. Commenting further
on solitary confinement, Dayan notes that "over the past two and a half
decades, an intimate dialogue between courts and prison administrators
has normalized what was once the most severe deprivation. The subject is
couched in euphemisms: first 'disciplinary segregation,' and later 'administrative segregation' (nominally based on security classification rather than
wrongdoing). Since prison officials claim that these units are non-punitive,
they are difficult to fight under either the Eighth or the Fourteenth Amendment. Since the 1980s, the United Nations Commission on Human Rights,
the United Nations Committee Against Torture, the Red Cross, human-
rights organizations such as Amnesty International and Human Rights
Watch, and civil-rights organizations such as the ACLU and the Center for
Constitutional Rights, have criticized the darkly authoritarian and abusive
conditions of prisons in the United States, focusing on super-maximum imprisonment, where inmates deemed incorrigible are locked down for 23 to
24 hours a day, their food delivered through a slot in the steel door of their
80-square-foot cell" (54–55). What makes the situation of Guantánamo in-

According to the Center for Constitutional Rights, of the 780 men imprisoned on the American base in Cuba since its opening in January 2002, nine have died while in detention (some of whom committed suicide), but fewer than nine have ever been convicted of a crime.[6] *Habeas corpus* — the constitutional right to know and challenge the reason for one's imprisonment — has thus been violated systematically over the last fifteen years.

Guantánamo, amas, amat

When in June 2004, Paul Muldoon published his poem "Hedge School" in the *New York Times,* the prison camp held 597 prisoners.[7] The lightheartedness of the expanded title given to the poem by the *New York Times,* alluding to the start of summer vacation around the country ("Out of School and Into Summer; Hedge School"), suggests that the editors might not have read much further than the poem's title before including it on the "Opinion" page of the newspaper's June 26, 2004 edition:

Hedge School[8]

Not only those rainy mornings our great-great-
        grandmother was posted at a gate
with a rush mat
over her shoulders, a mat that flashed
Papish like a heliograph, but those rainy mornings when my
        daughter and the rest

---

mates radically different from prisoners in US penal institutions is that the overwhelming number of the former have never been charged with a crime.

6   Center for Constitutional Rights, "Guantánamo by the Numbers." See also *The New York Times,* "The Guantánamo Docket" and Chapter 3 in this volume.

7   Ibid.; by then, 153 had been "transferred" to other countries or released. The overall population of the camp had been slowly decreasing since June 2003, which saw the highest number of inmates, 684.

8   Paul Muldoon, "Hedge School," in Muldoon, *Horse Latitudes* (New York: Farrar, Straus and Giroux, 2006), 94, originally published as "Out of School and into Summer; Hedge School," *New York Times,* June 26, 2004.

of her all-American Latin class may yet be forced to
    conjugate
Guantánamo, amas, amat
and learn with Luciana how "headstrong liberty is lash'd
with woe" — all past and future mornings were impressed

on me just now, dear sis,
as I sheltered in a doorway on Church Street in St. Andrews
(where, in 673, another Maelduin was bishop),

and tried to come up with a ruse
for unsealing the New Shorter Oxford English Dictionary
    back in that corner shop
and tracing the root of metastasis.

With the line "Guantánamo, amas, amat," Muldoon's poem
establishes first of all, as Armin Schäfer has observed, that
Guantánamo leaves its mark on language, that it has changed
language.[9] This is so not only because the policies responsible
for and resulting from the prison camp have given rise to hundreds of euphemisms of which Fred Halliday's book *Shocked
and Awed: A Dictionary of the War on Terror*[10] offers a meticu-
lous account. More insidiously, as Muldoon's poem suggests,
Guantánamo may "force" students to conjugate differently, and
to conjugate differently verbs such as the Latin *amare,* to love.
Guantánamo leaves its mark on the thesaurus of language, but
it may also affect and thus poison the grammar, the structural
rules that govern the use of that treasure.

If language, as Walter Benjamin argues in his essays on language, is a medium not of communication but a medium in
the literal sense, as a "space to which there is no outside,"[11] if
language is the medium *in which* we live as we live in the air

---

9 I thank Armin Schäfer for introducing me to Muldoon's poem and for the
    insights he shared with me.
10 Halliday, *Shocked and Awed.*
11 Following Wolf Kittler's fortuitous formulation in his *The Middle Voice,* 4.

we breathe, Guantánamo, by encroaching on language as Muldoon's poem suggests, will permeate everything. Muldoon's
poem ends with the word "metastasis" which rhymes with "dear
sis."[12] Just as the metastases of the cancer that would kill his sister have invaded the most intimate relationships and the words
for them, such as the endearing address used in and for one of
those relationships — "dear sis" — Guantánamo, by infringing
on the conjugation pattern of a verb, might "yet" uncontrollably
metastasize, especially if the point of entrance is "amare."[13] The
cancer "may yet" spread, fatally.

Following Muldoon's poem, two major areas affected by
Guantánamo can be named:

1) Guantánamo reveals that the conjugation of "amare," "to
love" needs a prefix in the language of Empire, "the Roman Empire," as Maria Johnston observed, "finding its continuation in
the present-day American one with the pointed reference to
Guantánamo."[14]

One reason for this necessity is what could be called the me-
tastasizing of Guantánamo: since the events of September 11,
2001, US citizens have learned "to acquiesce to," if not to love ideas and practices "once deemed so radical as to be unthinkable."[15]
The systematic violation of habeas corpus in Guantánamo can
be considered the centerpiece of those practices. The acceptability of torture, practiced for years at the camp and spreading
from there to places like Abu Ghraib, is another stark point in
case.[16] There is more. As Alfred McCoy wrote in 2012,

---

12 Helen Vendler, "Fanciness and Fatality," review of Paul Mudoon, *Horse Latitudes, The New Republic Online,* Nov. 9, 2006.

13 The last poem of *Horse Latitudes* speaks of the sister's losing battle against
the same cancer that killed her mother thirty years earlier (Muldoon, *Horse
Latitudes,* 99). See also Maria Johnston, "Tracing the Root of Metastasis,"
Contemporary Poetry Review, 2007; Jefferson Holdridge, *The Poetry of Paul
Muldoon* (Dublin: The Liffey Press, 2008), 186.

14 Johnston, "Tracing the Root of *Metastasis*".

15 Glenn Greenwald, "Extremism Normalized," *Salon,* July 31, 2012.

16 Greenwald: "'Torture' has been permanently transformed from an unspeak-
able taboo into a garden-variety political controversy" (ibid.). See also Mc-
Coy, "Tomgram: Alfred McCoy, Perfecting Illegality": "In […] late 2002,

after a decade of intense public debate over torture, in the last two years the United States has arrived at a questionable default political compromise: impunity at home, rendition abroad. [...]

[U]nchecked by any domestic or international sanction, Washington has slid down torture's slippery slope to find, just as the French did in Algeria during the 1950s, that at its bottom lies the moral abyss of extrajudicial execution.

The systematic French torture of thousands during the Battle of Algiers in 1957 also generated over 3,000 "summary executions" to insure, as one French general put it, that "the machine of justice" not be "clogged with cases."

In an eerie parallel, Washington has reacted to the torture scandals of the Bush era by generally forgoing arrests and opting for no-fuss aerial assassinations. From 2005 to 2012, U.S. drone killings inside Pakistan rose from zero to a total of 2,400 (and still going up) — a figure disturbingly close to those 3,000 French assassinations in Algeria. In addition, it has now been revealed that the president himself regularly orders specific assassinations by drone in Pakistan, Yemen, and Somalia off a secret "kill list." [...]

Absent any searching inquiry or binding reforms, assassination is now the everyday American way of war while extraordinary renditions remain a tool of state.[17]

Secretary of Defense Donald Rumsfeld appointed General Geoffrey Miller to head the new prison at Guantanamo, Cuba, and gave him broad authority to develop a total three-phase attack on the sensory receptors, cultural identity, and individual psyches of his new prisoners. After General Miller visited Abu Ghraib prison in September 2003, the U.S. commander for Iraq issued orders for the use of psychological torture in U.S. prisons in that country, including sensory disorientation, self-inflicted pain, and a recent innovation, cultural humiliation through exposure to dogs (which American believed would be psychologically devastating for Arabs). It is no accident that Private Lynndie England, a military guard at Abu Ghraib prison, was famously photographed leading a naked Iraqi detainee leashed like a dog" (*TomDispatch*, Aug. 14, 2012).

17 McCoy, "Tomgram." In *Torture and Impunity*, McCoy analyses this issue in detail.

Jennifer Gibson, one of the researchers of a 175-page study published in September 2012 by Stanford University and New York University, asserts that the drone war "has turned North Waziristan into the world's largest prison, a massive occupied zone. [...] The constant sense of terror is a feeling that knows no boundaries."[18]

Americans seem to have come to accept, if not to love, Guantánamo and what it spawned as indispensable for their national security.[19] That means, according to Muldoon's poem, that any "love," just like anything related to "school" is contaminated, tainted with Guantánamo. "Guantánamo" is now recited just as mindfully, mechanically, or mindlessly as one might conjugate a verb in school. The reason why Muldoon chooses Latin for this contamination is certainly because of the association of Rome with empire. But the use of Latin may also be read in the context of what Jacques Derrida has compellingly termed *mondialatinisation*, the essentially Christian "globalatinization," that is, the latinization not just of the globe, but of the world, including, to speak with Heidegger, of our "being-in-the-world."

In his analysis of the "two ages" of violence, which he sees to be at work in "our 'wars of religion,'" Derrida shows how the acts of violence that appear most "archaic" and those that are technologically most refined can both be described as "auto-immune" reactions and as such obey the same "terrifying but fatal logic."[20] According to Derrida, *globalatinization* produces in its heart that which threatens it from outside, for example terrorism that is carried out in the name of a specific religion. More precisely, *globalatinization* produces that which threatens it as auto-immune reaction, as a war against its own mechanisms of defense. As a consequence, the categories of inside and outside, of the center and the periphery, of friend and enemy lose their

---

18 Jennifer Gibson, "Living with Death by Drone," *Lincoln Journal Star*, Oct. 7, 2012. The Stanford/NYU study "Living under drones" is accessible online.

19 On the status of the prison camp in the waning days of the Obama presidency, see above, 134–35. The new administration has vowed to keep the prison camp open and to expand its operations.

20 Derrida, "Faith and Knowledge," 80, 88–89.

perspicuity. Derrida's concept is particularly useful for understanding how a democracy generates defense mechanisms that contradict its values in the most fundamental aspects, to the point of attacking its own set of "immunitary" defenses, such as the US constitution.

The second area affected by Guantánamo, according to Muldoon's poem, is the way in which it invades and reveals the meaning of *school* by subjecting the learning of a foreign language and of the canon of English-language literature (in this case Shakespeare) to the needs of what is termed "national security."[21] The first two stanzas of Muldoon's poem are all about school mornings: the past ones of the great-great-grandmother's "hedge school," one of defiance and resistance, vs. the future mornings of the daughter's "all-American Latin class," in which Shakespeare and Latin are forced into rhyme and complicity with Guantánamo.

The rhymes of Muldoon's poem delineate the contrasts between a hedge school of resistance and the "all-American," Latin learning school of co-optation:

"posted at a gate" vs. "forced to conjugate"
"with a rush mat" vs. "Guantánamo, amas, amat"
"a mat that flashed" vs. "headstrong liberty is lash'd"

As Antonia McManus explains, hedge schools "took root at the beginning of the eighteenth century, due to the strictures of the penal laws, which forced Catholic teachers to work

---

21 In this context, it is worth mentioning the "Critical Language Scholarship (CLS) Program" of the United States Department of State, Bureau of Educational and Cultural Affairs. According to its website, the program is "part of a U.S. government effort to expand dramatically the number of Americans studying and mastering critical foreign languages. Students of diverse disciplines and majors are encouraged to apply. Participants are expected to continue their language study beyond the scholarship period, and later apply their critical language skills in their future professional careers." Among the languages taught are Arabic, Persian, Azerbaijani, Bangla, Hindi, Indonesian, Korean, Punjabi, Swahili, Turkish, Urdu, Chinese, Japanese, and Russian.

underground."[22] Following the Williamite wars of 1690–91, "among the first penal laws to be enacted in 1695 during the reign of King William" had been those against Catholic education, one of which bore the telling title "An act to restrain foreign education," conceived to "limit contact between Irish Catholics and their continental allies." A "domestic provision" was also added, forbidding any "person whatsoever of the popish religion to publicly teach school or instruct youth in learning." McManus quotes P.J. Dowling's "pioneering work" on hedge schools which described the Catholic masters' defiance of the law "as 'a kind of guerrilla war' in education." The purpose of the anti-Catholic measures "was not so much to reduce Catholics to a state of ignorance and servitude [...] but rather to force their children to avail themselves of the Protestant education already on offer, an education guaranteed to train them up to be loyal Protestant subjects."[23] To visit a hedge school meant thus to defy the English crown, the Irish parliament and their "handmaid," the established church, in more than one way.[24]

The frontlines, however, were not clear-cut: Even before the repeal of the penal laws against Catholic education in 1782, the Catholic Church sided with the government in its fight against subversive and insurrectional groups in which hedge schoolmasters often played a leading role. As McManus explains,

> the main reason why so many hedge schoolmasters became involved in radical political organisations was firstly because they were sufficiently well educated to understand the radical writings of Thomas Paine, Jean Jacques Rousseau and William Godwin, and their relevance to the Irish political situation. [...] Secondly, hedge schoolmasters were independent of state control and to a certain extent of church control. While both bodies strongly disapproved of revolutionary

---

22 Antonia McManus, *The Irish Hedge School and Its Books, 1695–1831* (Dublin: Four Courts Press, 2002), 15.

23 Ibid., 15f.

24 Ibid., 17–18.

activity, they had no authority over the schoolmasters who selected that course of action, [and who did so at the risk of] being hanged, excommunicated or banished from their parishes.[25]

Moreover, in the case of the Irish hedge schools, Latin was not the language of empire. On the one hand, it was one of the most sought after disciplines, more than classical Greek and Hebrew, because in order to meet the entry requirements of catholic seminaries in Ireland or abroad, boys had to be fluent in Latin. On the other hand, Latin harbored the potential of sedition, with political leaders, contemporary writers, evangelists and landlords "far from happy" with "this quest for Latin learning by the ragged poor," and not wishing to see "young peasants [...] run about in rags with a Cicero or a Virgil under their arms."[26]

---

25 Ibid., 27–36, here 36.

26 According to McManus, there was a "strongly held conviction by political leaders, contemporary writers and evangelists that the poor should not be educated above their station in life [...]. The landlords and their agents were far from happy either with this quest for Latin learning by the ragged poor. [...] [Robert] Peel as home secretary (1822–27) expressed the view that such an education was unsuitable for 'young peasants.' He stated as much in the house of commons on 20 March 1826 in response to Spring-Rice, the MP for Limerick. He said that he: 'did not wish to see children educated like the inhabitants of that part of the country, to which the honourable member belongs, where the young peasants of Kerry run about in rags with a Cicero or a Virgil under their arms.' [...] Kerry was the county which contemporary writers repeatedly singled out as the centre of classical learning in Ireland, especially the famous classical hedge school at Faha. [...] George Holmes was astonished to meet 'amongst the uncultivated part of the country', 'good Latin scholars' who could 'not speak a word of English'. [...] [The hedge school teacher] O'Brien insisted that his students should speak the Latin language daily, as well as Greek, so that eventually they were as fluent in Latin and Greek as they were in English. In later life they corresponded through Latin and as one contemporary recollected, they even sold pigs at the fair through Latin. 'I recollect when, the scholars made by Kennedy, Cantillon, Buckley and O'Brien used keep up a regular correspondence, meet at the fairs, and buy pigs from each other without ever using a word but Latin'" (ibid., 125–26, 128–29). I thank Dr. Damian Shaw and Dr. Matthew Gibson of the University of Macao for discussing these matters with me.

The ruling class's opposition to any classical training and the fact that the soldiers of the English army didn't understand Latin turned the latter into a language that held a potential for revolution, for turning around or against, or, as we will see later, for *metastasis*.

Working in illegality, hedge school masters "taught at considerable risk to their own personal liberty," including the threats of exile and the death penalty. In Muldoon's poem this risk is alluded to in the description of the great-great-grandmother as being "posted at a gate." Indeed, hedge school students stood guard in order "to warn the master if a suspicious-looking stranger was approaching."[27] But the girl's position at a gate is not only one of defensive protection. The "rush mat" over the girl's shoulders flashing "*Papish* like a heliograph" is also a sign of defiance, appropriating against all odds the media-technology of the occupier, the heliograph, with its almost exclusively military use.[28] Muldoon opens here another historical perspective: in addition to the family history spanning from Bishop Maelduin to Muldoon's great-great-grandmother, his sister, himself, and his daughter, the mention of the heliograph points to the long

---

27 McManus writes that "a pupil was usually placed on sentry duty to warn the master if a suspicious-looking stranger was approaching. Appropriate arrangements were then made to reconvene at another location on the following day. During the winter months or periods of inclement weather, the master knew he could rely on the hospitality of the people, as he moved from one location to the next 'earning a little perhaps by turning his hand to farm work, or, when he dared, by teaching the children of his host.' The masters taught at considerable risk to their own personal liberty as there is ample evidence to show that prosecutions were brought against them, particularly during politically sensitive periods, such as the Jacobite scare of 1714. Corcoran in his study of the penal era, listed nineteen indictments against popish schoolmasters brought before the Limerick grand jury alone, between 1711 and 1722. A schoolmaster who contravened the penal laws was liable to three months' imprisonment and a fine of twenty pounds. He could be banished to the Barbadoes, and if he returned to Ireland, the death penalty awaited him. A ten pound reward was offered for his arrest and a reward of ten pounds for information against anyone harbouring him" (McManus, *Irish Hedge School and Its Books*, 16–17).

28 See Russell Burns, *Communications: An International History of the Formative Years* (Stevenage: The Institution of Electrical Engineers, 2004), 194–96.

history of Western military engagement in the geographic area so closely associated with Guantánamo: Pakistan and Afghanistan.[29] Developed by Christopher Mance of the British Army Signal Corps in the nineteenth century, the heliograph was first used "in a tactical situation" (a euphemism for the battleground) "during the Jowaki expedition" sent by the British-Indian government in 1877 and 1878 in the Peshawar district of what is now Pakistan, not far from the border of Afghanistan. The same source reports that "the first actual trial of the instrument was carried out during the Second Afghan War (1878–1880)."[30]

While an occupier can use the heliograph only in "good sunlight," the girl in Muldoon's poem uses the sign — via the process

---

29 The brutality of war is the theme of the poem that opens and lends its title to Muldoon's collection *Horse Latitudes*. In his review of the collection for *The Guardian*, James Fenton quotes an interview with the author: "Muldoon tells us that he started work on the 19 sonnets that form the title sequence of his new collection, *Horse Latitudes*, 'as the US embarked on its foray into Iraq. The poems have to do with a series of battles (all beginning with the letter 'B' as if to suggest a 'missing' Baghdad) in which horses or mules played a major role. Intercut with those battle-scenes are accounts of a 'battle' with cancer by a former lover, here named Carlotta, and a commentary on the agenda of what may only be described as the Bush 'regime.' This information, the sort of thing Muldoon is happy to tell an audience at a reading, is useful to the reader on the page, because these battles-beginning-with-B, in which horses or mules played a major role, are not all going to be very familiar (at least, they weren't to me). Here is the list: Beijing, Baginbun, Bannockburn, Berwick-upon-Tweed, Blaye, Bosworth Field, Blackwater Fort, Benburb, Boyne, Blenheim, Bunker Hill, Brandywine, Badli-Ke-Serai, Bull Run, Bronkhorstspruit, Basra, Bazentin, Beersheba, Burma." Fenton underscores Muldoon's comment that the 19 names of battles are "intended to suggest a 20th not yet mentioned" ("A Poke in the Eye with a Poem," *The Guardian*, Oct. 21, 2006).

30 Burns, *Communications*, 195. Major A.S. Wynne writes in March 1880 that "in the campaigns of the last two years in Afghanistan and Zululand" the heliograph "has been put to every possible test, with such satisfactory results that it must soon become an established addition to the Signalling Equipment of all armies" ("Heliography and Army Signalling Generally," *The Journal of the Royal United Service Institution*, vol. 24 [1881]: 235). The article gives many examples of the instrument's use in Afghanistan.

of analogy ("like") — in and in spite of the rain.[31] The occupier's mediatechnology is not only appropriated against all odds, but perfected to resist adverse conditions: another production, one could say, of an "auto-immune" reaction.

The girl's medium, the "rush mat," is no small matter for another reason, too. In his radio series *A History of Ireland*, produced for BBC North Ireland, the historian Jonathan Bardon describes the living conditions of the Irish in the eighteenth century, the majority of whom lived in humble dwellings,

> often no more than single-room cabins — there was no point in erecting more permanent houses for those who rented land from year to year, often forced to move on the following season. [...] [T]here were no beds but the whole family lying down on rushes strewn on the mud floor. Furniture consisted of little more than a deal table, an iron "cruisie" filled with fish oil to provide light, a couple of three-legged stools and an iron pot for boiling potatoes on an open fire. A rush mat served as a door and smoke had to find its way out without a chimney.[32]

In Muldoon's poem, the "rush mat" over the girl's shoulders thus indicates with her "papish" religion her family's poverty. But, flashing "like a heliograph," it also signifies something else. The rush mat door of the dirt-poor hut and the flash have in common that they function in the binary code: on–off, 1–0.

For Jacques Lacan, who, like Freud, was always mindful of "a constitutive overlapping of media-technology and

---

31 Burns, *Communications,* 195. Major Wynne also reports the occasional use of moonlight and of artificial light ("Heliography and Army Signalling Generally," 242–43).

32 Jonathan Bardon, "The Peasantry," in *A History of Ireland in 250 Episodes* (London: Gill and Macmillan, 2009), episode 131. For a similar description of Irish poverty, see McManus, *Irish Hedge School and Its Books,* 69–70, 108; for a description of the wretched conditions of hedge schools, see 72–73.

psychoanalysis,"[33] the binary code is "something articulated, of the same order as the fundamental oppositions of the symbolic register."[34] According to Lacan, cybernetics, the culmination of the binary code, "clearly highlights the radical difference between the imaginary and the symbolic orders."[35] The dimension of desire, that "function central to all human experience," can be grasped as constitutively dependent on the "oscillation" of presence and absence only within the symbolic order. "The fundamental relation man has to this symbolic order is very precisely what founds the symbolic order itself — the relation of non-being to being." In other words, contrary to the order of the imaginary, the symbolic order "is organized around the correlation of absence and presence," opening thereby the space for difference and desire.[36] The great-great-grandmother's flash then not only exposes the appropriation and subversive use of the imperial war-technology, but also the "alternating scansion that allows for the rendez-vous of presence and absence," the condition of possibility of desire.[37]

By contrast, in her "all-American Latin class," the imaginary "all-American" unity and coherence may be imposed onto the daughter. While the medium of the great-great-grandmother (the daughter's great-great-great-grandmother) depends on the "scansion," the caesura of an opening, the interruption or empty

---

33 Joseph Vogl, "Technologien des Unbewußten: Zur Einführung," in *Kursbuch Medienkultur,* eds. Claus Pias, Joseph Vogl, et al. (Stuttgart: Deutsche Verlagsanstalt, 1999), 374.

34 Jacques Lacan, *The Seminar of Jacques Lacan, Book II: The Ego in Freud's Theory and in the Technique of Psychoanalysis,* ed. J.-A. Miller, trans. S. Tomaselli (New York: W.W. Norton, 1991), 89.

35 Jacques Lacan, "Psychoanalysis and Cybernetics, or on the Nature of Language," in *The Seminar of Jacques Lacan, Book II,* 306. For Lacan's very instructive reflection on the door and its relation to cybernetics, see ibid., 301–2.

36 Lacan, "Psychoanalysis and Cybernetics, or on the Nature of Language," 308, 300.

37 Georg Christoph Tholen, "Platzverweis: Unmögliche Zwischenspiele von Mensch und Maschine," in *Computer als Medium,* eds. Norbert Bolz, Friedrich Kittler, and Christoph Tholen (Munich: Wilhelm Fink Verlag, 1994), 131; Lacan, *The Seminar of Jacques Lacan, Book II,* 223–24.

space that "remains in suspense as the distancing of non-being from being"[38] and that is constitutive of desire, the daughter, far from encountering such an opening of constitutive difference, may "be forced to conjugate" (literally "to bind together" and "to inflect"), to bend the word *amare* and to bind it together and lock it up with Guantánamo, to result in Guantánamare, in a schooling in which female liberty, insofar as it is "head-strong," as Muldoon quotes Shakespeare, is "lashed": "bound" and "flogged." Muldoon addresses here only the socialization of women: the opening of desire in the hedge school, in which girls participated in the "'guerrilla war' in education," vs. the imaginary identification through the bending and binding of love onto the identification with brutality in the name of national security — imaginary identification with empire. On the one hand, then, the great-great-grandmother of rebellion, on the other the daughter who might be forced into submissive obedience. In between the sister, whose invocation rimes with "metastasis."

The sister is in between, and with her, the metastasis interferes. For, in addition to the condensed media history, Muldoon's poem, by turning over or making off with the heliograph, conjures a meaning of "metastasis" that likely is as forgotten as the military beginnings of the heliograph in the area of what today is Pakistan and Afghanistan. According to Henry Peacham's rhetorics book of the sixteenth century, *The Garden of Eloquence*, "*Metastasis* is a forme of speech by which we turne backe those thinges that are obiected against us, to them which laid them to us. [...] This figure by the violence of his rebound driueth the edge of his enemies sword upon his enemies head, or as it were, taking up his enemies arrowe sendeth it backe from whence it came."[39] By effectuating the rhetorical meaning of "metastasis," the simile "like a heliograph" resonates with the American fears

---

38 Tholen, "Platzverweis," 131.

39 Henry Peacham, *The Garden of Eloquence: Conteining the most excellent ornaments, exornations, lightes, flowers, and formes of speech, commonly called the figures of rhetorike* (London: Field, 1593), 181–82.

that the Guantánamo poems could convey codes that might remain unrecognizable to the censoring authorities. Just like the language of one empire is, in the hedge schools, turned against another, and just like the mediatechnology of empire in the colony is turned against empire at home, the potential of code in the presumed enemy's language cannot be contained.

Peacham adds a "Caution" to his definition of *metastasis*: "This figure is of little force without a reason annexed to the obiection returned, for to denie the one, and to affirme the other without shewing reason of that is said, is a verie feeble manner of confutation or accusation, and is more meete for children and fooles then for men of understanding and wisedome."[40] The rhetorical figure *metastasis* is either potentially fatal to the adversary or, if used unwisely, exposes its author to ridicule. The question that Muldoon's poem formulates at the end is how to "come up with a ruse [...] to trace the root of metastasis." If it is too late to turn against the sister's cancer whose fatality is already sealed, it might not be too late to turn against the adversary "Guantánamo" whose devastating consequences extend in Muldoon's poem well into the future: "all past and future mornings." To turn the adversary's arguments against him and his media-technology, in a poem: the result could be a fatal blow to the adversary or being mocked as fool. This is the risk the poem runs.

---

40 Ibid., 182. Quintilian translates μετάστασις (*metastasis*) in his chapter on the defense against an accusation as "transference": "Sometimes, then, the blame is thrown on a person, as if Gracchus, being accused of concluding the Numantine treaty, (through fear of which accusation he seems to have passed his popular laws in his tribuneship) should say that he was sent to conclude it by his general. 14. Sometimes it is cast on some circumstance, as if a person who had been directed to do something in the will of another, and had not done it, should say that it was rendered impossible by the laws. This the Greeks call μετάστασις (*metastasis*), 'transference'" (*Institutes of Oratory*, ed. Lee Honeycutt, trans. John Selby Watson [1856], 7.413–14).

Rahim, Rahima, Rahma

For the Western, especially American reader, the question is how to live with Guantánamo, to love with Guantánamo, and, closely related to this question, how to teach and go to school with Guantánamo. Adapting Ariel Dorfman's reflection on torture to the prison camp and the systematic illegality it spawned, one can say that Guantánamo "corrupts the whole social fabric," because it can exist only at the condition of a pact of silence.[41]

For the prisoners, on the other hand, the question is how to survive in Guantánamo, physically, mentally, spiritually, and how to continue to love from Guantánamo. Mohamedou Ould Slahi's *Guantánamo Diary* and Murat Kurnaz's *Five Years of My Life: An Innocent Man in Guantánamo* give harrowing insight into the living conditions at the prison camp, the humiliations, interrogations, brutal abuse, sleep deprivation, solitary confinement.[42] In an essay he wrote in memory of his client Adnan Latif, Marc Falkoff described the "typical and often horrific" treatment his client received in the prison camp:

> Some of the indignities he suffered might seem trivial, but were in fact devious. For example, in the early years of his confinement, Adnan would occasionally have his trousers confiscated. The only reason for such bizarre treatment was to inflict religious torment, since his resulting immodest dress prevented Adnan from engaging in his daily prayers. Other treatment was more obviously barbaric, including the cell extractions to which he was occasionally subjected. Once, as punishment for stepping over a line painted on the floor of his cell while he was being served his lunch, Adnan

---

41 Ariel Dorfman, "Foreword," 5.
42 Mohamedou Ould Slahi, *Guantánamo Diary* (New York: Little, Brown and Co), 2015; Murat Kurnaz, *Five Years of My Life: An Innocent Man in Guantánamo* (New York: St. Martin's Griffin, 2008).

was visited by six guards dressed in riot gear. They pum-
meled him, leaving him bruised and bloodied.[43]

Composing poetry to reflect on experiences that assault the
poet's physical, mental, and cultural identity is in itself an act
of resistance especially in Arabic traditions, since the recitation
and production of poetry are an integral part not only of Arabic
culture, but of Arab identity.[44] Moreover, the poetic production
in Guantánamo can be understood as asserting a continuation
of a tradition, in which "protests and revolutions in the Arab
world have been accompanied, occasioned, and immortalized
by poetry."[45] Many of the poems in Falkoff's collection express
the longing for loved-ones not seen or touched in years of isolation. But another form of love plays a bigger role. Two motifs
may make it possible for the poems to reach English-speaking
readers in spite of the obstacles of structural censorship described above.

One of those motifs is the reference to tears in seven of the
twenty-two poems; the other is the complaint, in several poems,
that the jailors prevent the prisoners from caring for the elderly,
widows and orphans: those who are helpless. Protection of the
defenseless is one of the central obligations in all three monotheistic religions. The Qur'an gives it particular weight since
the prophet himself was "orphaned in a society in which status,
security, and life itself depended upon family connections."[46]
Especially the Suras of the early Meccan revelations offer, as
Michael Sells explains, "a critique of the human refusal to be
giving, to help the orphan and the person in want." "One of the

---

43 Marc Falkoff, "'Where is the World to Save us From Torture?'," in *The Routledge Companion to Literature and Human Rights,* eds. Sophia McClennen
and Alexandra Schultheis Moore (London: Routledge, 2016), 351.

44 Shawkat Toorawa, "Poetry," in *The Cambridge Companion to Modern Arab
Culture,* ed. Dwight Reynolds (Cambridge: Cambridge University Press,
2015), 97.

45 Ibid., 100. This fact may have contributed to the decision to lock up most of
the poems in a secure facility.

46 Michael Sells, *Approaching the Qur'an: The Early Revelations,* 2nd ed. (Ashland: White Cloud Press, 2007), 5.

fundamental messages of the early Meccan period" is the "condemnation of indifference and callousness toward the orphaned and the poor." Sura 90, "The Ground," describes the "steep pass" out of indifference: "To free a slave/ To feed the destitute on a day of hunger/ A kinsman orphan/ Or a stranger out of luck in need."[47]

In order to understand how "the spirit of those early Meccan verses [...] became central to the Qur'anic tradition," Sells invites the reader unfamiliar with the latter to consider that

> for Muslims, the Qur'an is first experienced in Arabic, even by those who are not native speakers of Arabic. In Qur'an schools, children memorize verses, then entire Suras. They begin with the Suras that are at the end of the Qur'an in its written form. These first revelations to Muhammad express vital existential themes in a language of great lyricism and beauty. As the students learn these Suras, they are not simply learning something by rote, but rather interiorizing the inner rhythms, sound patterns, and textual dynamics — taking it to heart in the deepest manner. Gradually the student moves on to other sections of the Qur'an. Yet the pattern set by this early, oral encounter with the text is maintained throughout life.[48]

The invocation of the orphaned and the helpless in the Guantánamo poems thus resonate with the prisoners' earliest childhood lessons of the Qur'anic understanding of justice. The "Qur'anic emphasis on helping the orphaned and the disinherited" is intrinsically a commandment to act.[49] Both motifs, tears and caring for the helpless, are closely linked in the experience of compassion.

Abdullah Thani Faris al Anazi describes Guantánamo as "a prison of injustice./ Its iniquity makes the mountains weep,"

---

47 Ibid., 79–83.
48 Ibid., 11–12.
49 Ibid., 91.

Ustad Badruzzaman Badr addresses "The Chief of the White Palace" writing that he, "Like other sinful chiefs,/ Cannot see our patience./ The whirlpool of our tears/ Is moving fast towards him."[50] Moazzam Begg invokes "years of tears," and Shaikh Abdurraheem Muslim Dost laments, "I am eating the bread of Eid with my tears."[51]

Sami Al Haj combines both motifs in his poem. After evoking America's "monuments to liberty/ And freedom of opinion, which is well and good," he adds "but [...] architecture is not justice./ America, you ride on the backs of orphans,/ And terrorize them daily." The accusation of failing or refusing to fulfill the commandment of compassion towards the weak (there isn't a more helpless member of the community than the orphan) is coupled in this poem with the evocation of the writer's tears that remain unanswered: "To Allah I direct my grievance and my tears [...] After the shackles and the nights and the suffering and the tears,/ How can I write poetry?/ My soul is like a roiling sea, stirred by anguish,/ Violent with passion."[52]

Othman Abdulraheem Mohammad asks his brother, to whom he addresses his poem, for forgiveness for not being able, in Guantánamo, to "help the elderly or the widow or the little child."[53] And Adnan Farhan Abdul Latif's "Hunger Strike Poem" describes his American jailors in the following terms: "They do not respect the law/ They do not respect men,/ They do not spare the elderly,/ They do not spare the baby-toothed child./ They leave us in prison for years, uncharged [...]."[54]

---

50   Falkoff, *Poems from Guantánamo,* 25, 28.

51   Ibid., 30, 36.

52   Ibid., 42–43. See Judith Butler's commentary on this poem in her *Frames of War,* 56.

53   "I am sorry, my brother,/ That I cannot help the elderly or the widow or the little child." (Falkoff, *Poems from Guantánamo,* 54).

54   Ibid., 52. The poem continues: "Because we are Muslims./ Where is the world to save us from torture?/ Where is the world to save us from the fire and sadness?/ Where is the world to save the hunger strikers?/ But we are content, on the side of justice and right,/ Worshipping the Almighty./ And our motto on this island is, *salaam."* On September 8, 2012, more than ten years after his incarceration without charge, Adnan Latif died at the age of

Abdulla Majid Al Noaimi writes, "The tears of someone else's longing are affecting me;/ My chest cannot take the vastness of

---

36 in Guantánamo Prison Camp. The cause of his death appears to be suicide. A few days after Latif's death, the Executive director of Amnesty International USA Suzanne Nossel described the circumstances of his detention: "The Department of Defense recommended Latif for transfer as far back as 2004, and again in 2006, 2008, and 2009. In July 2010, District Court Judge Henry Kennedy ruled that the government had not proved its case for holding Latif by 'a preponderance of the evidence' and concluded that Latif's detention was unlawful. But he remained detained. The conditions he faced at Guantánamo were horrendous and he had gone on a hunger strike to protest them. According to his attorney, Latif had been held in solitary confinement for the majority of his detention and had never received adequate treatment for medical problems he had suffered throughout his decade at the detention center. In a letter to his lawyers in March 2010, Latif alleged that Guantánamo's Immediate Response Force (IRF), '[entered] my cell on [a] regular basis. They throw me and drag me on the floor ... two days before writing this letter, [the IRF team] strangled me and pressed hard behind my ears ... I lost consciousness for more than an hour.' And in a meeting with his lawyer at Guantánamo on May 10, 2009, Latif cut one of his own wrists. He had previously made a number of suicide attempts. Writing to his lawyer from isolation in Guantánamo's Camp 5 in March 2010, he said that his circumstances make 'death more desirable than living.' On Oct. 14, 2011, nearly a decade after Latif was taken into custody, a divided panel of the D.C. Circuit ruled 2–1 for the government, overturning Judge Kennedy's order. The government argued that Judge Kennedy had failed to properly assess Latif's credibility and had been wrong in his assessment of the reliability of the intelligence report. Meeting with his lawyer in Guantánamo after the appellate ruling, Latif said 'I am a prisoner of death.' His lawyers appealed to the U.S. Supreme Court to review Latif's case. On June 11, 2012, the Court refused to do so, without comment" (Suzanne Nossel, "With the Death of Adnan Latif, So Must Come the Death of Guantánamo," *Huffington Post*, Sept. 12, 2012). See also Jason Leopold, "Sold Into 'A Piece of Hell': A Death of Innocence at Gitmo," *Truthout*, Oct. 18, 2012. See also Center for Constitutional Rights, "Adnan Latif – the Face of Indefinite Detention – Dies at Guantánamo. CCR blames Courts and Obama for Tragedy," Sept. 11, 2012. In its statement, CCR wrote: "Adnan Latif is the human face of indefinite detention at Guantánamo, a policy President Obama now owns. Mr. Latif, held without charge or trial, died a tragic and personal death — alone in a cell, thousands of miles from home, more than a decade after he was abducted and brought to Guantánamo Bay. Like other men, Mr. Latif had been on hunger strike for years to protest his innocence. His protests were in vain."

emotion."[55] As Judith Butler has noted, these tears "belong to everyone in the camp, perhaps, or to someone else," but they "impinge" on the speaker: "he finds those other feelings within him, suggesting that even in this most radical isolation, he feels what others feel."[56]

These poems thus closely associate justice and compassion, and I would venture to say that the kind of compassion at stake here would be called, in Arabic, *rahma,* which like its Hebrew relative, is closely related to the word for "womb."

In Arabic, *rahma* (رحمة, compassion) and *rahim* (رحم, womb) derive from the verb *rahima* (رحم, to have compassion). As George Williams explains, in the Hebrew Bible

> the most distinctive Hebraic word [for compassion] is derived from *rechem* "womb" that yields the plural *rachamim* "mercies" (once translated "bowels of mercy") and the verb *racham* "to love" or "to have mercy." [...] Although male-oriented interpreters of the Bible were formerly inclined to relate this word for mercy to the *brotherly* feeling of those born from the same womb, today scholars favor the [...] more convincing interpretation that roots this kind of mercy in the courageous and steadfast love of the mother for the offspring of her womb. [...] Mother-love, womb-love, womb-mercy in the Hebrew [Bible] eventually evolved into a generic word for steadfast love and was ascribed to God himself (cf. Psalm 25:6; Isaiah 49:15, 54:7; Hosea 2:19, 14:5; Zechariah 1:16) and then to men, such as the compassionate Joseph. [...] In Islam a man, like a woman, is enjoined to be merciful in one adjectival form of the noun for "womb" (*rahm, rahim*). More important, Allah is called the Merciful and the Compassionate, the two adjectives being both variants derived from womb-mercy, in the subtitle of every chapter of the Koran, except surah 9. And the Job of the Old Testament, taken over by the Koran in surah 40:07, speaks of Allah as "the most merci-

55 Falkoff, *Poems from Guantánamo,* 59.
56 Butler, *Frames of War,* 59.

ful of merciful ones," while Allah himself says in surah 7:156: "My mercy encompasses all things."[57]

Rahma is a compassion that cannot but act, because one's "womb" commands it and because God commands it. As Mouhanad Khorchide explains, the "straight road" or the "right path" consists in "accepting God's love and compassion and to give it reality in one's actions."[58] Sells writes that "holding or keeping the faith [...] includes not only intellectual assent to certain propositions but also engagement in just actions," such as "protecting those who are disinherited or in need." By contrast, "those who reject the reckoning [the final judgment] — which, in early Meccan revelations, is the foundation of religion — are those who abuse the orphan, who are indifferent to those suffering in their midst, and who are neglectful in performing the prayer."[59] Not helping the orphan and the widow, or worse, preventing others from helping the orphan and the widow is a fundamental rejection of the oldest and most ingrained obligation towards the other.

If one adds to this that in Genesis, Deuteronomy, and other places of the Hebrew Bible, as well as in the Gospels and the Qur'an, "the fatherless and the widows" are often named in the same verse, the same breath with "the aliens," foreigners, or strangers, it follows that in the foundational books of the three monotheistic religions the "mistreatment of strangers is a sure way to incur divine wrath."[60] Thus, what the Guantánamo po-

---

57 George H. Williams, "Mercy as the Basis of a Non-Elitist Ecological Ethic," in *Festschrift in Honor of Charles Speel*, eds. Thomas J. Sienkewicz and James E. Betts (Monmouth: Monmouth College, 1997), 31–32. I thank Aaron Gross for so generously sharing his erudition on the concept of *rachamim* with me. I also thank Racha El-Omari and Dwight Reynolds for their kind help and precious advice.

58 Mouhanad Khorchide, *Islam ist Barmherzigkeit: Grundzüge einer modernen Religion* (Freiburg: Herder, 2012), 87.

59 Sells, *Approaching the Qur'an*, 117, 125.

60 Miriam Schulman and Amal Barkouki-Winter, "The Extra Mile: The Ancient Virtue of Hospitality Imposes Duties on Host and Guest," *Ethics* 11, no. 1 (Winter 2000). Schulman and Barkouki-Winter quote Baker's *Evan-*

ems say of the widows and the orphans also applies to "aliens," "strangers" and therefore the inmates themselves, who, in Guantánamo, are profoundly "alien" in more than one sense.

Given the frequency of the theme of compassion in these poems, one might wonder to which extent its use follows mere convention. This, however, is not an argument against the poems. Susan Slyomovics reports how "Moroccan victims of torture hold poetry to be a deeply valued medium because it can communicate that which is too humiliating to acknowledge publicly, especially to relatives at home."[61] Precisely the conventions of poetry enable these voices not to be drowned in shame. In the Guantánamo poems, the invocation of the Qur'anic obligation to be compassionate without the expectation of reciprocity provides the anchor that makes suffering sharable without drowning in shame.

As two of the leading clinicians and scholars on torture, Françoise Sironi and Darius Rejali, have shown, the goal of torture is not only to destroy the victim's physical and mental health, but also to devastate the fabric that holds a community together. Intense shaming (such as what happened in Guantánamo and Abu Ghraib) achieves such devastation to the point of making it impossible for the victim to return to his/her community. The so-called "stealth" or "clean" torture is particularly ravaging since it leaves hardly, if any visible traces and thereby greatly reduces the ground on which sympathy and empathy — including with the "enemy" — flourish: the recognition of a shared vulnerabil-

gelical Dictionary of Biblical Theology which "associates hospitality with aliens or strangers in need, who were particularly vulnerable in the ancient Middle East: 'The plight of aliens was desperate. They lacked membership in the community, be it tribe, city-state, or nation. As an alienated person, the traveler often needed immediate food and lodging. Widows, orphans, the poor, or sojourners from other lands lacked the familial or community status that provided a landed inheritance, the means of making a living, and protection. In the ancient world, the practice of hospitality meant graciously receiving an alienated person into one's land, home, or community and providing directly for that person's needs.'"

61 Susan Slyomovics quoted in Flagg Miller, "Forms of Suffering in Muslim Prison Poetry," in Falkoff, Poems from Guantánamo, 15.

ity of the flesh.[62] The very methods perfected in Guantánamo and exported to places like Abu Ghraib thus combined intense shaming with a destruction of the basis of empathy.

In a different context, Myriam Revault d'Allonnes, following Hannah Arendt, describes compassion as relating to justice because it is about being "touched in the flesh" by the suffering of a singular other, contrary to pity which tends to "generalize," "homogenize," and thus indifferentialize.[63] Such being "touched in the flesh," in one's "womb," regardless of one's gender, is an obligation to act.

While Nietzsche fiercely criticized pity because it always threatens to shame its recipient, one will recall Rousseau, for whom pity needs the mediation of imagination, and is "nothing" if it doesn't prepare for the pursuit of justice.[64] Compassion as *rahma* in Arabic, or *rachamim* in Hebrew, is an act of resistance against both the shame of pity and against the shame of torture. And precisely through its formulaic invocation in the Guantánamo poems, it is an insisting call to action. As Judith Butler writes, these poems "communicate another mode of solidarity, of interconnected lives that carry on each others' works, suffer each others' tears, and form networks that pose an incendiary risk not only to national security, but to the form of global sovereignty championed by the US."[65] More than the secret messages suspected in the censored lines, the military censors might fear the code and the power of such "being touched in the flesh," regardless of one's gender, in one's womb.

---

62 Sironi, *Bourreaux et victimes*. See also Chapter 2 in this volume.

63 Myriam Revault d'Allonnes, *L'homme compassionnel* (Paris: Éditions du Seuil, 2008), 53–55. See also Paul Audi's masterful *L'empire de la compassion* (Paris: Les Belles Lettres, Encre Marine, 2011), 18–20.

64 See Audi, *L'empire de la compassion*, for example 77–78.

65 Butler, *Frames of War*, 62. Michael Richardson comments that the relationality expressed in the poems "constitutes a relation between bodies within a state of utter subjection, but also a relation of resistance." Such an "affective excess [...] resists consignment to the status of detainee, and suggests that no matter how much the biopolitical apparatus seeks to regulate affect, it cannot do so completely" (*Gestures of Testimony*, 71).

III.
DRONE
WARFARE

CHAPTER 5

Ages of Cruelty:
Jacques Derrida, Fethi Benslama, and their Challenges to Psychoanalysis[1]

Cruelty: Philosophy

In 1968, Jacques Derrida succinctly named the stakes implied in the neographism which gave his most famous text its name, "La différance." This word, he wrote, had "imposed itself" out of a double necessity: the necessity to think "what is most irreducible about our 'era,'" and the necessity that thought be "maintained in [...] a relationship with the structural limits of mastery."[2] All of Derrida's conceptual "provocation[s]" that followed in "La différance"'s wake obey the same impetus: "Not only is there no kingdom of *différance,* but *différance* instigates the subversion of every kingdom. Which makes it obviously threatening and infallibly dreaded by everything within us that desires a kingdom, the past or future presence of a kingdom."[3] From the first to the last text, Derrida's work raises the question: what is it that desires within us a kingdom and any avatar of "kingdom"? His interventions are inventive engagements whose apparent playfulness operates on the level of the signifier, challenging what one could call the repressed in Occidental philosophy. What

---

1   Originally published in *Mosaic* 48, no. 2 (June 2015): 1–27.
2   Jacques Derrida, *Margins of Philosophy,* trans. Alan Bass (Chicago: Chicago University Press, 1982), 7.
3   Jacques Derrida, "Provocation: Forewords," in *Without Alibi,* trans. Peggy Kamuf (Stanford: Stanford University Press, 2004), xv; Derrida, *Margins of Philosophy,* 22.

has sometimes been denounced by Derrida's detractors as futile word plays is anything but: for example, the term *hantologie* or "hauntology" is a conceptual "provocation" in the most radical sense insofar as it accomplishes at least three things:

- It undermines the traditional discourse of philosophy as ontology, the discourse of "being," that validates "presence" only, be it past, present, or future "presence," and thereby refuses to acknowledge the specters that always haunt it.
- It challenges philosophy to "show itself hospitable to the law of the ghost, to the spectral experience and to the memory of the ghost, of that which is neither dead nor alive, [...] hospitable to the law of the most imperious memory, even though it is the most effaced and the most effaceable, but for that very reason the most demanding."[4]
- It alludes to a *hontologie,* introducing the element of shame (*honte*) into the very business of philosophy.[5]

The first two aspects have garnered much scholarly attention, and I will not dwell on them, except to note that for Derrida, welcoming the law of the ghost is most explicitly at the heart of the philosopher's (or, as he writes, the "philosopher-deconstructor's") tasks, to the point that ignoring this would amount to the impossibility of thinking, if ever thinking is inspired by a "love" of "justice."[6] The provocation is here truly a call-for, and

---

4 Jacques Derrida, "Prolegomena" to "First Name of Benjamin," first presented in April 1990 at the opening of the colloquium held at UCLA, "Nazism and the 'Final Solution,' Probing the Limits of Representation." Published as Jacques Derrida, "Force of Law," in *Acts of Religion,* ed. Gil Anidjar (New York: Routledge, 2002), 259.

5 For a francophone ear, it is impossible to miss the homophony between *ontologie* and *hontologie.*

6 Jacques Derrida, *Specters of Marx,* trans. Peggy Kamuf (New York: Routledge, 1994), 221: "Could one address oneself in general if already some ghost did not come back?" (emph. in original). Referring to Shakespeare's *Hamlet,* Derrida continues: "If he [or she] loves justice at least, the 'scholar' of the future, the 'intellectual' of tomorrow" should "learn" to address him- or herself to the other, and to learn it "from the ghost."

a call-forward: toward a commitment that would open a different "futurity," a futurity in which those who have been silenced in death, and silenced beyond death, would teach the "scholar" how to address himself or herself to the other. As such, Derrida's thinking has always been deeply political. As Derrida's inventive interventions show, their provocations necessarily introduce elements of a new vocabulary of thought and new conceptual "sequences."[7] "Futurity," Amir Eshel writes, "marks literature's ability to raise, via engagement with the past, political and ethical dilemmas crucial for the human future."[8] The same goes for philosophy-deconstruction's ability, on the condition of not limiting this "future" to a "human" one.

As for the third aspect, philosophy as *hontologie,* or the "logos of shame," it needs to be considered in light of (at least) a triple *scandalon.*[9]

First, in his later work on sovereignty, Derrida underlines this "most stupefying" and most scandalous "fact about the history of Western philosophy": "never, to my knowledge, has any philosopher *as a philosopher, in his or her strictly and systematically philosophical discourse,* never has any philosophy *as such* contested the legitimacy of the death penalty. From Plato to Hegel, from Rousseau to Kant (who was undoubtedly the most rigor-

---

7   On the concept of "futurity," see Leslie Adelson, "Futurity Now: An Introduction," *Germanic Review* 88 (2013): 213 and Amir Eshel, *Futurity: Contemporary Literature and the Quest for the Past* (Chicago: Chicago University Press, 2013).

8   Eshel, *Futurity,* 5. Eshel discusses new "narrative sequences" (4).

9   Derrida opens his reflections in *The Animal That Therefore I Am* with the question of shame and of *pudeur,* modesty, or, as the English says it so tellingly, "self-consciousness," in a commentary on the second chapter of Genesis. Self-consciousness starts with shame. As David Wills writes in his commentary on Derrida's text, "Shame is precisely that complicated system of self-reflection that begins with consciousness of our nakedness. No animal knows it is naked [...] from this perspective, [shame] is the conceptual machinery itself, a machine set in motion by itself, always already on. Before being the automatism of blood rushing to the face, the pure life of spontaneous blush, shame is the originary technicity that is the origin of technology, for it is on the basis of it that we inaugurate the technological drive" ("The Blushing Machine," *Parrhesia* 8 [2009]: 39–40).

ous of them all), they expressly, each in his own way, and sometimes not without much hand-wringing ([as in] Rousseau), took a stand for the death penalty."[10] Later on, what "La différance" called "kingdom" is relentlessly pursued under the concept of "sovereignty," exemplified for Derrida by the death penalty. In his later seminars, Derrida comes to identify sovereignty as the "cement" or "solder" of the "onto-theological-political," which he links directly to "cruelty."[11] Noting the "terrible ambiguity" that lies in the fact that "sovereign power" is understood as "executing power," Derrida asserts that if one were to ask the question "What is the theologico-political?" the "answer would take shape thus: the theologico-political is a system, an apparatus of sovereignty in which the death penalty is necessarily inscribed. There is theologico-political wherever there is death penalty." This realization yields for Derrida, as a consequence, a new outline of deconstruction's scope: "Deconstruction, what is called by that name, is perhaps, *perhaps* the deconstruction of the death penalty, of the logocentric, logonomo-centric scaffolding in which the death penalty is inscribed or prescribed."[12] As Derrida shows, this is a "scaffolding" linked to the "Abrahamic and above all the Christian history of sovereignty, and thus of the possibility of the death penalty as theologico-political violence."[13] A departure from the theologico-political principle of sovereignty, which has marked the entire Western tradition in philosophy, politics, law, economics, education, etc., would indeed effect a "mutation." This "mutation," Derrida says in the context of a reflection on the "war on terror," "will have

---

10 Jacques Derrida and Elisabeth Roudinesco, *For What Tomorrow*, 146 (emph. in original).

11 "The keystone, or, if you prefer, the cement, the weld, as I just said, of the onto-theologico-political, the prosthetic artifact that keeps it upright" (Derrida and Roudinesco, *For What Tomorrow*, 148). The alternative translation is proposed by Elizabeth Rottenberg in "The 'Question' of the Death Penalty," *Oxford Literary Review* 35, no. 2 (2013): 267-69.

12 Jacques Derrida, *The Death Penalty*, Vol. 1, trans. Peggy Kamuf (Chicago: University of Chicago Press, 2014), 5 (emph. in original).

13 Derrida, *The Death Penalty*, 23.

to take place."[14] In Elizabeth Rottenberg's formulation, it is precisely because "philosophy (ontology) has been soldered (*soudée*), welded, *wedded* to the death penalty and to the principle of sovereignty from which it is inseparable" that a "'deconstruction' of what is most hegemonic in philosophy must [...] pass through a deconstruction of the death penalty."[15] Michael Naas places Derrida's observation in the context of two additional, and no less shameful, facts: "This sweeping claim about philosophy, however interesting in itself, might profitably be juxtaposed with Derrida's question in *Rogues* (2005), "why are there so few democrat philosophers (if there have been any at all), from Plato to Heidegger?" and his claim in *The Animal That Therefore I Am* (2008) that no philosopher qua philosopher has questioned the single, indivisible line distinguishing man from the animal." In short, Derrida invites us to

> ask along with him what notions of cruelty, sacrifice, or blood, what conception of the dignity of life or natural law, what *religion,* would allow philosophers across centuries, traditions, and languages — though particularly in European modernity — to maintain a discourse that is at once *pro-death penalty, anti-democratic,* and overwhelmingly *anthropocentric.* [...] What is it about philosophy, then, philosophy as opposed, perhaps, to literature, where Derrida finds all kinds of exceptions on each of these points, that leads to these positions?[16]

Naas surmises that Derrida's answer might

---

14 Derrida, "Autoimmunity," 106.

15 Elizabeth Rottenberg, "Cruelty and Its Vicissitudes," *Southern Journal of Philosophy* 50, Spindel Supplement (2012): 148 (emph. in original). The quote in the quote is from Derrida and Roudinesco's *For What Tomorrow* (146/88; trans. modified).

16 Michael Naas, "The Philosophy and Literature of the Death Penalty: Two Sides of the Same Sovereign," *Southern Journal of Philosophy* 50 (2012): 52 (emph. in original).

begin by pointing out a common call to sacrifice or minimize life in the name of a value or a life greater than life. From Plato's definition of philosophy as the practice of dying to Kant's identification of the priceless dignity of man beyond phenomenal life, to Heidegger's claim that only *Dasein* has a relation to death as such, philosophy identifies the confrontation or overcoming of death, the sacrifice of life, with the affirmation of a life beyond or greater than life, a life and thus a relationship to death that would be what is truly proper to man and not to any other form of animal life.[17]

In essence, what links philosophy's *pro-death penalty, anti-democratic,* and overwhelmingly *anthropocentric* stances for Derrida is their affirmation of what he calls "carno-phallogocentrism." "Carno-phallogocentrism" is as irreducibly driven by the desire of sovereignty as it is by cruelty.

In the following, I want to focus on the question of cruelty, specifically, inspired by Derrida, on two "ages" of cruelty: one, a high-tech version from which, at first sight at least, the cruor or blood seems to have been wiped away, and another, bloodily "archaic" one, reacting savagely to the first. As I will show through the analyses proposed by Derrida and the French–Tunisian psychoanalyst Fethi Benslama, these two "ages" of cruelty are closely intertwined, and for both of them, today's media play a crucial role.

Cruelty: Death Penalty without Trial, Remote-controlled

Today's news is awash in blood shed by the enemies of "the West" in the "war on terror" — the *cruor* of blood screams out of the headlines of news outlets. Yet the blood shed by the sophisticated, high-tech version of cruelty is all but erased from the news. If, as Derrida repeatedly asserts via Carl Schmitt, the sovereign is the one who decides over life and death, and the one who decides over the exception — that is, over the conditions in

---

17 Ibid. 53 (emph. in original).

which national or international laws no longer apply — then the war conducted with "armed unmanned aerial vehicles," commonly known as drones, is a deadly and triply remote assertion of sovereignty. This war is far-reaching, far away from public perception, and conducted via remote-control. The drone war has transformed a vast area in Pakistan into "the world's largest prison," with the constant "specter of death" looming inescapably from above, as described by American lawyer Jennifer Gibson, co-author of the Stanford University/New York University study *Living Under Drones*.[18] The non-profit organization Reprieve has described the "CIA killer drones programme" as "death penalty without trial, and the new face of state lawlessness in the name of counter-terrorism."[19]

According to data collected by Reprieve, to this date "the United States has used drones to execute without trial some 4,700 people in Pakistan, Yemen, and Somalia — all countries against whom it has not declared war. The US's drones programme is a covert war being carried out by the CIA" and the military.[20] As journalist and filmmaker Madiha Tahir, director

18 International Human Rights and Conflict Resolution Clinic, Stanford Law School, and Global Justice Clinic, NYU School of Law, "Living Under Drones: Death, Injury, and Trauma to Civilians from US Drone Practices in Pakistan," Sept. 2012.

19 Reprieve, "Investigations: Drones." See also Talk Nation Radio, "Jennifer Gibson: Drones Terrorize Populations, Victims Seek Justice at ICC," Feb. 24, 2014.

20 Reprieve, "Investigations: Drones." For the numbers of victims, see the regularly updated website of the Bureau of Investigative Journalism, "Get the Data: Drone Wars." See also Reprieve, "UN Expert: Lethal Use of Drones Must Be Curbed," June 19, 2014. On July 1, 2016, the US government published a long-awaited assessment of its drone war's casualties which put the count "between 64 and 116 civilians" killed during Obama's administration (Spencer Ackerman, "Obama Claims US Drones Strikes Have Killed Up to 116 Civilians," *The Guardian,* July 1, 2016). This number is a "fraction of the 380 to 801 civilian casualty range recorded by the Bureau of Investigative Journalism from reports by local and international journalists, NGO investigators, leaked government documents, court papers and the result of field investigations." (Jack Serle, "Obama Drone Casualty Numbers a Fraction of Those Recorded by the Bureau," The Bureau of Investigative Journalism, July 1, 2016). The official number also stands in stark contrast to an intelli-

of the November 2013 documentary *Wounds of Waziristan,* puts it, the US "sees itself as the center of the world," while Waziristan, the border region of Pakistan where most of the drones attack, "is at the margins of [the] margin." Pakistan's security forces and the insurgents "have killed many people here," she says, and nobody would use the words "precise" or "surgery-strikes." By contrast, drone attacks are "described as 'neat,' 'surgical' tactics in precision-based warfare," suggesting that "you can take out the bad without disturbing the good. No consequences for anyone. No sorrow. No loss." This is the reason why "drones are becoming acceptable among Americans as a way to kill in Yemen, in Somalia, and in Pakistan."[21] In an interview about her film, Tahir summarizes her conversations with psychiatrists who visited the region. Even though the Pakistani military and the insurgent groups are brutal, "whether it's true or not, people feel that with militants, there is some degree of control. You can negotiate. There is some cause and effect relationship. But there is no cause and effect with a drone, as far as people in the area are concerned. [Drone warfare] creates an acute kind of trauma that is not limited to the actual attack. It has to do with the constant threat flying above."[22]

The researchers and lawyers from Reprieve expand upon the reasons why the "constant threat" from drones is especially traumatizing:

> For communities living under drones, life is filled with constant terror. Nobody knows who the next target might be. Armed drones can hand down a death sentence simply because a person exhibited suspicious behaviour. Yet what that behaviour is, the United States refuses to say. Other times, the

---

gence report leaked in October 2015 according to which "Obama-led drone strikes kill innocents 90% of the time" (Andrew Blake, "Obama-led Drone Strikes Kill Innocents 90% of the Time: Report," *The Washington Times,* Oct. 15, 2015).

21 Madiha Tahir, *Wounds of Waziristan,* Parergon Films, 2013, 1'00"–5'00".

22 Alex Pasternack, "Life in the Dronescape: An Interview with Madiha Tahir," *Motherboard,* Oct. 29, 2013.

death sentence comes simply because the person fell within the target demographic: all males aged 18 to 65. According to the United States, these men are not deemed civilians unless they can prove their innocence — posthumously. The drones, sometimes as many as five or six at a time, constantly circle overhead, terrorising civilian populations, nearly half of whom are children. A recent study carried out in Yemen by clinical and forensic psychologist Dr Peter Schaapveld, reported severe post-traumatic stress disorder in children living in areas targeted for drone strikes.[23]

Under the title "Drone Penalty," David Wills analyzes the powerful link between the history of slave-trade, the perseverance of the death penalty in the us, and the latter's increasing use of drones in strikes that violate the sovereignty of other states and that are "illegal whether or not they have been consented to by the local government," since "a strike that takes place in an area [...] where there is no [declared] armed conflict, is by definition inflicted against civilians and constitutes a violation of international human rights law."[24] The so-called "kill list" is known to be consulted on a weekly basis by the us President himself, who decides, in sovereign fashion, "whom next to target on an ever-expanding extra-judicial death penalty list." Such absolute sovereignty is asserted by assuming "the prerogative of a universal right of inspection," the "power to see everything." As Wills writes, carrying all this out in secrecy reinforces "the sense of divine justice."[25] Indeed, Derek Gregory cites a drone pilot saying "sometimes I felt like a God hurling thunderbolts from afar," and Tom Engelhardt spells out "the metaphor's implications: 'Those about whom we make life-or-death decisions, as they scurry below or carry on as best they can, have — like any

---

23 Reprieve, "Investigations: Drones." See also Anon., "Drone Attacks 'Traumatising a Generation of Children," *Channel 4*, Mar. 5, 2013.

24 David Wills, "Drone Penalty," *SubStance* 43, no. 2 (2014): 176.

25 Ibid., 181–85.

beings faced with the gods — no recourse or appeal."[26] Gregory also shows that far from reducing "war to a video game in which the killing space appears remote and distant," the "new visibilities" provided by the latest drones' "macro-field of micro-vision" actually produce "a special kind of intimacy that consistently privileges the view of the hunter-killer, and whose implications are far more deadly."[27] "The high-resolution full-motion video feeds from the drones allow crews to claim time and time again that they are not thousands of miles from the war zone but just eighteen inches away: the distance from eye to screen. The sense of optical proximity is palpable and pervasive," so much so that journalist Mark Bowden could write that "'the dazzling clarity of the drone's optics' means that 'war by remote control turns out to be intimate.'"[28] This does not only affect the pilot. What Gregory calls the "time-space compression" entailed in drone warfare has brought all those in the "network" of what the US Air Force refers to as the "kill chain" "much closer to the killing space."[29]

As Tahir's testimony shows, the drone war exemplifies a cruelty that is all the more lethal because it is covert. Not at all or hardly monitored by the citizens whose taxes pay for it, it is the result of the highest technological sophistication, and is operated with the claim of "surgical precision."[30] Seen from the self-perceived "center" — which is very remote from the actu-

---

26   Derek Gregory, "From a View to a Kill: Drones and Late Modern War," *Theory, Culture & Society* 28, no. 7–8 (2011): 192. Gregory speaks of "the ultimate 'God-trick' whose vengeance depends on making its objects visible and its subjects invisible" (204). Engelhardt is quoted on 192.

27   Gregory, "From a View to a Kill," 194.

28   Derek Gregory, "Drone Geographies," *Radical Philosophy* 183 (2014): 9.

29   Gregory, "From a View to a Kill," 193, 196.

30   As Gregory points out, "the suite of four aircraft that constitutes a Combat Air Patrol capable of providing coverage twenty-four hours a day seven days a week involves 192 personnel, and most of them (133) are located outside the combat zone and beyond immediate danger." However, Launch and Recovery crews "are stationed to handle take-off and landing," and "large maintenance crews in-theatre" are on hand "to service the aircraft" ("Drone Geographies," 7).

al "theater of operation" — it is hardly perceived and certainly hardly ever referred to as "cruelty." Perhaps one could establish the following parallel: the destruction inflicted by drones in predominantly Muslim countries is perceived as acceptable in the United States and the West because of its asserted "surgical" nature, similar to the way that the death penalty is acceptable to many in the United States on the condition of being executed under anesthesia, or, as Peggy Kamuf provocatively puts it, on the condition of being an "anesthetic," "a drug, and an American drug *par excellence.*"[31] In both cases, "cruelty" is, in the public Western perception, numbed, anesthetized. In both cases, we need to raise, with Kamuf, the question of the "wholesale anesthetizing of public sensibility," and even of "anesthesia addiction."[32]

In contrast to the anesthetized experience at the "center," for the concerned population living at the "margins of the margin," drones are a permanent death threat looming above them. For them, drones mean state-sponsored terrorism conducted against them at the push of a button from thousands of miles away, brutally arbitrary, wanton, and bloody, always threatening, out of the blue sky, to tear loved ones, friends, and neighbors into bits. During a hearing on Capitol Hill on October 29, 2013, attended by only five members of Congress, Zubair Rehman gave an account of a drone strike that occurred on October 24, 2012, on an open okra field near a village in North Waziristan. His grandmother was killed while picking okra. Rehman, then twelve years old, and his sister, then eight, were injured while helping her. Rehman testified: "Now I prefer cloudy days when the drones don't fly. When the sky brightens and becomes blue, the drones return and so does the fear. Children don't play so often now, and have stopped going to school. Education isn't possible as long as the drones circle overhead."[33] Since the in-

---

31 Peggy Kamuf, "Protocol," 5.
32 Ibid., 12–13.
33 Karen McVeigh, "Drone Strikes: Tears in Congress as Pakistani Family Tells of Mother's Death," *The Guardian,* Oct. 29, 2013.

troduction, already in 2006, of a newer generation of American drones ominously named "Reaper," cloudy days no longer provide relief. The Reaper "has an all-weather, day or night radar, linked to a sensor ball that houses image-intensified and infrared cameras."[34] This surveillance ability pales however when compared to the "Persistent Wide-Area Airborne Surveillance (WASS) System" called "Gorgon Stare," deployed on the Reaper in 2015, which increased the previous single video feed to 10 or more.[35]

In *Wired for War: The Robotics Revolution and Conflict in the 21st Century*, P.W. Singer underscores that the rationale for war has always been linked to ideals such as ending tyranny or, today, ending "terrorism." Yet drone technology changes the stakes dramatically. "Robotics starts to take these ideals, so essential to the definition of war, out of the equation," to the point that Yale Law School professor Paul Kahn speaks of the "'paradox of riskless warfare.'" "As technologies have distanced soldiers more and more from the fighting, the risks, and the destruction," the sense of "equality and fairness" implied in a "sense of mutuality" between enemy soldiers becomes "harder to claim. When it

---

34 Nasser Hussain, "The Sound of Terror: Phenomenology of a Drone Strike," *Boston Review,* Oct. 16, 2013.

35 See the information given on the website of the Gorgon Stare's manufacturer, the Sierra Nevada Corporation: http://www.sncorp.com/AboutUs/ NewsDetails/618. In December 2015, the US Department of Defense confirmed that the Air Force uses drones equipped with the Gorgon Stare surveillance system. A December 2015 article by Gareth Jennings gives an indication of the speed with which surveillance systems are developed to feature ever greater capacities: "While the baseline system uses five monochrome charge-coupled device (CCD) daylight cameras and four thermal cameras built into a 25-inch EO/IR turret built by Exelis, the newer Increment II uses an EO sensor turret derived from the US Defense Advanced Research Projects Agency (DARPA) and BAE Systems' Argus technology (featuring 192 separate cameras), and an IR sensor manufactured by Exelis. While performance specifications for Increment II have not yet been released, SNC has previously stated that it provides a four-fold increase in area coverage and a two-fold improvement in resolution over the baseline Gorgon Stare." Gareth Jennings, "DoD Confirms Gorgon Stare to be Operational in Afghanistan," *HIS Jane's Defence Weekly,* Dec. 17, 2015.

becomes not just a matter of distance, but actual disconnection, as Kahn describes, it 'propels us beyond the ethics of warfare.'"[36]

The drone war thus exemplifies the utter delocalization and expropriation that Derrida associates with modern warfare and its tele-technoscience, and doubly so: for the victim, killed by someone via remote control, from thousands of miles away, and for the perpetrator, killing someone via remote control, thousands of miles away. For the pilot, however, the delocalization materializes as "the intimacy of the time-space compression from Nevada to Oruzgan," and oscillates between intense familiarity with the rhythms of the target's life and an identification with US forces in the actual combat zone. An Air Force investigation into a drone attack that caused more than twenty civilian casualties, among whom many were women and children, concluded that it was the Predator pilot's "desire to support the ground forces" that triggered "a strong desire to find weapons," and "converted civilians into combatants," detecting rifles where there were none.[37]

Gregory argues that the drone pilot's intimacy with his or her targets' life routines does not create a corresponding ethical intimacy: "'Intimacy' is thus cultivated within a culturally divided field […] in which crews are interpellated to identify so closely with their comrades-in-arms that they are predisposed to interpret every other action — which is to say every Other action — as hostile or sinister, sometimes with disastrous consequences for the innocent."[38] The drone pilot's "interpellation" is also very effective because it occurs, as Nasser Hussain observes, in a "mute world of dumb figures": While "the pilots can hear ground commands" from fellow US forces, the "lack of synchronic sound" in the footage "renders it a ghostly world in which the figures seem unalive, even before they are killed." Hussain points out another double asymmetry: "If drone operators can see but not hear the world below them, the exact oppo-

---

36 Singer, *Wired for War,* 432. Kahn is quoted on 432.

37 Gregory, "From a View to a Kill," 203.

38 Gregory, "Drone Geographies," 10.

site is true for people on the ground. Because drones are able to hover at or above thirty thousand feet, they are mostly invisible to the people below them. But they can be heard. Many people from the tribal areas of Pakistan (FATA) describe the sound as a low-grade, perpetual buzzing, a signal that a strike could occur at any time."[39] On the receiving end of the "war on terror," *this* is the "sound of terror."[40] Because of the perpetual buzzing, the locals refer to drones as "mosquitos," even though the sound triggers a "'wave of terror' coming over the community," and even though there is no chance of incapacitating them. On the other side, both the military and the CIA refer to those killed in a drone strike zone as mere "bugsplat."[41] The asymmetry of lethal force could hardly be stated more supremely.

Drones redefine war as "cynegetic," that is, as conducted primarily by "hunter-killers," replacing the "mutuality" model described by Singer and Kahn above. Consequently, "a new doctrine of state violence [has] emerged, finding its unity in the concept of the militarized manhunt."[42] This shift has far-reaching repercussions for the concept and assumption of sovereignty. As Grégoire Chamayou has argued, "the drone is the emblem of contemporary cynegetic war. It is the mechanical, flying and robotic heir of the dog of war. It creates to perfection the ideal of asymmetry: to be able to kill without being able to be killed; to be able to see without being seen. To become absolutely invulnerable while the other is placed in a state of absolute vulnerability. 'Predator,' 'Global Hawk,' 'Reaper' — birds of prey and angels of death, drones bear their names well."[43]

Even though the newest drone surveillance system carries lethal asymmetry to new heights, it bears its name "Gorgon Stare" less well. According to its manufacturer, "Gorgon Stare (GS) is

---

39 Hussain, "The Sound of Terror."
40 Ibid.
41 See the Introduction and Chapter 6 of this volume.
42 Grégoire Chamayou, "The Manhunt Doctrine," trans. Shane Lillis, *Radical Philosophy* 169 (2011): 2. In his brilliant *A Theory of the Drone* (New York: The New Press, 2013), Chamayou develops his analyses in great depth.
43 Ibid., 4.

a one-of-a-kind Persistent Wide-Area Airborne Surveillance (WAAS) System. A Multi-Mission/Multi-Mode Intelligence, Surveillance and Reconnaissance (ISR) platform with a unique Electro-Optical/Infrared (EO/IR) toolset providing wide-area (city-sized), continuous 'stare' coverage."[44] What the specifications don't include is that the terror of the original Gorgon's stare was caused by its inescapable deadliness, but only when the victim looked directly at the Gorgon's face. Avoiding a direct face-to-face no longer protects from the Gorgon's deadly reach. As Maj. Gen. James O. Poss, the Air Force's assistant deputy chief of staff for intelligence, surveillance, and reconnaissance, explained, "Gorgon Stare will be looking at a whole city, so there will be no way for the adversary to know what we're looking at, and we can see everything."[45]

Consequently, in Chamayou's succinct analysis, "the zone of armed conflict, fragmented into micro-scale kill-boxes, reduces itself in the ideal-typical case to the single body of the enemy prey: the body as the field of battle."[46] In line with this new doctrine, the military and the CIA argue that, in effect, "because we can target our quarry with precision [...] we can strike them wherever we see fit, even outside a war zone." The result is, in Gregory's words, a "drone geography" definable as a "global hunting ground produced through and punctuated by 'mobile zones of exception.'"[47]

If it is true, as Chamayou cautions in an elaboration of a thought by Nietzsche, "that this form of compromise that human societies call justice cannot exist without a certain balance of forces and a certain reciprocity of the power of aggression, it may be that the pretensions for just cynegetic war cannot become effective without terrible retaliation. This is in any case," Chamayou continues, "the path opened, unwittingly, by those

---

44 Sierra Nevada Corporation, "Gorgon Stare: Persistent Wide-Area Airborne Surveillance (WASS) System," Sierra Nevada Corporation, June 9, 2014.

45 Ellen Nakashima and Craig Whitlock. "With Air Force's Gorgon Drone 'We Can See Everything," *Washington Post,* Jan. 2, 2011.

46 Chamayou quoted in Gregory, "Drone Geographies," 14.

47 Ibid.

today who seek to legitimate the drone attacks by a certain 'right to anticipatory self-defence against non-state actors.'"[48] The "new" cruelty inflicted by technoscience, of which drone warfare is the epitome, is countered by what Derrida calls "reactive savagery." To decipher either of them, one needs the tools of psychoanalysis, on the condition that "psychoanalysis" opens itself to be challenged in some of its fundamental assumptions.

Cruelty: Interventions in Psychoanalysis

While the drone war exemplifies the delocalization and expropriation of tele-technoscience and its weapon systems, it also exemplifies one of the two "ages" of cruelty that manifests, according to Derrida, in our "wars of 'religion.'" In 1994, Derrida was already calling upon psychoanalysis to understand the "new cruelty" of today's wars, and he wrote about the then-contemporary wars in ways that are profoundly illuminating for a reflection on today's wars as well. Today, Derrida writes, our "wars of religion" are characterized by a "new cruelty" in which an

> archaic and ostensibly more savage radicalization of "religious" violence claims, in the name of "religion," to allow the living community to rediscover its roots, its place, its body and its idiom intact (unscathed, safe, pure, proper). [This new cruelty] spreads death and unleashes self-destruction in a desperate (auto-immune) gesture that attacks the blood of its own body: as though thereby to eradicate uprootedness and reappropriate the sacredness of life safe and sound. [...] *A new cruelty* would thus ally, in wars that are also wars of religion, the most advanced technoscientific calculability with a reactive savagery that would like to attack the body proper directly, the sexual thing that can be raped, mutilated or simply denied, desexualized — yet another form of the same violence. Is it possible to speak today of this double rape, to speak of it in a way that wouldn't be too foolish, uninformed

---

48 Chamayou, "The Manhunt Doctrine," 5.

or inane, while "ignoring" "psychoanalysis"? To ignore psychoanalysis can be done in a thousand ways, sometimes through extensive psychoanalytic knowledge that remains culturally disassociated. Psychoanalysis is ignored when it is not integrated into the most powerful discourses today on right, morality, politics, but also on science, philosophy, theology, etc.[49]

The "new cruelty" is, in sum, one facet of a desperate attempt to return to the purity of origin, the "proper" (*le propre*), both in the sense of what is clean, unscathed, and of what is one's own, in response to the radical expropriation in the wake of globalization, the accelerated capitalization of economies, and the explosion of media-technology. One question that needs the most urgent attention is why, in the words of the French–Tunisian psychoanalyst Fethi Benslama, the "urge to return to one's origins," in the sense of one's mythical original past, is accompanied "by a terrifying wish for vengeance in the present."[50]

For Derrida, it is indispensable to engage with psychoanalysis on these questions, since "the very *aim,* and I do say the aim, of the psychoanalytic revolution is the only one not to rest, not to seek refuge, in principle, in [...] a theological or humanist alibi."[51] However, it must be acknowledged that this is not an unproblematic decision, especially when psychoanalysis risks remaining, as Derrida puts it, "culturally disassociated." Such

---

49 Derrida, "Faith and Knowledge," 89, emphasis and quotation marks around the words religion and religious Derrida's. The wars that received the greatest media coverage at the time were the Persian Gulf War (1990–1991), the Rwandan Civil War (1990–1993), the Algerian Civil War (1991–2002), the Somali Civil War (1991–present), the Croatian War of Independence (1991–1995), the Bosnian War (1992–1995), and the civil war in Afghanistan (1992–1996).

50 Fethi Benslama, *Psychoanalysis and the Challenge of Islam,* trans. Robert Bononno (Minneapolis: University of Minneapolis Press, 2009), 10.

51 Jacques Derrida, "Psychoanalysis Searches the State of its Soul: The Impossible Beyond of a Sovereign Cruelty," in *Without Alibi,* trans. Peggy Kamuf (Stanford: Stanford University Press, 2004), 240. See also Elizabeth Rottenberg, "Cruelty and its Vicissitudes" (155).

"dissociation" not only includes ignorance of another culture's foundational texts and modes of interpretation, but also occurs when the institutional representatives of psychoanalysis remain silent about abuses such as the practice of torture, one of the "most spectacular ways in which psychoanalytical authorities compromise with political or police authorities," of which Derrida accused the International Psychoanalytical Association in 1981 with regard to its public discourse — and silence — on Latin America. In this text, "Geopsychoanalysis," Derrida also warns of "more invisible abuses" in which psychoanalysis "may serve as a conduit" for "new forms of violence." He writes: "Inasmuch, indeed, as psychoanalysis does not analyze, does not denounce, does not struggle, does not transform (and does not transform *itself* for these purposes), surely it is in danger of becoming nothing more than a perverse and sophisticated appropriation of violence or at best merely a new weapon in the symbolic arsenal."[52]

This passage is quoted by Joseph Massad in his critique of Benslama's book *Psychoanalysis and the Challenge of Islam*, accusing the latter of conducting a "foreign policy" of psychoanalysis via a fortification of the "language of individualism, freedom, and human rights" which accepts as "the only tolerable Islam [...] a liberal form of Islam that upholds all the liberal values of European maturity" and individualism.[53] In the same 2009 special issue of the psychoanalytically oriented journal *Umbr(a)*, Stefania Pandolfo goes as far as to accuse Benslama's book of conveying "a specific political position, one that participates actively in the ideological apparatus of the 'war on terror.'"[54] Certainly, Benslama takes considerable risks in ap-

---

52 Jacques Derrida, "Geopsychoanalysis: ... and the Rest of the World," *American Imago* 48, no. 2 (1991): 211 (emph. in original).

53 Joseph Massad, "Psychoanalysis, Islam, and the Other of Liberalism," *Umbr(a)* (2009): 58. Massad's second main argument is that Benslama speaks of "Islam" in terms that are too undifferentiated and thus make him conflate in strategic places "Islam" and "Islamism."

54 Stefania Pandolfo, "'Soul Choking': Maladies of the Soul, Islam, and the Ethics of Psychoanalysis," *Umbr(a)* (2009): 76.

proaching not only "Islam" and Muslim culture from the experience of psychoanalysis, but he does so compelled by the events that rock the entire Middle East, and that have profound repercussions in the Western hemisphere.[55] In the midst of the risks taken, Benslama's work suggests that psychoanalysis has a productive — rather than reductive — role to play in our understanding of today's conflicts. Nathan Gorelick's assessment seems thus more just, when he points out that Benslama's *Psychoanalysis* "attempts to *inaugurate* the analytic relationship, to suspend the impulse toward solutions and to establish the terms of this absolutely vital confrontation within a rubric that both resists closure and at least attempts to evade complicity with the reductive and violent manifestations of either one of its objects of concern." Moreover, Gorelick underlines Benslama's steadfast refusal of the often assumed "dichotomy through which the Islamic philosophical tradition and its European 'counterpart' are held in total distinction [...]. The effect of an encounter between psychoanalysis and Islam jeopardizes, through the very discomfort to which it gives rise, the self-assured identities of either party, causing the cultural and historical terms through which they have both been rendered intelligible, to themselves and to each other, to tremble with disquieting intensity."[56]

In addition, in the very text Massad turns against Benslama, Derrida castigates the psychoanalytical establishment for the "utter dissociation of the psychoanalytical sphere from the sphere of the citizen or moral subject in his or her public or private life," a dissociation which he characterizes as "one of the most monstrous characteristics of the *homo psychoanalyticus* of

---

55 Speaking about his book *Soudain la révolution! De la Tunisie au monde arabe: La signification d'un soulèvement,* Benslama himself writes that "I have taken the risk of writing this small book in closest proximity of the event, in order to contribute to take it out of the gossip, but also in order not to let drop again the unthinkable that is this event's radiant kernel" (*Soudain la révolution! De la Tunisie au monde arabe: La signification d'un soulèvement* [Paris: Denoël, 2011], 10–11).

56 Nathan Gorelick, "Fethi Benslama and the Translation of the Impossible in Islam and Psychoanalysis," *Umbr(a)* (2009): 190–91 (emph. in original).

our time" and "a ghastly deformity."[57] Invoking the shameful silence by psychoanalytic institutions on the torture committed
at the time in Latin America, Derrida goes on to remind his
audience (mostly psychoanalysts from all over the world) that

> this is precisely the subject of your theory, your practice,
> and your institutions. You ought to have essential things to
> say — and to do — on the matter of torture. Especially on
> the matter of the particularly modern aspect of torture [...].
> Surely it is here that a properly psychoanalytical intervention
> should absolutely be set in motion — provided, of course,
> that there is such a thing as the "properly psychoanalytical"
> in this sphere. And if ever there were not, very grave conclu-
> sions would have to be drawn on all sides from that fact. Can
> one say that such an intervention, either direct or indirect, is
> occurring? I don't think so, for the moment. Is it possible? I
> don't know — I put the question to you. [...] The question is
> still open, but one thing is already certain: if the dominant
> and representative forces of psychoanalysis in the world to-
> day have nothing specific to say or do, nothing original to
> say or contribute to the thinking and the struggle that are
> proceeding in connection with the concepts and the crude
> or refined realities of torture, then psychoanalysis, *at least
> within the dominant forces that have currently appropriated its
> representation* [...] is nothing more and probably much less
> than those traditional medical health organizations to which
> the IPA distributes its principled protest.[58]

Benslama's very considerable merit thus is to confront "psychoanalysis" with that "other" to which, as Benslama points out,
Freud, regretfully admitting his ignorance, dedicated only a few
sentences.[59] Benslama attempts to decipher the cruelty committed in the name of "Islam" with the concepts and experience of

---

57 Derrida, "Geopsychoanalysis," 215.
58 Ibid., 217–18 (emph. in original).
59 Benslama, *Psychoanalysis and the Challenge of Islam*, 68–72.

"psychoanalysis," thus taking up Derrida's challenge to refuse the "dissociation of the psychoanalytical sphere from the sphere of the citizen or moral subject." If psychoanalysis wants to remain relevant today, it has to name Egypt, Syria, Iraq, and all the other countries in which cruelty and sovereignty are most intimately intertwined, which would certainly include the United States as well. While in his 2000 address to the "States General of Psychoanalysis" (*États généraux de la psychanalyse*) Derrida seemed to limit the "proper affair of psychoanalysis" to "nonbloody cruelty, psychical cruelty," his reflections on auto-immunity and the "war on terror" make it clear that he also considers psychoanalysis an indispensable discourse for understanding forms of cruelty other than the purely psychic.[60] Benslama, then, accepts Derrida's challenge to the "States General of Psychoanalysis." Can the Freudian logic on "cruelty," Derrida asks,

> induce, if not found (and if so, how?), an ethics, a code of law, and a politics capable of measuring up, on the one hand, to this century's psychoanalytic revolution, and, on the other hand, to the events that constitute a cruel mutation of cruelty, a technical, scientific, juridical, economic, ethical and political, ethical and military, and terrorist and policing mutation of our age? What remains to be thought *more psychoanalytico* would thus be a mutation of cruelty itself — or at least new historical figures of an ageless cruelty, as old and no doubt older than man.[61]

The difficulty of the task of thinking *more psychoanalytico* the "cruel mutation[s] of cruelty" of our age cannot be overstated, since it concerns not only psychoanalysis with regard to Muslim culture and the violence the Muslim world and, in different

---

60 As Elisabeth Roudinesco writes, "the States General brought together a thousand participants from thirty-three countries in the large amphitheater of the Sorbonne in Paris" (Derrida and Roudinesco, *For What Tomorrow*, 233n7). See Rottenberg. "Cruelty and its Vicissitudes," 155.

61 Derrida, "Psychoanalysis Searches the State of its Soul," 270 (emph. in original).

ways, the Western world are experiencing, but psychoanalysis in general. As Derrida underlined in that same address, psychoanalysis has not yet given any answer "in the very place where one expects the most specific response from psychoanalysis — in truth, the only appropriate response." He elaborates: "As I see it, psychoanalysis has not yet undertaken and thus still less succeeded in thinking, penetrating, and changing the axioms of the ethical, the juridical, and the political, notably in those seismic places where the theological phantasm of sovereignty quakes and where the most traumatic, let us say in a still confused manner the most cruel events of our day are being produced."[62] It is no consolation, Derrida continues, that psychoanalysis "is not alone, far from it," in not having thought through the concept of "cruelty," and its mutations, in those "seismic places." It is no consolation "especially for those who, like myself, believe that psychoanalysis, having announced as much at its birth, should have something indispensable and essential not just to say but also to do on this subject. Without alibi. The decisive thing that there would be to say and to do on this subject should register the shock wave of one or more psychoanalytic revolutions. Notably on the subject of what is called, therefore, sovereignty and cruelty."[63]

Benslama's undertaking is thus enormous. For that very reason, his approach is inspired by what Adorno called "minima moralia," namely, the sense that "one can no longer tackle with monumental frescos the domains of human reality." The "short essay," by contrast, "that is linked to personal experience," may constitute "a mode of resistance to the great theoretical brutali-

---

62 Ibid., 244–45.

63 Ibid., 245. A bit later, Derrida pushes the question and the challenge even further: "What new forms of cruelty would a psychoanalyst of the year 2000 have to interpret at renewed expense, outside or within the institution? With regard to the political, the geo-political, the juridical, the ethical, are there consequences, or at least lessons to be drawn from the hypothesis of an irreducible death drive that seems inseparable from what is so obscurely called cruelty, in either its archaic or its modern forms? Would there also be, a few steps further beyond the principles, a beyond of the beyond, a beyond of the death drive and thus of the cruelty drive?" (257–58).

ties in which one prefers to gaze at oneself as in a mirror, in a cosmic system in order not to see the facts and effects of human desire which can be tracked down in the detail." Benslama explains that his experience as a psychoanalyst has led him "to think the subjective and the political dimensions together. The clinical work with migrants and the confrontation with one of today's most severe crises of civilization, the crisis of Islam, have convinced me that there is a geopsychoanalytical research field in which I deposit as I go along what I find that is related to this articulation of the individual and collective 'psychical.'"[64]

One example of what Adorno also called "micrology" offered by Benslama is an analysis of the self-immolation of Mohammad Bouazizi that triggered the "hurricane" of the "Arab Spring," and an analysis of possible reasons why this particular "self-sacrifice," but not similar suicides that had preceded it, set a revolution in motion.[65] Could it be, Benslama asks, that the name *Bouazizi* provided the "original scene of the Tunisian revolution with a powerful symbolic charge?"

Benslama conjectures that

> in pronouncing the name Bouazizi, Tunisians spoke of the man who had immolated himself but in doing so, they received without knowing a word whispered from the conjunction of the act and the signifiers of the name, that could be articulated as *the son of the priceless, cherished father has sacrificed himself for dignity.* Such a resonance is the fruit of an interpretation that assumes that language moves human beings between the possible and the necessary. The possible is the contingent, otherwise put what can be or cannot be. In order for an upheaval to occur, the necessary, which is always looking for its chance, must encounter words which confer to it the possibility of a poignant truth.[66]

---

64 Benslama, *Soudain la révolution,* 12 (emph. in original). All translations of *Soudain la révolution* are mine.

65 Ibid., 20, 32–33.

66 Ibid., 33–34.

Benslama, then, seeks to find in the power of the signifier what moves people to acts that would be unthinkable under other circumstances. In the case of Bouazizi, the "martyr" was "constructed" after the fact, but this was only possible because he introduced "the possibility of a reversal of the relations by showing how a man can find power in his very impotence, can exist while disappearing, can make his right prevail while losing everything."[67]

Bouazizi's act was motivated by utter despair and "the shame of being human," by his realization that he was crushed by a recklessly arrogant and brutally oppressive government. When the tyrant, forced by the revolutionary events, visited the severely burnt Bouazizi in the hospital, the image circulating on social media confronted "the first personality of the State and the last of the last," the sovereign and the "one who is nobody." This scene caused the "human community's gaze to squarely face the gap between the figure of cruel power and the figure of the burnt person reduced to almost nothing on his death bed. The opening of this gaze creates a decisive separation from the master of their alienation. This is why we say here that the unconscious cannot not be political."[68]

Cruelty: Media's Pervertibility

The so-called war on terror is conducted on more than one front. Within the US and other Western countries, civil liberties are curtailed; in Iraq, Afghanistan, Pakistan, Somalia, Yemen, and Syria — predominantly Muslim countries — military operations are conducted in the form of undeclared wars.

Given that the "resistance to the intelligibility of Islam" is widespread throughout the history of Western Europe and the US, and given that, as Benslama puts it, this "ignorance has even increased, finding new pretexts in our tortured present," a

---

67 Ibid., 26.
68 Ibid., 27, 30.

"metapsychological translation" of psychoanalysis is as difficult as it is urgent.[69]

A short detour to the question of media is here necessary. As indicated above, media provide the link between the two "ages" of cruelty and testify with particular clarity to the fact that the perpetrators of archaic cruelty are, in Abdelwahab Meddeb's words, "as much children of their time and of a world transformed by Americanization as they are the product of an internal evolution, unique to Islam." That is, they are also the children of the most media-savvy modernity.[70] In the interview with Giovanna Borradori, given shortly after 9/11, Derrida underlined the "mutation" and (to use a concept introduced by W.J.T. Mitchell) the "cloning" of cruelty through endless repeatability via visual media. He argued that "the maximum media coverage was in the *common* interest of the perpetrators of 'September 11,' the terrorists, and those who, in the name of the victims, wanted to declare 'war on terrorism.' Between these two parties, such media coverage was, like the good sense of which Descartes speaks, the most widely shared thing in the world." This autoimmune "pervertibility" of media, while perhaps not taking the "form of an evil intention," is, *as* virtuality, "enough to frighten, even terrify. It is the ineradicable root of terror and thus of a terrorism that announces itself even before organizing itself into terrorism. Implacably. Endlessly."[71]

Since that bright September morning, the "'central nervous system' of the social body," in Marshall McLuhan's language, or the "technoeconomic power of the media," in Derrida's, has "been traumatized by an image — the spectacle, the word, above all the *number as enigmatic name*: 9/11. The image, the spectacu-

---

69 Benslama, *Psychoanalysis and the Challenge of Islam,* ix.

70 Abdelwahab Meddeb, *The Malady of Islam,* trans. Pierre Joris and Ann Reid (New York: Basic, 2003), 147.

71 Derrida, "Autoimmunity," 108–9. Emphasis Derrida's. Derrida adds a note of caution: "Let me add here as a reminder: there is nothing purely 'modern' in this relation between media and terror, in a terrorism that operates by propagating within the public space images or rumors aimed at terrifying the so-called civilian population" ("Autoimmunity," 109).

lar destruction of the twin towers, has been cloned repeatedly in the collective global nervous system. The mediatizing of the event was, in fact, its whole point."[72] This has become brutally clear again in recent years with the use of social media as a weapon. Commenting on videos showing the beheadings of two American journalists (and a few months later, one had to add the videos of the beheadings of a British aid worker, a French mountaineer, a Japanese adventurer, a Japanese journalist, the burning alive of a Jordanian pilot, and the beheading of twenty-one Egyptian workers), David Carr wrote in the *New York Times* in September 2014 that "the videos deliver in miniature the same chilling message as the footage of the towers falling 13 years ago: Everything has changed, no one is safe and the United States is impotent against true believers. It is a memo from a foe that has everything to gain by goading America into a fight in a faraway land where its enemies are legion. The tactic worked back then." Carr adds: "Video beheadings are a triple death — murder and defilement in a public way — and YouTube becomes the pike on which the severed heads are displayed" — endlessly.[73]

Carr's analysis confirms a thesis Derrida underlined in the interview given right after 9/11, in which he argued that the temporalization of trauma needs to be thought in terms of the future: "The wound remains open by our terror before the future and not only the past. [...] There is traumatism with no possible work of mourning when the evil comes from the possibility to come of the worst, from the repetition to come — though worse. Traumatism is produced by the *future,* by the to *come,* by the threat of the worst *to come.*"[74] In this sense, too, "the traumatic event is its future," as Cathy Caruth writes in *Literature in the Ashes of History*; it "is its repetition as something that returns but also returns to erase its past, returns as something other than what one could ever recognize."[75] Derrida's concept of "au-

72 Mitchell, *Cloning Terror,* 51 (emph. in original).

73 David Carr, "With Videos of Killings, ISIS Sends Medieval Message by Modern Method," *New York Times,* Sep. 7, 2014.

74 Derrida, "Autoimmunity," 96ff (emph. in original).

75 Caruth, *Literature in the Ashes of History,* 87 (emph. in original).

to-immunity" encapsulates the stakes: While the "new cruelty" justifies itself in a discourse of return to the purity of the origin, it uses the most advanced media to clone its archaic ferocity, and clone it endlessly, in the name of "a future reduced to a concluded past."[76] Derrida's concept captures this terrifying, terrorizing cycle. Mitchell explains in his book *Cloning Terror* while in the immediate aftermath of 9/11, and then during the anthrax attacks of fall 2001, the "equation of terrorism with literal or metaphoric bioterrorism was unavoidable," Derrida offered, in that very moment, "an alternate biopolitical metaphor," which, rather than focusing "on the usual picture of terrorism as a foreign invasion by alien microbes," focused on the "defense mechanisms of the organism itself."[77] The notion of "immunity" is all the more useful for Derrida because, as Mitchell points out in quoting the medical historian Arthur Silverstein, rather than stemming from a biological discourse, it originated in a sociopolitical one: "The Latin words *immunitas* and *immunis* have their origin in the legal concept of an exemption," a sense reflected in the notion of "diplomatic immunity." Mitchell comments on the importance of the word's genesis:

> The whole theory of the immune system, and the discipline of immunology, is riddled with images drawn from the sociopolitical sphere — of invaders and defenders, hosts and parasites, [...] borders and identities that must be maintained. In asking us to see terror as autoimmunity, then, Derrida is bringing the metaphor home at the same time he sends it abroad [...]. The effect of the "bipolar image" is to produce a situation in which there is *no literal meaning,* nothing but the resonances between two images, one biomedical, the other political. The impossibility of a literal meaning, of course, means that we literally "do not know what we are talking about" or what we are "literally" talking about. [...] For Derrida, this admission of ignorance is crucial, because the real

---

76 Benslama, *Psychoanalysis and the Challenge of Islam*, 10.
77 Mitchell, *Cloning Terror*, 45.

politics of the autoimmunity metaphor, beyond its power to deconstruct all the easy, Manichean binary oppositions that have structured the War on Terror, is the restaging of terrorism as a condition that needs to be thought through analytically, systemically, and without moral tub-thumping [...]. Even more far-reaching is the implication that "a mutation will have to take place" in our entire way of thinking about justice, democracy, sovereignty, globalization, military power, the relations of nation-states, the politics of "friendship" and enmity, in order to address terrorism with any hope of an effective cure. In other words, we have something to learn here.[78]

Derrida's reflections on September 2001 are just as relevant for understanding the "terror" of our day and age:

"Terrorist" acts try to produce psychic effects (conscious or unconscious) and symbolic or symptomatic reactions that might take numerous detours [...]. The *quality* or *intensity* of the emotions provoked (whether conscious or unconscious) is not always proportionate to the number of victims or the amount of damage. In situations and cultures where the media do not spectacularize the event, the killing of thousands of people in a very short period of time might provoke fewer psychic and political effects than the assassination of a single individual in another country, culture, or nation-state with highly developed media resources. And does terrorism have to work only through death?[79]

Derrida rejects the Western bias that attributes much greater attention to death inflicted by "terrorism," as defined and portrayed by mainstream media, than to deaths that are not seen as such or that are presented as justified for reasons of "national security." After enumerating a long list of examples, including

---

78 Mitchell, *Cloning Terror,* 47–48 (emph. in original).
79 Derrida, "Autoimmunity," 107–8 (emph. in original).

letting millions of people die of hunger and disease, Derrida concludes: "All situations of social or national structural oppression produce a terror that is [...] organized, institutional, and all these situations depend on this terror without those who benefit from them ever organizing terrorist acts or ever being treated as terrorists. The narrow, too narrow meaning commonly given today to the word 'terrorism' gets circulated in various ways in the discourse that dominates the public space, and first of all through the technoeconomic power of the media."[80] As Derrida points out in the same interview, "one doesn't count the dead in the same way from one corner of the globe to the other. It is our duty to recall this."[81] Among many possible examples, one may recall that the drone war conducted in remote areas in Pakistan and Afghanistan occurs in "situations and cultures where the media do not spectacularize the event," with the result that the killing of hundreds or thousands of people goes almost unnoticed in the very countries whose taxpayers finance the lethal operations.

Cruelty: Our Day, Our Age

Benslama's analysis of today's atrocities and their *mise-en-scène* (again, the acts cannot be separated from their mediatized calculation) is, I argue, an example of what Derrida may have had in mind when he underlined the necessity of psychoanalysis for a reflection on auto-immunitarian cruelty. Indeed, Benslama approaches those "seismic places" where cruelty is taking on new forms and qualities. He turns his attention, to use Derrida's words, to places "where the theological phantasm of sovereignty quakes and where the most traumatic, let us say in a still confused manner the most cruel events of our day are being produced," thus confronting the question "what new forms of

---

80 Ibid., 108.
81 Ibid., 92.

cruelty" a psychoanalyst of this day and age would have to "interpret at renewed expense, outside or within the institution."[82]

Benslama describes several major political conditions that form the broader context of the "civilizational mutation" taking place in the Islamic world that resonate with Derrida's analysis and are often neglected in the public debates in Western nations.[83]

First, there is the fact that in the beginning, the encounter of Muslim countries and modernity occurred through the brutal experience of colonialism: "Enlightenment arrived with gunboats. We need not forget that the culture of enlightenment, together with its scientific and technological apparatuses disembarked with military expeditions (Egypt 1798, Algiers 1831…), implanted themselves with colonialism and that they shook the very foundations, both material and symbolical, of the Muslim world. In a very short lapse of time, Islam became the reference of a dislocated civilization, whose members are dominated at home."[84]

Further, the importation of Western capitalism did not advance political self-determination for the peoples of the Middle East. Rather, it allowed the ruling families of oil-rich monarchies to "ferociously" exploit their countries' resources, on the one hand transforming them "into a product of consumption for a minority," and on the other, leaving "desolate urban landscapes" in which an "unheard-of demographic explosion" left "masses of people abandoned without care by those who govern them, human matter ready to be molded in all the forms of desperate and unregulated expression."[85] In other texts, Benslama frequently underlines the people's despair in Middle Eastern countries, in particular in Tunisia, where the regime had achieved a "political

---

82 Derrida, "Psychoanalysis Searches the State of its Soul," 244, 257.

83 Benslama, *Psychoanalysis and the Challenge of Islam*, 51.

84 Fethi Benslama, *La guerre des subjectivités en Islam* (Paris: Lignes, 2014), 18. All translations of *La guerre des subjectivités en Islam* are mine.

85 Benslama, *Psychoanalysis and the Challenge of Islam*, 51, and Benslama in Hella Lahbib, "Entretien avec Fethi Benslama," *La Presse de Tunisie*, Aug. 30, 2014. Translation mine.

despair" so deep that the political speech of its opponents "limited itself to declarations of political impotence."[86] In the wake of the destruction of the Caliphate by Atatürk in 1924, and of the struggle for liberation from colonial power, ruthless dictatorships were established, able to survive only with the complicity of the West, stripping their populations of justice and imposing draconian censorship on cultural productions and political expression. The most egregious example, Saudi Arabia, is "the only state in the world whose name bears that of its leading family." For more than thirty years, the Saud family "has continued to eradicate argument, opposition, and creativity through the use of imprisonment, torture, murder, the corruption of elites, and the imposition of the most brutal norms on the planet [that include] aggravated archaic forms of male domination and sexual repression."[87] Other analysts underline this factor as well, including the acclaimed Middle East correspondent for *The Independent*, Patrick Cockburn, the French-Tunisian poet, scholar of Islam, and novelist Abdelwahab Meddeb, and the Algerian writer, novelist, and newspaper editor Kamel Daoud.[88] As a consequence of this political circumstance, the cultural process of modernization for many predominantly Muslim countries has been vastly different compared with the European context. Benslama notes that "the acceptance of science and technology did not occur through a process of creative integration [...]. In the absence of any critical function, without any accompanying ethics or aesthetics, [...] modernization took place without the necessary work of culture (*Kulturarbeit*, as Freud expressed it)," resulting in an "expulsion of the function of language in the name of science."[89] Fast-forwarding to a time closer to the present, two pivotal decisions by Paul Bremer also need to be listed

---

86 Benslama, *Soudain la révolution,* 49.

87 Benslama, *Psychoanalysis and the Challenge of Islam,* 65.

88 Patrick Cockburn, *The Jihadis Return: ISIS and the New Sunni Uprising* (New York: OR Books 2014), 21; Meddeb, *The Malady of Islam,* 188; Kamel Daoud, "Saudi Arabia, an ISIS that Has Made It," *New York Times,* Nov. 20, 2015.

89 Benslama, *Psychoanalysis and the Challenge of Islam,* 45.

here, which he made in May 2003 as the top civilian adminis-
trator for the Coalition Provisional Authority, and thus Iraq's
chief executive authority who was permitted to rule by decree.
Among the first and the most calamitous decrees were Coalition Provisional Authority Order Number 1, which barred Iraqis
who ranked in the higher levels of Saddam Hussein's Baath Party
from government work for life, and CPA Order No. 2, which dis-
banded the Iraqi Army, putting at least three hundred thousand
men out of work in a country plagued by high unemployment.
As James Pfiffner shows, both decrees were made "against the
advice of military and CIA professionals and without consulting
important members of the President's staff and cabinet."[90] It is
now well-documented that many soldiers of the former Iraqi
army joined the insurgency, and many former officers have been
providing military expertise to the self-declared "caliphate" of
the "Islamic State."[91]

For Benslama, one of the causes of Islamist extremism is "the
widespread liquidation of speech and political meaning" that
has been enforced for decades, and the resulting "catastrophic
collapse of language": according to Benslama, language was "no
longer able to translate for people a particularly intense historical experience, that of the modern era."[92]

The combination of all these factors prepared fertile ground
for the Islamist discourse, "a discourse that promises justice
through identity, that offers vengeance and reparation through
the reappropriation of the proper [*le propre*: the clean/one's

---

90 James Pfiffner, "US Blunders in Iraq: De-Baathification and Disbanding the
Army," *Intelligence and National Security* 25.1 (2010): 76. See also Scott An-
derson, "Fractured Lands: How the Arab World Came Apart," *New York
Times Magazine,* Aug. 11, 2016.

91 See also Ben Hubbard and Eric Schmitt, "Military Skill and Terrorist Technique Fuel Success of ISIS," *New York Times,* Aug. 27, 2014; Michael Gordon,
"Fateful Choice on Iraq Army Bypassed Debate," *New York Times,* Mar. 17,
2008. Linking the former to the latter, Kamel Daoud writes: "Daesh [the
acronym for the Islamic State in Arabic] has a mother: the invasion of Iraq.
But it also has a father: Saudia Arabia and its religious-industrial complex"
("Saudi Arabia, an ISIS that Has Made It").

92 Benslama, *Psychoanalysis and the Challenge of Islam,* 4.

own]," and promises "access to the 'originary plenitude of politics'" by means of a "return to the golden age of the founding of Islam."[93]

As an example of Derrida's "auto-immunity," Benslama explains how Islamist clerics in large numbers invoke science to prove the truth of the foundational religious texts. The revealed signs of the religious system whose truth "remains hidden from all proof" are replaced by religious writings "in which the discourse of science continuously vouches for revelation." Thus, "contrary to popular conceptions, what we are witnessing, far from being a simple return of the religious, is the confused manifestation of the decomposition of religion and its recomposition as a new, modern totalitarian ideology: national-theo-scientism."[94] Given the crucial role of mass and social media, one may insert another specification and speak of national-theo-media-scientism.

When the "rupture" or "caesura" in the "identificatory anchorages" that "characterizes modernity as such" occurs without the corresponding cultural work, "it is transformed into a disastrous process of subjective revocation on a large scale [*révocation subjective à grande échelle*] which triggers the despair of the masses."[95] Benslama underlines that such ruptures in identificatory anchorages are, wherever they occur, "high-risk process[es]." While poverty and the destruction of living spaces render this despair more devastating, its causes "lie in the loss of unconscious individual-collective anchorages and are expressed in the identificatory fear of losing face." However, the "aggravated forms of the aptitude at annihilation" Middle Eastern countries are witnessing result for Benslama not from this despair, but from the latter's "denial."[96]

Benslama offers several perspectives on the ensuing violence, and its particular brand of cruelty. One of the factors

---

93 Benslama in Hella Lahbib, "Entretien avec Fethi Benslama"; *Psychoanalysis and the Challenge of Islam*, 4.

94 Benslama, *Psychoanalysis and the Challenge of Islam*, 49–50.

95 Ibid., 54.

96 Ibid., 55; Beslama, *Soudain la révolution*, 44.

fueling them is an extraordinary literalism that is assumed to move backwards in time, in order to simultaneously produce the origin of Islam, the end of time, and divine vengeance. The radical Islamist response to the massive and collective "subjective revocation" is to "re-Islamicize" Muslims, sanctioning along the way "violent extremist groups to kill and massacre" people denounced as "simulacra of Muslims whose deaths will be a service to Islam." In this logic, the accused pseudo-Muslims "have evolved backward and crossed the wall of time to a period before their beginning." As a consequence, "the emirs who are 're-Islamicizing' Muslims assume the position of being wrapped in a collective primal scene and clinging to the gateway of beginnings, where they can control death by taking the tithe of life and flesh."[97]

Benslama's analysis resonates with the one offered by Sohaira Siddiqui who rejects the "authenticity debate" on whether or not "ISIS" is Islamic and instead examines ISIS's juridical claims in relation to the Islamic juridical tradition. Siddiqui argues that publications such as a 2004 book with the telling title *The Management of Savagery* and ISIS's own recruitment materials advocate a "constant cosmic war which requires the use of violence by every Muslim against anyone considered non-Muslim." "From the totality of the images, articles, and statements of ISIS, their use of violence is guided by the basic principle that it is unrestricted and should be practiced with utmost brutality to not only physically defeat the enemy, but to psychologically impair" him or her.[98] While some commentators note the "literalism" and "seriousness" with which ISIS ideologues profess to read the sacred texts, Siddiqui shows that they can claim "historical precedence to justify their actions [only] by manipulating the legal tradition and using *non-majoritarian,* often *rejected* juristic opinions of the past. For ISIS, spreading violence and expanding the Caliphate, irrespective of the loss of life, is the goal. Their

---

97 Benslama, *Psychoanalysis and the Challenge of Islam,* 26.
98 Sohaira Siddiqui, "Beyond Authenticity: ISIS and the Islamic Legal Tradition," *Jadaliyya,* Feb. 24, 2015.

legal architecture is created to fulfill this mission, regardless of what the majoritarian opinions are within the totality of Islamic juristic thought."[99]

The literal adoption of seventh-century practices repudiated by the juridical majority can happen only on the condition, as Siddiqui shows, of ignoring the "plurality of legal rulings" and the underlying acceptance that the "law could evolve," and of enforcing a "top-down model" of the law, "imposed upon the masses irrespective of society or custom."[100] In Benslama's terms, such literal adoption occurs at the condition of the "uprooting of metaphor and the destruction of interpretation"; in Meddeb's assessment, at the condition of moving "away from a voice that

---

99 Siddiqui is highly critical of the analysis proposed by Graeme Wood and Bernard Haykel who insist that the fighters of the Islamic State faithfully reproduce the norms of war of early Islam, including "a number of practices that modern Muslims tend to prefer not to acknowledge as integral to their sacred texts," such as "slavery, crucifixion, and beheadings." What is striking about Islamic State fighters, according to Haykel, "is not just the literalism, but also the seriousness with which they read these texts" (Graeme Wood, "What ISIS Really Wants," *The Atlantic*, March 2015, Haykel is quoted by Wood). Siddiqui, by contrast, shows, that those practices cannot be categorized as "norms of war of early Islam," but that they need to be considered marginal. For example, the majority of jurists agreed on the prohibition of mutilation, including the mutilation by fire, "on the basis that bodies, regardless of faith, should be treated with dignity" (Siddiqui, "Beyond Authenticity"). Amal Ghazal and Larbi Sadiki accuse Wood and Haykel of "crude Orientalism," when they cite "coherent and even learned interpretations of Islam." "To the contrary," Ghazal and Sadiki write, "ISIS' interpretations are neither coherent nor learned, fall outside of juristic consensus and betray historical precedents. The author's emphasis on ISIS' "medieval religious nature" fails to see the complicity of modernity and modern institutions in the creation of phenomena like ISIS" (Amal Ghazal and Larbi Sadiki, "ISIS: The 'Islamic State' between Orientalism and the Interiority of MENA's Intellectuals," *Jadaliyya*, Jan. 19, 2016).

100 One of the authors Siddiqui quotes is Ahmad Atif Ahmad who concludes his analysis of "war" in the Qur'an and the Islamic theories of the rights of war and peace by "reject[ing] singling out the jihad tradition as a uniquely good example of bad wars. If anything, jihad theories and practices may be examples that deserve mention for their restrained quality and limited scope" (Ahmad Ahmad, *Islam, Modernity, Violence, and Everyday Life* [New York: Palgrave, 2009], 146).

veils the text in a strangeness all the more delightful for its excess, and toward an articulation of triumphant meaning, a reign of terror that divides all acts between reward and punishment."[101] Benslama's work has the great merit of taking into consideration both the Islamic tradition and the geopolitical history of the region, thus building its analyses "on the intertwining of politics and theology, not their dualism."[102] According to Benslama, from its early days on, Islamism has assimilated "Enlightenment" with "new crusades" and found

> confirmation of its thesis of the ablation of the Muslim subject from his/her confessional community. This is why the recurrent reactive figure of the subject at war in the modern Muslim world has not ceased to be that of the *avenger of the divinity*. The agony for justice does not have another meaning in this context than that of accomplishing Allah's vengeance. The mechanism of voluntary death hinges here on a decision by which the subject fulfills himself in the perspective of a last judgment, through the sacrifice of his life for the survival of his God and the restoration of his empire. This means in the end that the subject is responsible *before* God only by having become responsible *for* God."[103]

As a number of scholars have noted, many jihadists joining ISIS understand their mission to be to bring about the end of time.[104] Benslama explains why, from a psychoanalytic perspective, such assumed responsibility *for* God paves the path for cruelty. Cruelty, he writes, "supposes the sadist *jouissance* [sc. excessive pleasure or enjoyment] of the other's suffering." But in order for such *jouissance* to materialize, the sadist subject must imagine

---

101 Benslama, *Psychoanalysis and the Challenge of Islam*, 26; Meddeb, *Islam and the Challenge of Civilization*, 8.

102 Ghazal and Sadiki, "ISIS."

103 Benslama, *La guerre des subjectivités*, 18–19 (emph. in the original).

104 For example, William McCans, *The ISIS Apocalypse: The History, Strategy, and Doomsday Vision of the Islamic State* (New York: St. Martin's Press, 2015).

that through the other's suffering, he, the perpetrator, causes the absolute Other's, i.e., God's, *jouissance*.[105] Reflecting on the "profound political breakdown" of the Arab world over the last decades, Benslama cautions against attributing this breakdown exclusively to "victimization" or "humiliation by outside forces." Instead, he ascribes the breakdown to the fact that "the cruelty associated with the destruction of politics shatters human dignity," leaving behind "derisory things [*choses dérisoires*]." Since the 1960s, the ruling families have "financed the emergence of radical Islamist movements in order to destroy progressive forces, suspend the interpretation of ancient texts, and disseminate their own [corrupt] values."[106] The reduction of their subjects to "derisory things" deprived of the dignity of political self-determination is replicated and exploited by

> instigators who lead the masses on a path littered with worn-out values, where the imperative is to reanimate those values by transforming oneself into their living fetishes. [...] The current proliferation of parades that exhibit bodies marked by the stigmata of subjection, and dress codes of disguise that wipe out personal identity to produce the gesticulation of religious automatons, [illustrate] that the desire of the avenger of the divinity correlates to being the instrument of God's *jouissance* and, in many cases, to make his law. This is where the reversal occurs that allows the subject to pass from derision to the grandiose.[107]

It is the assertion of absolute sovereignty, the sovereignty thought to be meted out by a cruelly punishing God. Benslama observes that in Arabic, the word for "sovereignty," *siyaada,* shares its roots with the word for "blackness," *sawaad*: "This is the archaic meaning of this sovereign power: it wants to govern as the night that falls onto the world." In a footnote, Benslama

---

105 Benslama in Hella Lahbib, "Entretien avec Fethi Benslama."
106 Benslama, *Psychoanalysis and the Challenge of Islam,* 64, 66.
107 Benslama, *La guerre des subjectivités,* 19.

recalls that the etymology of the word "sovereign" in the Latin tradition is just as foreboding: *superanus* "indicates the most elevated, i.e. the solar position. The one who makes the day makes the night."[108]

The quasi-divine power of making the day or the night is asserted in both the archaic and the techno-scientific manifestations of sovereignty which in both theaters of war descends cruelly, often lethally. The task of the deconstructor-philosopher is thus clear, as is that of the psychoanalyst: to disturb that which *desires within us* a kingdom, in all the forms this desire might take, in all the forms the "us" might take, and to analyze, without alibi, the cruelty that is intrinsic to all of them. This is for Derrida specifically the task of scholars working in the humanities, as can be deduced from the way he described the necessary work on the history of the death penalty:

> We are not here to simplify. We are here — permit me to recall this because it is essential and decisive at this point — neither in a courtroom or on a witness stand, nor in a place of worship, nor in a parliament, nor in print, radio, or televised news. And neither are we in a real theater. To exclude all of these places, to exit from all of these places, without exception, is the first condition for *thinking* the death penalty. And thus for hoping to change it in some way."[109]

Something similar could be said of terror and its wars.

108 Benslama, *Soudain la révolution,* 46, 46n.
109 Derrida, *The Death Penalty,* 27 (emph. in original).

CHAPTER 6

Kill Boxes:
Kafka's Beetles, Drones

Any "living together" supposes and guards, as its
very condition, the possibility of this singular, secret,
inviolable separation, from which alone a stranger
accords himself to a stranger, in hospitality.
— Jacques Derrida[1]

The first sentence of Kafka's "Die Verwandlung" ("The Metamorphosis") famously reads: "When Gregor Samsa woke up one
morning from unsettling dreams, he found himself changed in
his bed into a monstrous vermin [*ein ungeheures Ungeziefer*]."[2]

---

1 Derrida, "Avowing," 28.
2 Franz Kafka, "Die Verwandlung," in *Drucke zu Lebzeiten*, eds. Hans-Gerd
  Koch, Wolf Kittler, Gerhard Neumann (Frankfurt: S. Fischer, 1994), 113;
  The Metamorphosis, trans. and ed. Stanley Corngold (New York: Modern
  Library Classics, 2013), 3. Susan Bernofsky translates the first sentence as
  follows: "When Gregor Samsa woke one morning from troubled dreams,
  he found himself transformed right there in his bed into some sort of monstrous insect" (Franz Kafka, *The Metamorphosis*, trans. Susan Bernofsky
  [New York: W.W. Norton, 2016], 3). The literary criticism on this short story
  is enormous. The main purpose of this chapter is not to provide an in-depth
  scholarly analysis of Kafka's text, but to place it in a new context. Therefore, I will be able to refer only to a very limited number of critical studies.
  On the importance of the German prefix *un-* in this first sentence ("from
  unsettling," "uneasy," or "troubled dreams" reads in German *aus unruhigen
  Träumen*), see for example Michael Levine, "The Sense of an *Unding*: Kafka,
  Ovid, and the Misfits of Metamorphosis," in *Franz Kafka's The Metamorphosis,* New Edition, ed. Harold Bloom (New York: Bloom's Literary Criticism,
  2008), 126–28.

This beginning is captivating evidence for an assertion reported by K., the protagonist of Kafka's novel *The Trial*. Someone had told him once that "the riskiest instant of the day was the instant of awakening."[3] Indeed, at the beginning of "The Metamorphosis," Gregor Samsa first tries to explain to himself his transformed state as a byproduct of the ruinously irregular sleeping hours caused by his profession as a traveling salesman. In his inner monologue, he implies that temporal disruption and spatial displacement are responsible: the necessity of "getting up so early" and "the agony of traveling" — Corngold even translates with "the torture of traveling" — "worrying about train connections" and "human intercourse that is constantly changing, never developing the least constancy or warmth" or "cordiality" — they all contribute to a lack of sleep.[4] We know the havoc sleep deprivation can wreak.

The instant of awakening is the riskiest instant of the day, because it is on the threshold from one state to the other, the instant, in German "der Augenblick," "the glance of an eye" — no longer than the movement of an eyelid — in which the transition happens from a world over which the sleeper had no control, to a presumably familiar world. It is a risky, potentially dangerous moment because the sleeper may awaken, against expectations, into a radically unknown world. His "unsettling dreams" notwithstanding, Gregor has no idea of what happened while he was asleep. Sleep is abandonment, utter trust.

As the verb form of the English present participle shows, awakening "does not have a point in time [...], it never falls into *this* time, *now*; the digits of [measured] time are foreign and exterior to it as they can always only show 'too late' and only measure the inner distance, which the event [of awakening] encloses in itself."[5] By contrast, as K.'s unknown source asserts, once the

---

3   Franz Kafka, *Schriften-Tagebücher-Briefe. Kritische Ausgabe: Der Prozeß. Apparatband,* vol. II, ed. Malcolm Pasley (Frankfurt: Fischer, 1990), 168.

4   Kafka, *Metamorphosis,* trans. Bernofsky, 4; trans. Corngold, 4.

5   Joseph Vogl, "Vierte Person: Kafkas Erzählstimme," *Deutsche Vierteljahrsschrift für Literaturwissenschaft und Geistesgeschichte* 68, no. 4 (Dec. 1994): 745.

instant of awakening is "overcome, without one having been pulled away to somewhere from one's place, one can be confident ['comforted' or 'consoled': *getrost*] during the entire day."[6]

The temporal deferral encapsulated in the instant of awakening corresponds to a spatial displacement, particularly evident when the awoken one is disoriented from a lingering dream.

Still, however displaced and deferred in itself, awakening is but the beginning in Kafka's array of experiences that appear out of place.

Kafka's texts are populated with undefinable things like the living and laughing Odradek who or that resembles a living thread spool; they feature singing, piping, or whistling, but certainly speaking mice, discoursing apes and dogs that (or who) are engaged in research, and they feature dancing celluloid balls and a crossbreed between a lamb and a kitten. These texts lead into a world that not only undermines the "categorical order of things and creatures," but also ignores the limits of the anthropomorphic altogether. "This is a world of crossings and transitional beings that includes animated things, composite creatures, lignified organisms, living machines, animal people, and human animals in equal measure and which above all registers the mutual mutations and metamorphoses."[7] One reason why Kafka's texts are so fresh to today's reader, almost as if still "unread," is that they register the role media technology plays in the displacements, deferrals, and shocks they record.

The moment of awakening, as "The Metamorphosis" shows, is, indeed, the riskiest, because the estrangement from oneself, in spite of the very recognition thereof by the one concerned, might be irreversible. Given Kafka's astute awareness of the interdependency of organic life and inorganic objects and tech-

---

6 "Darum sei auch der Augenblick des Erwachens der riskanteste Augenblick im Tag, sei er einmal überstanden, ohne daß man irgendwohin von seinem Platze fortgezogen wurde, so könne man den ganzen Tag über getrost sein" (Kafka, *Schriften*, 168).

7 Joseph Vogl, "Kafkas Komik," in *Kontinent Kafka: Mosse-Lectures an der Humboldt Universität zu Berlin,* ed. Klaus Scherpe, Elisabeth Wagner (Berlin: Vorwerk 8, 2006), 80. All translations of "Kafkas Komik" are mine.

nology, the well-known literary topic of "I is another" does not exhaust the dynamic of his texts. Rather, one has to take into consideration what Walter Benjamin described as the deep penetration of technology into the "fabric of the given [*das Gewebe der Gegebenheit*]" that transforms the "apparatus of apperception" of the human body.[8] In that vein, Joseph Vogl has read some of Kafka's texts along the logic of the slapstick. The slapstick performs the "entanglement of mechanisms and organisms"; it encroaches on the area where "the mechanic or machine-like in life and the inorganic life of objects encounter each other and wrestle with each other."[9] What cinema in general does with bodies, such as subjecting them to chain-reactions, making them "function like rubber balls or parts of machines," or "follow the laws of ballistics," is displayed and exaggerated in the slapstick, with the result that "organic nature is transformed into a machine for the production of mechanical movements."[10]

For Benjamin, film is *"the art form corresponding to the increased threat to life that faces people today.* Humanity's need to expose itself to shock effects represents an adaptation to the dangers threatening it. Film corresponds to profound changes in the apparatus of apperception — changes that are experienced on the scale of private existence by each passerby in big-city traffic, and on a historical scale by every present-day citizen."[11]

---

8   Walter Benjamin, "The Work of Art in the Age of Its Reproducibility (third version)," in *Selected Writings, vol. 4, 1938–1940,* eds. Howard Eiland and Michael Jennings, trans. Edmund Jephcott et al. (Cambridge: Belknap Press, 2003), 263, trans. slightly modified. The English translation of *das Gewebe der Gegebenheit* reads "reality."

9   Vogl, "Kafkas Komik," 78.

10 Ibid. For Vogl, this is the "first metamorphosis." The second metamorphosis is the one in which objects become ob-jects: rebellious things that are no longer "there" but become autonomous and "acquire their own, non-organic life." Reiner Stach points out that "in Kafka's works, 'The Metamorphosis' marks the beginning of a series of thinking, speaking, and suffering animals, of learned dogs and voracious jackals, psychotic moles, worldly-wise apes, and vainglorious mice" (Reiner Stach, *Kafka: The Decisive Years,* trans. Shelley Frisch [Orlando: Harcourt, 2005], 195).

11 Benjamin, "Work of Art in the Age of Its Reproducibility," 281n42. Benjamin's emphasis.

Those are among the shocks and corresponding changes Kafka, who reportedly went to the movies often, registers in his writing.[12] Reading Kafka's story through Benjamin's lens, John Zilcosky notes that the "shocks of modern technology increase, as does the thickness of our 'shields.' Like Samsa, we develop 'armor,' but, in so doing, become dialectically intertwined with the technology we had wanted to ward off."[13]

The time frame in which Kafka wrote "The Metamorphosis" and, about six months later, "prepared the typescript," is noteworthy: it falls within the Balkan War, which lasted from October 1912 to May 1913.[14] Kafka's biographer Reiner Stach acknowledges the difficulty "to assess the effects" of the war on Kafka, especially given the fact that a catastrophe, "that shape[d] the destiny of millions of people [left] almost no trace in [his] autobiographical documents." Nevertheless it is a well-founded assumption that the war "must have hit an exquisitely sensitive nerve in Prague, where public life was subject to the constant tension between Germans and Czechs." A letter of November 1, 1912, to Felice Bauer quoted by Stach shows that "the images of soldiers, which Kafka had evidently studied long and hard, started following him into his sleep." Even though in the "Central European collective memory" the Balkan war may have been "overshadowed by the four-year nightmare of World War I[,] many people later saw it as a kind of rehearsal; in fact, the armaments industry was using the Balkans as a welcome testing ground for its newest products."[15] This war was so brutal that it came to be known as the "Balkan slaughterhouse." According to Stach, it is possible that Kafka heard "firsthand" war reports from Egon Erwin Kisch who had "traveled through the Balkans for the Prague newspaper *Bohemia* in May 1913," which were atrocious to the point of being "unprintable." In any case, the

---

12 See for example Hanns Zischler, *Kafka Goes to the Movies*, trans. Susan Gillespie (Chicago: Chicago University Press, 2003).

13 John Zilcosky, "Samsa Was a Traveling Salesman," in Kafka, *The Metamorphosis*, ed. Corngold, 264.

14 Stach, *Kafka*, 200. Kafka wrote the short story in November 1912.

15 Ibid., 228–30.

creation of the story of the armored body of Gregor Samsa falls within a time in which the Austro-Hungarian Empire, and with it the city of Prague, was awash with "shattering images" and graphic reports of war.[16]

With this context established, let us approach the strange creature, the enigmatic beetle, the "enormous" or "monstrous vermin" with its "back as hard as armor plate," into which — or rather, perhaps, into whom — Gregor Samsa has been transformed.[17] His strangeness, and the openly horrified, disgusted reactions to him by his immediate family and his supervisor, may cause the reader to overlook that he is actually surrounded by objects that also have a life of their own. In the second sentence, an inanimate object, a blanket, is described as if it were on the edge of being alive: it is "about" or "prepared [*bereit*]" to "slide off completely," "just barely managing to cling" to or "sustain itself [*sich erhalten*] on" the beetle's "vaulted brown belly" that is "segmented by rigid arches."[18] The blanket has more potential for initiative than the armored, stiffly arched body of the beetle. The room, ominously called a "human room," also seems to breathe — I will return to this point.

As has been noted by several commentators, this beetle has a predecessor in Kafka's oeuvre. Between 1907 and 1909, Kafka worked on a novel he later abandoned. The surviving text fragment describes Eduard Raban, a man around thirty, who takes a trip by train to visit his fiancée "on the countryside." Among the people in the train car are a number of business travelers

16 Ibid., 230.

17 Kafka, *Metamorphosis*, trans. Corngold, 4. Bernofsky translates with "hard, like a carapace" (3).

18 I combine here Corngold's and Bernofsky's translations, resp. 3, 3. The translation of *bereit* with "prepared" is my own. Corngold translates "about to slide off completely." The German "auf dessen Höhe sich die Bettdecke, zum gänzlichen Niedergleiten bereit, kaum noch erhalten konnte" implies much stronger agency (Kafka, "Die Verwandlung," 115). Joyce Crick's translation reads: "he could see his curved brown abdomen, divided by arch-shaped ridges, and doomed so high that the bedspread, on the brink of slipping off, could hardly stay put" (Franz Kafka, *The Metamorphosis*, trans. Joyce Crick [Oxford: Oxford University Press, 2009], 29).

(*Geschäftsreisende*), whose profession is thus the same as Gregor Samsa's in "The Metamorphosis."[19] Given his strongly ambivalent feelings towards his fiancée, Eduard Raban actually dreads the trip, and before undertaking it, experiments with a fantasy:

Can I not act as I always did as a child in dangerous transactions [*bei gefährlichen Geschäften*]? I don't even have to travel to the country myself, that's not necessary. I send my clothed body [*Körper*]. [...] If he staggers out [*wankt er...hinaus*] of the door of my room, then the staggering does not indicate fear, but his nothingness [*Nichtigkeit*]. Nor is it agitation [*Aufregung*] when he trips [*stolpert*] on the stairs, when he travels sobbingly [*schluchzend*] to the countryside and eats his dinner there, weeping [*weinend*].[20] For I, in the meantime, I am lying in my bed, smoothly covered over with the yellow-brown blanket, exposed to the air that wafts through the slightly opened room. As I lie in bed, I have the form of a big beetle, of a stag beetle or a May beetle, I believe. [...] The large form of a beetle, yes. I would pretend that it was a matter of hibernation [*Winterschlaf*], and I would press my little legs to my bulbous body [*Leib*]. And I would whisper a small number of words, those are instructions to my sad body [*Körper*], which stands right next to me and is bent over. Soon I'll be done, he bows, leaves quickly and will manage everything in the best manner possible, while I rest."[21]

This "rest," however, is a complicated one. The hibernation Raban imagines would, for a beetle, be what in German is called *Winterstarre* (winter torpor or winter numbness) as distinct

---

19 Zilcosky devoted a detailed analysis to the traveling salesman in Kafka's texts: Zilcosky, "Samsa Was a Traveling Salesman," 245–71.

20 In German, the word for "body," Körper, is masculine, thus the personal pronoun "he" in the present translation.

21 Franz Kafka, *Nachgelassene Schriften und Fragmente I,* ed. Malcolm Pasley (Frankfurt: Fischer, 1993), 17–18; Kafka, "From Wedding Preparations in the Country," in *Metamorphosis,* trans. Susan Bernofsky, 51, trans. slightly modified and partially quoted from Stach, *Kafka,* 195.

from *Winterschlaf* (winter sleep). This particular variety of hibernation, found in insects, puts them in a state of complete rigor, a death-like condition which they cannot regulate internally and from which only the exterior temperature change can awaken them, similar to a machine that needs an external stimulus to be set into motion.[22]

Therefore it is all the more noteworthy that in Kafka's fragment the beetle body is designated with the word *Leib*, usually reserved for the body of humans or of animals of higher orders (such as primates, large carnivores, and animals in close contact with humans, especially horses), that is, for bodies considered endowed with a soul, which implies that they are also endowed with a face. On the other hand, the dispatched clothed body is called a *Körper*, a noun that may be used for all living creatures, but, contrary to *Leib*, needs to be used for lifeless forms: a cube is a *Körper*, and cannot be designated as *Leib*.

Both beetles mentioned by Kafka are, in the German-speaking cultural context, associated with fighting or war. In particular, the May beetle plays a prominent role in a famous traditional children's song that describes the ravages and bereavement brought on by war. While in the song the beetle is called on to fly, and thus take flight away from a child whose father is fighting a war and whose mother is "in burned-down Pomerania" (or, as in one variation of the song, "(Gun-)Powderania"), in Raban's fantasy, the figure that, in spite of his "sobbing" is a mere shell of a clothed body, is sent out to fight as a proxy, while the beetle stays in bed. Raban's preference for the death-like torpor of the winter-struck May beetle over the trip to the countryside is motivated by the fear of hostility and certain misery. It is the dread of "all those who want to torment me and who have now occupied the entire space around me"

---

22 This is one of the reasons why the scarab, which belongs to the same lineage as May and stag beetle, was chosen as a symbol of metamorphosis. During wintertime, only a chemical substance produced by their bodies prevents beetles from freezing in sub-zero temperatures.

that triggers the memory of the child's strategic imagination.[23] The body endowed with a soul that has taken on the form of a faceless beetle goes into frigid hibernation and numbness. The weeping, thus face-endowed, but machine-like body is sent out as a proxy.

The specific beetles mentioned in Kafka's fragment are not the only connection to war. As John Zilcosky has shown, there is another trembling, shaking, and sobbing man in the train car, a salesman who sits across from Raban: "This shaking and sobbing man prefigures the post-First World War 'war tremblers' — *Kriegszitterer* — and echoes [...] the 'clothed body' that Raban had always sent on journeys in his stead" in his imagination.[24] Zilcosky surmises that Kafka stopped writing about "mechanized bodies" after 1916, because his

> literary premonitions have come true. The streets of Prague, Vienna, and Berlin are now shot through with bodies that twitch nervously [...]. With the mechanically damaged body now in public view, it no longer belongs to Kafka's nighttime fiction but rather to the daylight of political action. Just ten days before Kafka read "In the Penal Colony" aloud in war-torn Munich, he completed a newspaper appeal calling attention to the injured soldiers who now "twitch and jump with nerves in the streets of our cities." Like Raban's staggering "clothed body," these men signify only their own damage, simulated or not, and they require scientific — not literary — help.[25]

In "The Metamorphosis," the child's daydream and response to dangerous situations has become the nightmarish reality: "It was no dream."[26] Zilcosky reads Gregor Samsa's "armor-like" body as "redolent" of medieval knights "but also of the armored trains

---

23 "Alle, die mich quälen wollen und die jetzt den ganzen Raum um mich besetzt haben" (Kafka, *Nachgelassene Schriften,* 17).

24 Zilcosky, "Samsa Was a Traveling Salesman," 247.

25 Ibid., 265–66.

26 Kafka, *Metamorphosis,* trans. Bernofsky, 3; trans. Corngold, 3.

and tanks that first appeared on battlefields in 1916," which had been in development already during the preceding decade.[27] The room in which the transformation has occurred is recognized by the insect as a "proper human room" (*Menschenzimmer*), albeit a somewhat too small one, that "lay quiet between the four familiar walls."[28] Again, an inanimate object's description implies its quasi-animation, almost an ability to act: the room lay calmly (*ruhig*) between the walls, as if, in contrast to the enormous beetle, it could get up and move. The room does not consist of four walls, but lays between them, quietly. The next time the room is described, the reader learns that three of the walls have doors, behind each of which stands a different family member voicing expectations: mother, father, sister. Gregor's room is thus a space under surveillance from three potentially open sides, it is a passage or a thoroughfare. Gregor's life as a traveler in constant transition reaches into the most intimate sphere, his bedroom. In spite of the three doors, or, rather, because of them, because of the surveillance from three sides that, soon enough, will morph into an attack from the air, Gregor's room has been transformed from a passageway into a trap: "this high-ceilinged room [the German reads 'this high, free room'], in which he was forced to lie flat on the floor, distressed him [*ängstigte ihn*], without his being able to determine the cause — after all, it was his room, which he had been living in for five years now — and with a half-unconscious motion, and not without a twinge of shame, he scurried beneath the couch [...]."[29]

The cause for Gregor's apprehension becomes clear enough a bit further: in a lofty room, being pinned on the floor makes a

---

27 Zilcosky, "Samsa Was a Traveling Salesman," 265.

28 "Sein Zimmer, ein richtiges, nur etwas zu kleines Menschenzimmer, lag ruhig zwischen den vier wohlbekannten Wänden" (Kafka, "Die Verwandlung," 115). Corngold translates "His room, a regular human room, only a little on the small side, lay quiet between the four familiar walls" (Kafka, *Metamorphosis,* 3). Bernofsky: "His room a proper human room, if admittedly rather too small, lay peacefully between the four familiar walls" (Kafka, *Metamorphosis,* 3).

29 Kafka, "Die Verwandlung," 145; *Metamorphosis,* trans. Bernofsky, 18–19; trans. Corngold, 25.

creature extremely vulnerable to being assailed from above. One of the turning points of the story is when the beetle assesses with his unwaveringly human thinking the threatening "gigantic size" (*Riesengröße*) of the father's boot-soles and the fact that in the time and space in which the father performs only one step, he, Gregor, has to perform *eine Unzahl von Bewegungen,* "a non-number of movements," in other words, countless insect movements in his frenzied attempt to avoid becoming "bug splat."[30] Even though the "vermin," as the transformed Gregor is called, is huge, too wide to fit under the couch or through a door, the beetle's perception is that of a standard-sized small insect for which the size of a human sole is gigantic. A few moments later, the terrified Gregor is indeed hit by a rain of projectiles, apples with which the father, the sovereign inside the house, "bombards," as the narrator puts it, the insect who understands that now, "further running was pointless," and who is severely and permanently wounded in his back, the insect-armor being no match for the father's projectiles. He describes himself feeling "as if nailed fast" or "nailed to the spot" (*festgenagelt*) — just like an insect in a showcase, in a shadow box.[31] A radical asymmetry is established: even though the family feels under siege, they are the ones who are able to kill without being able to be killed; they are able to see without being seen. As the story goes on, the more the father and sister become invulnerable, the more Gregor approaches a state of utter vulnerability.

As Stanley Corngold has remarked, quoting earlier Kafka scholars, etymologically translated, the German noun *Ungeziefer,* "vermin," derives from a "late Middle High German word

---

30 Kafka, "Die Verwandlung," 170; *Metamorphosis,* trans. Bernofsky, 31: "each time his father took a step, he himself had to execute any number of motions"; trans. Corngold, 42: "whenever his father took one step, Gregor had to execute countless movements": again the prefix *un-*. See above, note 2.

31 Kafka, "Die Verwandlung," 171; *Metamorphosis,* trans. Bernofsky, 31, trans. Corngold, 43. Mark Anderson reads the word "festgenagelt" as confirming the "Christian overtones of this death" which "support the basic narrative of conflict between father and son" (Mark Anderson, "Aesthetic Autonomy in The Metamorphosis," in *Franz Kafka's The Metamorphosis,* 90).

term originally meaning 'the unclean animal not suited for sacrifice.'[32] Under the conditions of modern hygiene, the revulsion triggered by vermin is the harbinger of an unquestioned because preordained fate: extermination. This explains the feeling of "shame" with which Gregor hides underneath the couch. As *Ungeziefer*, Gregor Samsa isn't even worthy to be pinned in a shadow box. He only deserves to be exterminated without memory, apprehended in a miniaturized zone of exception, a "microcube of death," not unlike what in current US military parlance would be called a "kill box."

What determines a kill box is not a space determined by physical borders, such as geographical or national borders or even (as in Kafka's story) the physical borders of walls. A kill box is determined only by the location of the prey.

If, as the German philosopher Hans Blumenberg developed in the mid-1970s, the trap is the concept's "prototype" and "first triumph," because it unites in one contraption the mastery over distance and the mastery over absence, given that during its engineering, the prey is absent, and during the capture or kill, the engineer can be absent or remote, the "kill box" brings the concept truly and literally to new heights. The assertion of mastery and of sovereignty is for Blumenberg *in essence* one that acts *at a distance*. Consequently, Blumenberg observed that "it is not by chance that throwing devices and projectiles continue to dominate the history of human actions."[33]

Today, "unmanned" or "uninhabited" aerial vehicles combine the assertion of absolute mastery over distance and space, and the assertion of absolute sovereignty over life, to the point that those killed via remote control from at least twelve airbases

---

32 Stanley Corngold, *The Commentators' Despair: The Interpretation of Kafka's Metamorphosis* (Port Washington: National University Publications, 1973), 10. Corngold also notes that Kafka studied medieval German literature at the University of Prague and that he "assiduously consulted Grimm's etymological dictionary" (258n14). See also Levine, "'The Sense of an Unding,'" 127; Zilcosky, "Samsa was a Traveling Salesman," 268.

33 Hans Blumenberg, *Theorie der Unbegrifflichkeit,* ed. Anselm Haverkamp (Frankfurt: Suhrkamp, 2007), 13.

distributed over at least nine US states (and exclusively in predominantly Muslim, not "evenly matched" countries) are in the vast majority of cases not indicted or even identified.[34]

Both the military and the CIA refer to those killed in a drone strike zone as "bug splat." A computer program called *Bugsplat* is available to calculate the "likely destruction with various missiles and angles of attack," a strike with many civilian casualties being referred to as "causing 'heavy bugsplat.'"[35] Under the title *Bugsplat*, the British Channel 4 ran in May 2015 a pilot episode of a sitcom set at a Royal Air Force base "where a squadron that used to fly bombers in Basra were now stuck in a Portakabin, remotely controlling hi-tech drones."[36] On the one hand, entire populations terrorized by drones, on the other, a sitcom referring to the casualties as crushed insects: the unmitigated asymmetry of lethal force and the casualness of language resulting from the "moral hazard" that accompanies it are here in plain sight.[37] President Obama himself thought it appropriate to use drone strikes or the threat thereof as comedy material at the White House Correspondents Association Dinner on May 1, 2010, when he warned three famous pop stars against "get[ting] any

34 See Chapter 5 above, 170–72. As of June 2012, 64 drone bases were in operation in 27 US states. Of these, twelve bases distributed over nine states (Arizona, California, Georgia, New York, New Mexico, Nevada, North Dakota, South Dakota, Texas) were housing Predator and Reaper UAVs, which can be armed. As of June 2012, 22 additional bases were being planned. (Lorenzo Franceschi-Bicchierai, "Revealed: 64 Drone Bases on American Soil," *Wired,* June 13, 2012). The list can be found here: https://publicintelligence.net/dod-us-drone-activities-map/.

35 Gusterson, *Drone*, 38. See also Jennifer Robinson, "'Bugsplat': The Ugly US Drone War in Pakistan," *AlJazeera*, Nov. 29, 2011; Brandon Bryant, "'Numbing & Horrible': Former Drone Operator Brandon Bryant on His Haunting First Kill," *Democracy Now!*, Nov. 20, 2015: "And we fire the missile. And the safety observer is counting down. He counts down to zero, and he says, 'Splash!'"

36 Michael Hogan, "Bugsplat!, Channel 4, Review: 'Current,'" *The Telegraph*, May 6, 2015.

37 See David Wills, "Drone Penalty," 183. Like other commentators, Wills also notes that in spite of the geographical distance of the killing zones, "reservist terminators" at Hancock and Creech Air Bases in New York and Nevada, report post-traumatic stress symptoms (184).

ideas" involving his young daughters, and his audience obliged with applause and laughter.[38] One might wonder what the President's or his audience's reaction would be if their children were referred to and hunted down as "fun-sized terrorists."[39]

John Kaag and Sara Kreps have proposed to apply the concept of "moral hazard" to weigh on ethical decisions regarding drone operations. The term stems from the insurance industry and designates "a situation in which greater risks are taken by individuals who are able to avoid shouldering the cost associated with these risks."[40] Drones have made it possible to some governments to "obviate, most, if not all, of [the] costly risks" that in the history of warfare have been associated with military activities, including, first and foremost, the lives of soldiers, but also "public censure" of casualties and possible retribution.[41] Kaag and Kreps argue that such "moral hazard" is a result of technological feasibility that is not accompanied by the neces-

---

38 "The Jonas Brothers are here. (Applause.) They're out there somewhere. Sasha and Malia are huge fans. But, boys, don't get any ideas. (Laughter.) I have two words for you — predator drones. (Laughter.) You will never see it coming. (Laughter.) You think I'm joking. (Laughter.)" Barack Obama at the White House Correspondents Association Dinner, May 1, 2010, You-Tube video posted by Michael Moore. As Alex Pareene remarked sarcastically, "it's funny because predator drone strikes in Pakistan have killed literally hundreds of completely innocent civilians, and now the president is evincing a casual disregard for those lives he is responsible for ending by making a lighthearted joke about killing famous young celebrities for the crime of attempting to sleep with his young daughters. (Really, everything about the joke is inappropriate...)" (Alex Pareene, "Obama Threatens Jonas Brothers with Drone Strikes," *Salon,* May 3, 2010). See also Benjamin, *Drone Warfare,* ch. 1 ("A sordid love affair with killer drones"), para. 2–3.

39 A former drone operator described a scene "when a series of smaller black shadows would appear across their screens — telling them that kids were at the scene. They called them 'fun-sized terrorists'" (Ed Pilkington, "Life as a Drone Operator: 'Ever Step on Ants and Never Give It Another Thought?,'" *The Guardian,* Nov. 19, 2015).

40 John Kaag and Sara Kreps, "The Moral Hazard of Drones," *New York Times,* July 22, 2012.

41 Kaag and Kreps, *Drone Warfare,* 109.

sary ethical deliberations (which would also need to include moral and legal training of soldiers).[42]

As Grégoire Chamayou writes in *A Theory of the Drone,* if "classical military doctrines used to rely on 'the horizontal projection of power across an essential[ly] "flat" and featureless geopolitical space,'" this mode of projection has today been "replaced or supplemented" by another: we have "switched from the horizontal to the vertical, from the two-dimensional space of the old maps of army staffs to geopolitics based on volumes."[43] Moreover, the "twofold principle of intermittence and scalar modulation for the kill box" makes it possible to "extend" the three-dimensional model "beyond the zones of declared conflict. Depending on the contingencies of the moment, temporary lethal microcubes could be opened up anywhere in the world if an individual who qualifies as a legitimate target has been located there."[44]

In a publication of the National Research Council, "Micro Air Vehicles" or MAVs were defined, in 2000, as "having characteristic dimensions of less than 15 cm."[45] An army strategy manual of 2010 shows greater ambition: the drone of the future is imagined as a nano-drone no bigger than an insect, "capable of marauding in a swarm and 'navigating in increasingly confined spaces."[46] Under the title "Fast Lightweight Autonomy" (FLA), one of the 2015 programs of the Defense Advanced Research Projects Agency (DARPA), pursued the goal "to develop and demonstrate the capability for small (i.e., able to fit through

---

42 Ibid., 135 et passim.

43 Chamayou, *Theory of the Drone,* 54. The quote in the quote is from Stephen Graham. As an example, in 2009, for an area at 10,000 feet mean sea level (MSL) the standard height of a kill box was determined at 25,000 feet. See Army, Marine Corps, Navy, Air Force, *Kill Box: Multi-Service Tactics, Techniques, and Procedures for Kill Box Employment* (Air Land Sea Application Center, 2009), 43. The internet site *Public Intelligence* has made this publication available to the public.

44 Chamayou, *Theory of the Drone,* 56.

45 National Research Council, *Uninhabited Air Vehicles. Enabling Science for Military Systems* (Washington, DC: National Academy Press, 2000), 63.

46 Chamayou, *Theory of the Drone,* 56.

windows) autonomous UAVs to fly at speeds up to 20 m/s with no communication to the operator and without GPS waypoints."[47] The FLA's director, Mark Micire explained in early 2015 that "birds of prey and flying insects exhibit the kinds of capabilities we want for small UAVs (unmanned aerial vehicles) [...]. Many insects [...] can dart and hover with incredible speed and precision. The goal of the FLA program is to explore non-traditional perception and autonomy methods that would give small UAVs the capacity to perform in a similar way, including an ability to easily navigate tight spaces at high speed [...]."[48] With devices such as these, Chamayou remarks, "armed violence could be unleashed in tiny spaces, in microcubes of death. Rather than destroy an entire building in order to eliminate one individual, a miniaturized [weapon] could be sent through a window, and the impact of the resulting explosion could be confined to one room or even one body. Your [bed]room, [your] study could become a war zone." [49]

In the drone war of the near future, insect-like machines will be sent out, as proxies, to kill outside the legal frames governing the by now largely obsolete law of warfare. The development of ever smaller drones impacts their range to the point of "dislocat[ing]" the "spatio-legal notion of an armed conflict [...] almost completely." Chamayou describes this "paradoxical dismemberment" as governed by two principles:

(1) The zone of armed conflict, having been fragmented into miniaturizable kill boxes, tends *ideally* to be reduced to the body of the enemy or prey. That is, his body becomes the battlefield. This is the principle of *precision* or *specification*. (2) In order for the pursuit and surgical strikes to be carried out, this mobile microspace must be able to be aimed wherever

---

47 Jean-Charles Ledé, "Fast Lightweight Autonomy (FLA)."

48 Mark Micire, quoted in Anthony Cuthbertson, "DARPA Plans Autonomous 'flying insect' Drones with Skills to Match Birds of Prey," *International Business Times,* Jan. 2, 2015.

49 Chamayou, *Theory of the Drone,* 56 (trans. slightly modified).

necessary — so the whole world becomes a hunting ground. That is the principle of *globalization* or *homogenization*.[50]

These two principles have turned the drone into "the emblem of contemporary cynegetic war."[51] In the words of General T. Michael Moseley, "we've moved from using UAVs primarily in intelligence, surveillance and reconnaissance roles before Operation Iraqi Freedom, to a true hunter-killer role with the Reaper." His comments about how this name was chosen for the MQ-9 UAV reflect full awareness of the absolute asymmetry involved: "The name Reaper is one of the suggestions that came from our Airmen in the field. It's fitting as it captures the lethal nature of this new weapon system."[52] As Chamayou notes, the badge of the MQ-9 Reaper drone shows a black-hooded skeletal grim reaper, "with its disturbing grin and blood dripping from its blade, accompanied by the motto 'That others may die.'"[53] In the name of the missiles fired from the Reaper, "Hellfire," the absolute asymmetry of deadly force is asserted to reach beyond death into an infernal afterlife.

While the actual kill boxes might get smaller and smaller, the effect on the populations at the receiving end is in inverse proportion gigantic. As Chamayou writes, "drones are [...] petrifying. They inflict mass terror upon entire populations. It is this — over and above the deaths, the injuries, the destruction, the anger, and the grieving — that is the effect of permanent lethal surveillance: it amounts to a psychic imprisonment within a perimeter no longer defined by bars, barriers, and walls, but by the endless circling of flying watchtowers up above." Similar to Gregor's realization during his flight from the father's projectiles, in the drone war, "further running [is] pointless." In the village Datta Khel in North Waziristan, Pakistan, a village that made headlines in March 2011 because an American drone strike had

---

50   Ibid. 56–57.
51   Chamayou, "The Manhunt Doctrine," 4. See Chapter 5 above, 178.
52   Anon., "'Reaper' Moniker Given to MQ-9 Unmanned Aerial Vehicle," US *Airforce News*, Sep. 14. 2006.
53   Chamayou, *Theory of the Drone*, 92.

killed 44 people, many of whom civilians, and because it has been "hit more than 30 times by drones in the course of [...] three years," neighbors are described to "have lost their mental balance [and] are just locked in a room. Just like you lock people in prison, they are locked in a room."[54] With the latest generation of drones, however, not leaving one's house or avoiding being outside on a sunny day no longer provides protection; entire areas are transformed into open-air prisons.[55] The Yemeni writer Ibrahim Mothana's warning that the drone war leads to "the Talibanization of vast tribal areas and the radicalization of people who could otherwise be America's allies" should thus not come as a surprise.[56] Four former drone operators echoed the same concern when they urged President Obama in an open letter in November 2015 to consider that "targeted killings and remote-control bombings fuel the very terrorism the government says it's trying to destroy."[57] In sum, "while drones are tactically effective, their strategic effectiveness is limited. Drones may kill terrorists with ruthless efficiency, but they leave the fundamental drivers behind terrorism unaddressed — and they may even exacerbate those motivations."[58]

---

54 Quoted in ibid., 45.

55 See Chapter 5.

56 Ibrahim Mothana quoted in Gusterson, *Drone*, 110.

57 Amy Goodman and Juan González, "Exclusive: 2 Air Force Vets Speak Out for First Time on Why They Want the Drone War to Stop," *Democracy Now!*, Nov. 20, 2015. In their letter the four former men took responsibility for the killings they had committed or contributed to. One of them opened the Air Force issued letter from which former service members learn the number of killings to which they have contributed. In his case, the number itemized 1,626 killings. In an interview with *The Guardian*, Michael Haas, one of the former drone operators, asked: "Ever step on ants and never give it another thought? That's what you are made to think of the targets — just as black blobs on a screen. You start to do these psychological gymnastics to make it easier to do what you have to do – they deserved it, they chose their side. You had to kill part of your conscience to keep doing your job every day — and ignore those voices telling you this wasn't right" (Ed Pilkington, "Life as a Drone Operator").

58 Kaag and Kreps, *Drone Warfare*, 138.

The spaces of slaughter caused by weapons described to be "surgical," clean, and thus just, but which end up imprisoning entire populations in terror, are, for the most part, not visible to people in high-tech societies, who react, understandably, strongly to the spectacular assaults of combatants physically entering the civilian places they have chosen as zones of combat. But the latter's spectacular, bloody attacks are intimately connected to the presumably surgical ones, to what Jacques Derrida has called the delocalization and expropriation of tele-techno-science and its weapon systems. As explained in the previous chapter, the drone war exemplifies one of the two "ages" of cruelty which for Derrida characterize today's wars. More than twenty years ago Derrida underlined the necessity to understand the "new cruelty" of today's wars which allies "the most advanced technoscientific calculability with a reactive savagery" that, in response to the delocalization imposed by tele-techno-science, attacks "the body proper directly, the sexual thing that can be raped [and] mutilated," and does so in the name of the reappropriation of "the sacredness of life safe and sound."

One glaring piece of evidence for such "delocalization" is the physical absence of the drone pilot from the battle field, resulting in the above-mentioned asymmetry of absolute vulnerability on one side, combined with absolute invulnerability on the other. Hugh Gusterson calls this process the "respatialization" of the battlefield, Klem Ryan goes a step further and suggests "delocalization," echoing Derrida's reflections on the effects of techno-science. Such delocalization, Ryan writes,

> undermines important assumptions of IHL [international humanitarian law] (as it is conceived in the Hague and Geneva Conventions), namely that belligerents mutually occupy a distinct physical space in which war is conducted. In IHL, the battlefield is a space separate from the civilian sphere where the military representatives of the belligerent parties assume the identities of combatants and the privileges and costs that accompany this identity. [...] It was so obvious to most eighteenth and nineteenth-century theorists

and jurists that war occurred on battlefields that were clearly distinguishable from other spaces that this did not warrant explicit mention. It was only in the late nineteenth and early twentieth centuries, as new weapon technologies developed, especially the development of aerial warfare, that the need to define the battlefield became evident. For without the clear physical distinction of the battlefield, concepts essential for the effective functioning of the laws (such as the identity of combatants and what constitutes a military target) lose their clarity.[59]

Ryan cautions that the stark asymmetry and delocalization of drone operations lead to at least three forms of "dissociation," each "exacerbated as the distance between belligerents increases: dissociation of agents from their violent acts, dissociation of the targets from the source of the violence directed against them, and dissociation of the public from the violence committed on its behalf." With Lisa Hajjar, we can add to the delocalization a de-temporalization: the "dronization of war sets the conditions for perpetual war *because* of the technology's risklessness to US soldiers."[60]

According to a 2004 report by the International Committee of the Red Cross quoted in Ryan's essay, "many studies have shown that people find it difficult to kill their fellow human beings at close range and that special conditioning is needed to overcome this inhibition. Conflicts in which recourse is had to advanced technologies which permit killing at a distance or on the computer screen prevent the activation of neuro-psychological mechanisms which render the act of killing difficult." Ryan

---

59 Klem Ryan, "What's Wrong with Drones? The Battlefield in International Humanitarian Law," in *The American Way of Bombing: Changing Ethical and Legal Norms, from Flying Fortresses to Drones,* ed. Matthew Evangelista and Henry Shue (Ithaca: Cornell University Press, 2014), 211–12. Ryan recalls that the "Hague Conventions of 1907 represent the first major overt attempt in IHL to expressly separate combatant and civilian spaces."

60 Lisa Hajjar, "Drone Warfare and the Superpower's Dilemma," Part 2, *Jadaliyya,* Sept. 21, 2015.

concludes that when "belligerents are thousands of miles apart, the relationship required for reciprocal rules to limit war simply does not exist. We should not be surprised, then, if the use of drones tends to produce hostility and continued violence, as opposed to restraint, engagement, concession, and peace." [61]

This analysis echoes the dire warning Paul Kahn expressed in 2002 in his examination of the "paradox of riskless war:"

> For the asymmetrically powerful to insist on the maintenance of the combatant/noncombatant distinction has the appearance of self-serving moralizing. Just as it is practically intolerable to suffer an asymmetrical use of force, it is intolerable to suffer an asymmetrical risk to a civilian population. There is likely to be a cycle of escalation, as each side responds to the other's infliction of risk upon noncombatants. [...] This means that the asymmetrical capacities of Western — and particularly U.S. forces — themselves create the conditions for increasing use of terrorism. This, in turn, creates a cycle of destruction outside of the boundaries of the battlefield, with its reliance on the distinction of combatants from noncombatants. [62]

Richard Falk draws the conclusion that "the embrace of state terror to fight against non-state actors makes war into a species of terror and tends toward making limits on force seem arbitrary, if not absurd." [63] Kahn's and Falk's assessments capture in nuce the stakes: massive asymmetry of lethal force exposes

---

61 Ryan, "What's Wrong with Drones?," 213, 219.

62 Paul W. Kahn, "The Paradox of Riskless Warfare," *Faculty Scholarship Series,* Paper 326 (New Haven: Yale Law School, 2002), 6. Kahn asserts that "the same motivations are powering the Intifada. If the Palestinians cannot hope realistically to create a reciprocal risk for the Israeli military, they will direct the risk of injury at civilians. And, of course, the character of the attack on September 11 was itself a response to the asymmetry in conventional forces."

63 Richard Falk, "Why drones are more dangerous than nuclear weapons," in *Drones and Targeted Killing: Legal, Moral and Geopolitical Issues,* ed. Marjorie Cohn (Northampton: Olive Branch Press, 2015), 45. As its title announces, Falk's essay lies out the reasons why in his view drone warfare is

the boundary between the battlefield and civilian space on *both* sides to the danger of being erased.[64] It recreates, according to what Derrida described as the "terrifying but fatal logic" of "auto-immunization," the violence it declares to fight.[65] While in countries targeted by drones, kill boxes abolish *de facto* the distinction between military targets and civilian spaces, the "removal of military pilots from bases abroad to bases within the United States that are physically distant but experientially proximate to the killing zones accomplishes a parallel erasure of the distinction between combat and noncombat spaces" at home.[66] Again, we can apply the Derridean concept of auto-immunization: the very same military decisions that abolish civilian space abroad have a similar effect on the "homeland," even if the scales of visibility and destructiveness are vastly different. Gusterson calls this the "flip side of globalization" in the described process of "respatialization." While asymmetry of lethal force has characterized many other colonial contexts in the past, drones constitute an "imperial border-control technology for the age of late capitalism."[67]

Not so much in spite of, but, along the lines of Derrida's auto-immune process, rather *because of* the radical asymmetry endemic to a neocolonial counterinsurgency context, there are other parallels between the methods used by insurgents and those expected to fight them. Quoting Talal Asad's observation that American soldiers "need no longer go to war expecting to die, but only to kill," Gusterson notes that this in itself "destabilizes the conventional understanding of war as an activity in which human dying and killing are exchanged." The resulting "absence of reciprocity of bodily exposure" makes drone war-

---

"likely to become more destructive of international law and world order" than the "reliance on nuclear weapons."

64 Gusterson, *Drone*, 48.

65 Derrida, "Faith and Knowledge," 80.

66 Gusterson, *Drone*, 48.

67 Ibid., 47–48, 148. Gusterson notes that drones would never be used against "evenly matched adversaries" like China or Russia or in Western countries like Germany or France (56–57).

fare not only "dishonorable" but also causes a "perverse parallel-
ism, or mirror imaging, between drone warfare and the tactic of
suicide bombing" of insurgents: "Drone operators and suicide
bombers, either by preemptively destroying their bodies or by
absenting their bodies, deprive their adversaries of the opportunity to capture or kill them, thus undermining the structural
reciprocity that conventionally, or at least ideally, defines war."[68]

Moreover, even if killing by remote control appears to be
"the antithesis of the dirty, intimate work of interrogation," and
if the deployment of drones was dramatically expanded to solve
"the stubborn problem presented by the indefinite detention
of terrorist suspects,"[69] there is an element of continuity or of
contamination (if indeed, interrogation is "dirty" in the sense of
"enhanced," i.e., employing illegal methods). Citing Elaine Scarry's description of war as a "contest" in which "the participants
must work to out-injure each other," Gusterson again underlines
the decisive feature of structural reciprocity, even if it is only
potential. By contrast, the drone war, like torture and indefinite
detention without indictment, let alone trial, "involve a unilateral infliction of pain."[70]

In passing, Gusterson establishes a fourth disturbing parallel: "like blindfolds, hoods, darkened cells, or isolation tanks,
the air-conditioned trailers seal off drone operators from the
nearby physical environment and make them suggestible to
other cues."[71] This is a noteworthy observation for two reasons:
not unlike torture, drone operations devastate the social fabric, because the "terrorizing effects" of the persistent presence
of drones are not limited to the lives of individuals, but profoundly alter and disrupt communal life: "given the perception
that drones are more likely to attack people when they gather
in groups," customary practices such as "political gatherings of
elders, [...] important tribal dispute-resolution bodies," burials,

---

68 Ibid., 57–58.
69 Kaag and Kreps, *Drone Warfare*, 127.
70 Gusterson, Drone, 106, 145–46. This is why Gusterson surmises that drone
   operations might not deserve to be called "war."
71 Ibid., 61.

and the education of children in schools have been affected or destroyed.[72] Medea Benjamin, who visited the border region of Pakistan and Afghanistan already starting in 2002, reports that "one of the most troubling consequences [of drone operations] is the erosion of the *Jirga* system, a community-based conflict-resolution process that is fundamental to Pashtun society." Funerals are impeded in two ways: they are dangerous because public gatherings are particularly vulnerable to drone attacks. But in addition, "since drone victims are often incinerated, with body parts — if indeed there are any — left in pieces and unidentifiable, traditional burial processes are impossible."[73]

Children in affected areas have been described as "hollowed out shells [...], sullen looking, with no spark, whose dreams are of drones and dead persons." In fact, Tom Reifer concludes, "there is a particular aspect of drone strikes that is tantamount to torture, which in classic definitions includes being subjected to a fear of imminent death. While in general the context for torture is the physical captivity of the victim, with drone strikes, whole communities are subjected to an imminent fear of death, without being formally in the control of others."[74]

Gusterson's observation hints also at a damaging effect on the drone operators' own social fabric at home: surreptitiously, they too are isolated from their surroundings, friends, and families. A number of studies have shown that drone operators suffer from "similar levels of depression and PTSD" as "military personnel deployed to the battlefield."[75]

---

72 Ibid., 42–43.

73 Medea Benjamin, "The Grim Toll Drones Take on Innocent Lives," in *Drones and Targeted Killing: Legal, Moral and Geopolitical Issues,* 95.

74 Tom Reifer, "A Global Assassination Program," in *Drones and Targeted Killing: Legal, Moral and Geopolitical Issues,* 82–83.

75 Ed Pilkington, "Life as a Drone Operator." However, Gusterson notes that "this evidence is open to dispute" (*Drone,* 79). The effects on domestic life on the "homefront" are described in George Brant's play *Grounded.* See also Gusterson, *Drone,* 48–51. Kaag and Kreps cite a 2011 Pentagon study which "showed that nearly 30 percent of drone pilots experience what the military calls 'burnout,' defined by the military as 'an existential crisis'" (Kaag and Kreps, *Drone Warfare,* 116). See also Woods, *Sudden Justice,* 186–89.

Given the structural, auto-immune proximity to the insurgency tactics it seeks to destroy (attack on civilian spaces and similarity to suicide bombings) and the contamination by the illegal practices they were meant to supplant (indefinite detention and torture), one should not be surprised that drone warfare has "replaced Guantánamo as the recruiting tool of choice for militants."[76] In the drone war, the hooded man from Abu Ghraib continues to haunt American counterinsurgency operations. Hence, rather than being "set aside in the name of expediency," as happens too often, "sustained ethical reflection" about drone warfare should be imperative and pressing.[77]

The majority of American taxpayers appear to support the drone war, albeit with rather vague notions about where and how drones operate.[78] The lack of a public discussion focusing on ethical questions might be due to the unawareness of the US public vis-à-vis the "prevalence or nature of drone strikes," which for Kaag and Kreps cannot "simply be attributed to willing ignorance" but is also the result of a secrecy justified by government agencies as necessary in the face of "exceptional threats" which, in turn, is met with "deference" on matters of national security on the part of the public.[79] Steven Levine goes a step further and postulates an "essential fit between drones and covert operations." In his view, secrecy is not a "contingent feature of U.S. drone policy" but is "endemic to the technology and its *likely*, i.e. not ideal, use." Therefore, Levine warns, "drones do not just make war too tempting, they also make assassina-

---

76 Jo Becker and Scott Shane, "Secret 'Kill List' Proves a Test of Obama's Principles and Will," *New York Times*, May 29, 2012. See also Gusterson, *Drone*, 109.

77 Kaag and Kreps, *Drone Warfare*, 106. "Expediency, convenience, calculability, security — this sums up the U.S. drone program" between 2003 and 2016 as one that presents itself as both reasonable and rational, as Kaag and Kreps note (*Drone Warfare*, 120). Kaag and Kreps use Herbert Marcuse's 1941 analysis of a dynamic in national-socialist Germany "that subjugate[d] human autonomy to the direction of machines." However, they repeatedly underline that the "rising drone culture" is not the same as Nazi Germany.

78 Ibid., 63–64, 123.

79 Ibid., 123, 131.

tions and secret intelligence operations too tempting." Secrecy, for Levine, is not an accidental or contingent feature of drones. Rather, it is "essential," that is, inseparable from the technological capacities. This leads him to assert that the very features of drones "undercut" democratic accountability."[80]

The "moral hazard" analyzed by Kaag and Kreps results, then, from technological rationality and reasonableness one the one hand and from "habituation" on the other, especially given the official discourse of and public trust in "surgical precision." Mindful of the vastly different historical and political circumstances, Kaag and Kreps analyze the public's "habituation" with the help of Hannah Arendt's concept of the "banality of evil." Aided by secrecy, habituation has made "drone strikes in the last decade became 'terribly and terrifyingly normal." If indeed, as Kaag and Kreps surmise, "Obama's policy of targeted killings may be more popular with the American public *because* it does away with the stubborn problem presented by the indefinite detention of terrorist suspects," this constitutes another piece of evidence for the refusal of facing the hooded man from Abu Ghraib, the origins of his brutal treatment and the lingering aftermath. Such refusal, conscious or unconscious, also expressed in the public's acceptance of being kept in the dark, has a cost. Towards the end of their book, which includes military considerations in favor of drone warfare, Kaag and Kreps, inspired by Arendt, reach the conclusion that "the banality of evil emerges in the tyranny of the thoughtless majority." They also embrace Arendt's assertion that "in general the degree of responsibility increases as we draw further away from the man who uses the fatal instrument with his own hands."[81] Lack of awareness does not dispense from responsibility. Similar to the acceptance of the death penalty at the condition of it being administered under anesthesia, in order for the condemned person not to feel

---

80 Steven Levine, "Drones Threaten Democratic Decision-making," quoted in ibid., 131–32. The issue of secrecy that is "endemic" to the very technology of drones is central in Levine's important essay, but cannot be further developed here.

81 Kaag, Kreps, *Drone Warfare*, 124–27.

it, the public may accept drone operations at the condition that they kill "quickly and surreptitiously," "much like the use of poison."[82]

The reasons why already Immanuel Kant categorically and unequivocally condemned such surreptitious killing methods in his 1797 reflections on international right and the laws of war should give today's citizens pause:

> The attacked state is allowed to use any means of defence except those whose use would render its subjects unfit to be citizens. For if it did not observe this condition, it would render itself unfit in the eyes of international right to function as a person in relation to other states and to share equal rights with them. It must accordingly be prohibited for a state to use its own subjects as spies, and to use them or indeed foreigners, as poisoners (*Giftmischern*) or assassins (to which class the so-called sharpshooters who wait in ambush on individual victims also belong), or even just to spread false reports. In short, a state must not use such treacherous methods as would destroy that trust (*Vertrauen*) which is required for the future establishment of a lasting peace.[83]

The perspective of the future, that is, the imagination of a common future, of a future living together with past or present enemies, and the faith or trust that is indispensable for such an imagination, determines for Kant what a state is permitted to do. Certain belligerent actions make a person unfit to be a citizen, and must therefore be unconditionally prohibited. Chamayou, after quoting Kant's analysis, explains:

> The principle of citizenship forbids the state from ordering its soldiers to assassinate an enemy, employing weapons that

---

82 Ibid., 131.

83 Immanuel Kant, *Political Writings*, ed. H.S. Riess (New York: Cambridge University Press, 1991), 168 (trans. slightly modified). Quoted in Chamayou, *Theory of the Drone*, 196.

a priori deprive the enemy of any chance of fighting back. The underlying idea is that what a state can make its subjects do is limited by what that would make them become. Whatever we are made to do makes us what we are, but some metamorphoses are forbidden to a state. Kant declares that a state does not have the right to turn its own citizens into assassins. Combatants, yes; assassins, no.[84]

Some metamorphoses are forbidden to a state, because of the metamorphosis it forces upon its citizens. Until 2000, the acronym UAV also stood for "uninhabited aerial vehicle."[85] The elimination of this name has the advantage of clarity, of reflecting awareness of what is at stake. Inhabiting means dwelling, in both senses of "to live in" and "to think at length about." To paraphrase Heidegger, dwelling is a fundamental trait of "mortals," his term for human beings: "Mortals dwell in that they initiate their own essential being — their being capable of death as death — into the use and practice of this capacity, so that there may be a good death."[86] Drone warfare destroys noncombat zones, dwelling spaces, on both sides of the conflict, on the one side, lethally, on the other surreptitiously. The language of drone operators reduces human beings' death to the elimination of vermin. At the same time, in the allusions to the operators' godlike power, it rejects the consideration of the latter's own mortality, denying a common, *shared* mortality.[87] That drones prevent communities from burying their dead in communal funeral practices extends the destruction of dwelling beyond death.

In Kafka's story, the son and brother transformed into a bug is soon enough no longer recognized as a family member. Little

84 Ibid., 196–97.
85 See above, note 45.
86 Martin Heidegger, "Building Dwelling Thinking," in *Basic Writings*, ed. David F. Krell (San Francisco: Harper, 1992), 352.
87 "'Sometimes I felt like God hurling thunderbolts from afar,' and 'I truly felt a bit like an omnipotent god with a god's seat above it all.' Such turns of phrase are a common trope in commentary about drones" (Gusterson, *Drone*, 62).

by little, his room is no longer recognized as a dwelling, transformed as it is from his bedroom into a storage space into which "useless" things, "dirty junk," the "ash can and the garbage can from the kitchen" are discarded, "whatever was not being used at the moment was just flung into Gregor's room."[88] As an insect, Gregor has been robbed of his face. Consequently he is no longer considered worthy of address or memory. The cleaning woman, who discovers Gregor's lifeless body one early morning, "shouted at the top of her voice into the darkness: 'Come and have a look, it's croaked; it's lying there, dead as a doornail!'," or, as the German reads: "croaked through and through" [*ganz und gar krepiert*], foreboding Heidegger's verdict that "only man dies. The animal perishes [*verendet*]."[89] Gregor's death is marked by his parents and sister only in its bare facticity, with relief and even gratitude: "'Well,' said Mr. Samsa, 'now we can thank God!'," after which the three cross themselves, the latter signaling more their gratitude towards God than their mourning over the son and brother. When the cleaning woman sets out to recount how she got "rid of the stuff next door," the father harshly interrupts her, and as the sole witness to the disposal of Gregor's remains, she is fired the same evening.[90] Gregor's body, having become faceless, is not considered worthy of a burial. There is no sign of mourning. The oblivion is to be complete. There is to be no memory of "bug splat."

In our drone wars, the work of destruction beyond death is completed by faceless but all-seeing drones inspired by the agility of insects. But it is executed by operators and their commanders who have a face, against victims who have a face. It is executed in our name, by our proxies. "We're allowing this to happen. And by 'we,' I mean every American citizen who has access to this information now, but continues to do nothing about

---

88 Kafka, *Metamorphosis,* trans. Corngold, 50.
89 Kafka, "Die Verwandlung," 194; *Metamorphosis,* trans. Corngold, 60. Martin Heidegger, "The Thing," in *Poetry, Language, Thought,* trans. Albert Hofstadter (New York: Harper & Row, 1971), 176.
90 Kafka, *Metamorphosis,* trans. Corngold, 63.

it."[91] We have to face our responsibility in murder, and face the consequences.

---

91 The "source" quoted in Scahill, *The Assassination Complex*, 222.

by Richard Falk

The United States emerged from World War II with a triumphal sense that its military power had defeated evil political forces in Europe and Asia, and should not be subject to scrutiny despite causing massive civilian casualties along the way to victory. There were few tears shed as a result of the firebombing of Dresden, an occurrence given a long literary life thanks to Kurt Vonnegut's *Slaughterhouse Five,* or in reaction to the firebombing of Tokyo, or even in reaction to the atomic bombings of Hiroshima and Nagasaki. These two Japanese cities were selected because they had not been previously bombed in the war, as they contained no important military targets and would provide ideal sites to convey the extent of devastation caused by this new hyper-weapon.

There is little doubt that if Germany or Japan had developed the bomb and used it in a similar fashion, and then despite this, lost the war, their leaders would have certainly been charged with war crimes and held accountable. What the United States learned from this major wartime experience was that military superiority ensured the triumph of justice, as well as gained for the country diplomatic ascendancy and enormous economic benefits. The unpleasant fact that the vehicle for such success included recourse to genocidal tactics of warfare was put aside as irrelevant, or worse, a demeaning of a just war and those who fought it. Ever since World War II there has been this psychotic doubling of moral consciousness that fractures the coherence of any legal regime by violating its imperative first principle: treating equals equally. The contrary approach of "victor's justice" is to grant impunity to the victor, while imposing accountability on the loser as by way of the Nuremberg and Tokyo trials.

Visiting North Vietnam in June of 1968 to view what the American Secretary of Defense, Robert McNamara, had described as the most "surgical" bombing campaign in all of history, I was shocked by the indiscriminately devastated cities that had been targeted from air. I was even more shocked by the awareness of total vulnerability of Vietnamese society to the onslaught of what was then almost limitless high-tech superiority in weaponry, which translated into total American domination of air, sea, and land dimensions of the Vietnam War. An aspect of the vulnerability of this essentially peasant society to high tech one-sided warfare, which disturbed me deeply at the time, was the relative helplessness of the Vietnamese to do anything by way of retaliation. In this respect, the war was relatively one-sided, with war thinkers at such think tanks as RAND openly advocating a gradual escalation of the pain being inflicted on Vietnamese society until the political leadership in Hanoi came to their senses and surrendered as Germany and Japan had finally done two decades earlier. After lesser forms of punishment failed to achieve their desired result, American political and military leaders pondered whether to bomb the dikes in the Red River Delta that would cause flooding in heavily populated areas, thus likely producing several million civilian casualties, or use nuclear weapons with even worse results, but held back, not because of moral or legal inhibitions, but because they feared a severe political backlash at home and internationally.

It would be misleading to suppose that the Vietnamese were entirely helpless. The Vietnamese had the capacity to rely on relatively low-tech weaponry and the advantages of fighting in their territorial homeland against a foreign enemy, to inflict significant casualties on American ground forces and even to shoot down American planes now and then, often capturing and imprisoning the pilot. Unable to overcome this Vietnamese resilience and faced with a growing political discontent at home, the US government began as early as 1968 to search for an exit strategy to cut their losses in Vietnam. The highest priority of American diplomacy was to cover up the startling reality that despite the American military juggernaut, the United States still lost the Vietnam War. This effort also failed as the outcome in Vietnam eventually became clear enough for all to see, although Washington's effort to save face prolonged the combat for seven long years, causing tens of thousands of superfluous casualties on both sides. Of course, this was not the first time that the political resolve of a mobilized native population shifted the balance against a Western state that enjoyed a decisive military superiority. All the colonial wars after 1945 exhibited a similar pattern, perhaps most spectacularly in India, where Gandhi led a massive nonviolent movement to induce the United Kingdom to abandon its most prized colonial possession.

Unlike the European colonial powers that came to understand that the imperial age was over, the United States was not prepared to cut back on its global security role. Instead, it made three sets of adjustments to the Vietnamese experience so that it might carry on as previously: (1) it did its best to undermine citizen opposition to non-defensive wars of choice by professionalizing the armed forces, eliminating the draft, and managing the media to minimize adverse comment during the course of a war; (2) it worked hard to find tactics and weaponry that enabled one-sided warfare, avoiding battlefield casualties for American troops while inflicting heavy damage on the adversary; (3) it struggled politically to demonstrate to the American people that its military power could again be efficiently used to achieve geopolitical goals (disguised as "security") and by so doing overcome what Washington policymakers derisively referred to as "the Vietnam Syndrome," that is, a post-Vietnam reluctance of the citizenry to back a distant overseas war that had nothing to do with self-defense. The United States finally found an ideal war in 1991 to rehabilitate global militarism, when with UN blessings it restored Kuwaiti sovereignty by forcing an Iraqi withdrawal from Kuwait in the First Gulf War, experiencing more American casualties due to "friendly fire" than from enemy resistance. This reinstatement of American military credibility was further reinforced, again rather brutally, by the Kosovo War (1999), in which NATO achieved its political goals entirely through air power without suffering a single casualty, while causing substantial civilian casualties on the ground in Kosovo. After Serbia withdrew from Kosovo, Washington think tanks began boasting about the new tactical wonders of "zero casualty wars," seeming unaware of the vast differences of the vast differences between types of warfare, thus paving the wave for frustrating repetitions of Vietnam in Afghanistan, Iraq, and Libya.

When approaching Elisabeth Weber's extraordinary group of essays on how war is being waged beneath the shadows cast by the 9/11 attacks, I find this background relevant. It especially shows how reliance on one-sided warfare was achieved by technological and tactical innovations at the close of World War II and later by a series of adjustments to the American defeat in Vietnam. There were two important changes between the wars that occurred before and after 9/11. Perhaps the most important of these changes was the determination and capacity of the militarily inferior enemy to retaliate in ways that inflicted important symbolic harm on their militarily superior adversary and gave rise to intense fear and anger among the civilian population.

In the period between 1945 and 2001 the wars fought could be described as "Westphalian Wars," that is, wars either between territorial sovereign states or within one such state, and mainly wars involving Northern countries seeking to retain their positions of dominance in the South. In these wars the combat zone was confined to the South. After 9/11, the ensuing wars were more properly understood as engaging North/South interaction with reactive violence by the South directed at targets in the North, sometimes with great effect, as in the 9/11 attacks. True, battlefield military superiority, although taking new forms thanks to technological and tactical innovations, remained concentrated in the North, particularly the United States, but the other side developed the will and capacity to retaliate effectively, although in a manner that was accurately perceived as immoral and illegitimate, and characterized as "terrorism."

The second fundamental change in the nature of warfare, also of a post-Westphalian character, was to make the whole world a potential battlefield including, or even particularly, the homeland. In effect, the United States developed weapons and tactics to hunt for the prey wherever on the planet they might be hiding, including within "sleeper cells" in its own society. Similarly, the adversary used what ingenuity it possessed to find soft spots in "homeland security" and deliver violent blows wherever it might inflict harm and cause fear, a kind of low-tech "shock and awe." The entire world, without much respect for boundaries and sovereign rights, has become a global battlefield in which the so-called "War on Terror" is being waged between two non-Westphalian political entities. On one side is the United States as the first "global state" in history with a network of hundreds of foreign military bases, navies in all oceans, militarization of space, and many allies among foreign countries. On the other side are a variety of non-territorial extremist networks (Al Qaeda, IS) spread across the globe, and capable of attracting followers in the heartland of its enemies who are willing to undertake suicide missions either by following orders or spontaneously.

Weber's brilliant essays shine the bright light of philosophical, cultural, and psychological interpretation on these new patterns of violent conflict that have completely overwhelmed the outmoded Westphalian political consciousness. Her approach is heavily influenced by the complex illuminations of Jacques Derrida, especially his electrifying insights into the inevitability of living together on this planet either badly, maybe disastrously, but also possibly living together well. Weber takes account of Derrida's profound application of the autoimmune mechanism to the kind of monstrous political behavior that these post-9/11 shockwaves have produced, and his depictions of the unnerving equivalencies between the sophisticated cruelties of the "civilized" countries and the "barbaric" cruelties of their supposedly primitive enemies.

These are fundamental realities that elude the conscience, and even the consciousness, of the political class that devises the war policies for the West, which, above all, claims the high moral and legal ground for its counterterrorist campaigns often under the deeply deceptive banner of "humanitarian intervention," what Noam Chomsky has labeled as "military humanism."

It is helpful to remember that the consciousness of the politicians and decision-makers has been shaped for centuries by a form of cynical realism misleadingly attributed to Thucydides and Machiavelli that allegedly adopts the simplistic amoral formula of "might makes right," which has the secondary effect of marginalizing considerations of law and ethics. Henry Kissinger, the arch-realist of our era, makes no secret in various writings of his annoyance with ill-tutored aides that remind him of legal or moral constraints that should be considered when contemplating policy choices. For the Kissingers of this world, the only considerations that count are effectiveness and the minimization of risks and costs to our side, underpinned by the idea that the principal agency of history is military power, the results of which tended to be mostly vindicated by nationally oriented historians, although also challenged by a few historians with revisionist interpretations.

What Weber's essays of exploration help us understand is that this Kissinger worldview directly leads to torture, kill boxes, indefinite detention, and drone attacks in response to the post-Westphalian non-territorial reconfiguration of conflict that currently controls the political imagination in the West. Put more explicitly, the conventional Westphalian geopolitical constructs of deterrence, defense, and retaliation do not work in non-territorial struggles in which the combat soldiers of the enemy engage in suicide missions, lack high-value targets to destroy, and do not threaten invasion or occupation. What works, then, is gaining information as to the intentions and location of the potential attackers, places of refuge, and the leaders. Given this understanding, normalized recourse to torture was an irresistibly attractive option for those who saw the world through a realist optic. As well, preventive war and preemptive tactics of taking out anyone deemed by word or deed to pose a threat to compensate for the absence of an effective reactive option; this circumstance contrasts with Westphalian patterns of warfare where the stronger side militarily always retained a retaliatory capability even if the adversary struck first. An exemplary victim of a drone strike was the extra-judicial, presidentially approved killing of Anwar al-Awlaki, accused of delivering extremist radio broadcasts from his Yemen hideout that allegedly inspired "homegrown terrorists" to launch lethal attacks against Americans. The realist mentality has a hard time accepting social science findings that question the utility of torture as the preferred means to gather information, and since there is only lip service given to normative considerations, it is not surprising that torture persists despite being unconditionally criminalized internationally. True, torture is sanitized to some extent for the sake of modern liberal sensibilities by leaving the victim unscarred or transferring the suspect to a CIA "black site" or to a torture-friendly foreign government by way of "extraordinary rendition." We are perceptively reminded in two of Weber's essays how the CIA relied extensively on the secret use of torture during the Cold War, having made a great effort to develop methods of torture that did not leave the victim physically disfigured.

Another puzzle of these post-Westphalian challenges involves figuring out how to retain the strategic and tactical benefits of military superiority in essentially non-territorial contexts of conflict and political inhibition. The main goal becomes how to find and destroy the enemy while losing as few lives as possible on the technologically advanced side. Drone warfare, at first glance, seems like the ideal solution, a technology that puts to "battlefield" use the information procured through torture and bribery, in a manner that identifies and locates suspects in the most remote parts of the planet, and delivers precise lethal blows with supposedly minimal collateral damage to civilians nearby. Yet as Weber so well shows the reader, the real circle of devastation is far broader than the "kill box" within which the targeted individuals are closeted. Studies have now confirmed that the entire surrounding communities are literally terrorized and so acutely alienated as to become receptive to extremist recruitment efforts. It is revealing that a mainstream film, *Eye in the Sky,* claimed to address the morality of drone strikes by limiting the civilian collateral damage to one young female street vendor in an African town, while the use of the drone was justified to avoid a terrorist attack on a crowded local market that if allowed to go forward was estimated to have killed eighty persons. What was occluded from the movie watcher was the realization that the entire surrounding community would be indefinitely traumatized by this attack launched from the sky.

On further reflection, drone warfare may turn out to be a Pandora's Box for the United States. Already there are reports of IS making use of drones, and, unlike nuclear weaponry, the idea of a nonproliferation regime for drones is generally dismissed as utterly fanciful. But the seductive short-term appeal of drone warfare seems irresistible even to a Nobel Peace Prize recipient like Barack Obama. What drones offer is a way of ignoring sovereignty and geography without provoking widespread protests likely to erupt if either lots of civilians died (civilian casualties were not even counted in Iraq and Afghanistan by the Rumsfeld Defense Department *as a matter of policy,* creating an impression that either there were no such deaths, or if civilians died it was irrelevant to the conduct of military operations, while the Obama presidency ignores completely the community terrorization caused by drone strikes) or American pilots were occasionally shot down or captured. Reliance on drones also avoids, or rather evades, the Guantánamo range of problems associated with capturing terrorist suspects. Drone operators can sit comfortably in their Nevada office complex thousands of miles from the target, and yet have an eerily intimate and disorienting relationship to the human damage done due to the vividness of remote visualization technology. Weber's commentary here tells us much about the paradoxically unnerving relationship between distance and proximity in this new era.

The greatest blow to our Westphalian sensibilities is undoubtedly what Derrida describes as the dynamics of the "autoimmune response." It is here that horror is reproduced by adopting methods to protect the threatened political organism, the homeland, that are no less cruel than what has been experienced. In effect, terrorism begets terrorism, and humane values, always precarious and subject to rights of exception, are explicitly subordinated to the alleged requirements of "security." The post-Westphalian turn encroaches upon the rights of the threatened society by making everyone a potential suspect, and especially implicates those who share a religious and ethnic identity with the assailants, and become too often designated as secondary targets. Weber shows the rather grotesque equivalence between the suicide bomber and the drone operator, simultaneously inflicting death and situating their bodies outside the zone of retaliatory violence.

One of the greatest contributions made by Weber takes the form of indicating the extreme censorship imposed on the publication of poems written by those detained at Guantánamo. The justification given was that poems might transmit coded messages, although it is hard to imagine what useful information could be conveyed by those held in conditions of prolonged captivity. A better explanation might be the reluctance of Guantánamo officials to give these prisoners an opportunity to bear witness to their sufferings and often personal and spiritual aspirations, which would undermine security by "humanizing" terrorists that need to be thought of as "the worst of the worst" to sustain homeland morale. Such a line of interpretation adds weight to Weber's central claim that the humanist sensibility poses a real challenge, if not a threat, to the militarized mentality that allows the modern forms of cruelty to pass undetected through the metal detectors of "civilized societies."

I think a reading of *Kill Boxes* is particularly valuable at this time to unmask the inhumane features of post-Westphalian forms of violent conflict. We are left to ponder whether it is too late to wish for a humane future in which there is respect for and deference to the dynamics of self-determination in the non-West. We need also to seek to have the deadly mechanisms of the post-9/11 autoimmune reactive politics pass through ethical filters before carrying out their deadly missions, sometimes in foreign countries that are remote from the declared combat zones. At the very least, the challenges posed throughout this book point to an urgent need to reconstruct international humanitarian law in light of the realities of these non-territorial patterns of transnational conflict.

It now seems that all the features of armed conflict so disturbingly depicted and interpreted in *Kill Boxes* are in the process of being grossly magnified by the onset of the Trump presidency. Without shame, the new American leader calls for the resumption, and intensification, of torture, and promises to eliminate "radical Islam" from the face of the earth, which amounts to issuing a declaration of war against the entire Muslim world, with the accompanying irony that such advocacy is the surest way to convince young Muslims that only violent resistance can protect their cultural space from American aggression. The credibility of Trump's extreme approach is reinforced by so ardently seeking to impose a temporary ban on all immigration from seven Muslim majority countries, although the simultaneous opportunism of the pledge is revealed by excluding Saudi Arabia from the ban despite supplying most of the perpetrators of the 9/11 attacks and continuing to fund and encourage jihadism throughout the world. The Trump leadership seems unwittingly intent on carrying the Kissinger worldview to its apocalyptic omega point, which will surely test the resilience of the human species in the face of such unprecedented threats to its physical and spiritual survival.

BIBLIOGRAPHY

Ackerman, Spencer. "Obama Claims US Drones Strikes Have Killed Up to 116 Civilians," *The Guardian*. July 1, 2016. https://www.theguardian.com/US-news/2016/jul/01/obama-drones-strikes-civilian-deaths.

———. "Rare Photographs Show Ground Zero of the Drone War." *Wired*. Dec. 12, 2011. https://www.wired.com/2011/12/photos-pakistan-drone-war/.

Adelson, Leslie. "Futurity Now: An Introduction." *Germanic Review* 88 (2013): 213–18.

Agamben, Giorgio. *Remnants of Auschwitz: The Witness and the Archive*. Translated by Daniel Heller-Roazen. New York: Zone Books, 2002.

———. *State of Exception*. Translated by Kevin Attell. Chicago: Chicago University Press 2005.

Ahmad, Ahmad. *Islam, Modernity, Violence, and Everyday Life*. New York: Palgrave, 2009.

Akçam, Taner. *A Shameful Act: The Armenian Genocide and the Question of Turkish Responsibility*. New York: Metropolitan Books, 2006.

Al-Awlaki, Nasser. "The Drone That Killed My Grandson." *New York Times*. July 17, 2013. http://www.nytimes.com/2013/07/18/opinion/the-drone-that-killed-my-grandson.html.

Améry, Jean. *At the Mind's Limits: Contemplations by a Survivor on Auschwitz and its Realities*. Translated by Sidney Rosenfeld and Stella P. Rosenfeld. Bloomington: Indiana University Press, 1980.

———. *Werke,* vol. 2. Edited by G. Scheit. Stuttgart: Klett-Cotta, 2002.

———. *Werke,* vol. 6. Edited by G. Scheit. Stuttgart: Klett-Cotta, 2004.

Anderson, Mark. "Aesthetic Autonomy in The Metamorphosis."
In *Franz Kafka's The Metamorphosis*, New Edition, ed.
Harold Bloom. New York: Bloom's Literary Criticism, 2008.

Anderson, Scott. "Fractured Lands: How the Arab World Came
Apart." *New York Times Magazine.* Aug. 11, 2016. http://
www.nytimes.com/interactive/2016/08/11/magazine/isis-
middle-east-arab-spring-fractured-lands.htm.

Anidjar, Gil. *Semites: Race, Religion, Literature.* Stanford:
Stanford University Press, 2008.

———. *The Jew, the Arab: A History of the Enemy.* Stanford:
Stanford University Press 2003.

Anon. "A Giant Art Installation Targets Predator Drone
Operators." *#NotABugSplat.* https://notabugsplat.com/.

———. "Drone Attacks 'Traumatising a Generation of
Children.'" *Channel 4.* Mar. 5, 2013. http://www.channel4.
com/news/drone-attacks-traumatising-a-generation-of-
children.

———. "Drone Strike That Killed Awlaki 'Did Not Silence
Him,' Journalist Says." *NPR.* Sept. 14, 2015. http://www.npr.
org/2015/09/14/440215976/journalist-says-the-drone-strike-
that-killed-awlaki-did-not-silence-him.

———. "'Reaper' Moniker Given to MQ-9 Unmanned Aerial
Vehicle." *US Airforce News.* Sep. 14, 2006. http://www.af.mil/
News/ArticleDisplay/tabid/223/Article/129780/reaper-
moniker-given-to-mq-9-unmanned-aerial-vehicle.aspx.

Army, Marine Corps, Navy, Air Force, *Kill Box: Multi-
Service Tactics, Techniques, and Procedures for Kill Box
Employment.* Air Land Sea Application Center, 2009.
https://publicintelligence.net/fm-3–09–34-kill-box-tactics-
and-multiservice-procedures/.

Asad, Talal. *On Suicide Bombing.* New York: Columbia
University Press, 2007.

Audi, Paul. *L'empire de la compassion.* Paris: Les Belles Lettres,
Encre Marine, 2011.

Avelar, Idelber. *The Letter of Violence: Essays on Narrative,
Ethics, and Politics.* New York: Palgrave MacMillan, 2004.

Balakian, Peter. *The Burning Tigris: The Armenian Genocide and America's Response.* New York: HarperCollins, 2003.

Bardon, Jonathan. "The Peasantry." In *A History of Ireland in 250 Episodes.* London: Gill and Macmillan, 2009.

Bataille, Georges. *Eroticism: Death and Sensuality.* Translated by Mary Dalwood. San Francisco: City Lights Books, 1986. Originally published as *L'érotisme. Oeuvres complètes,* vol. 10. Paris: Gallimard, 1987.

Baumann, Nick. "The American Teen Whose Death-by-Drone Obama Won't Explain." *Mother Jones.* April 23, 2015. http://www.motherjones.com/kevin-drum/91-982015/04/abdulrahman-al-awlaki-obama-drone.

Becker, Jo, and Scott Shane. "Secret 'Kill List' Proves a Test of Obama's Principles and Will." *New York Times.* May 29, 2012. http://www.nytimes.com/2012/05/29/world/obamas-leadership-in-war-on-al-qaeda.html.

Benjamin, Mark, and Michael Scherer, "Electrical Wires." "The Abu Ghraib Files," Chapter 4. *Salon,* Mar. 14, 2006. http://www.salon.com/2006/03/14/chapter_4/.

Benjamin, Medea. *Drone Warfare: Killing by Remote Control.* New York: OR, 2012, Kindle Edition.

———. "The Grim Toll Drones Take on Innocent Lives." In *Drones and Targeted Killing: Legal, Moral and Geopolitical Issues,* ed. Marjorie Cohn, 91–98. Northampton: Olive Branch Press, 2015.

Benjamin, Walter. "The Work of Art in the Age of Its Reproducibility (third version)." In Walter Benjamin, *Selected Writings, vol. 4, 1938–1940,* eds. Howard Eiland and Michael Jennings, trans. Edmund Jephcott et al. Cambridge: Belknap Press, 2003.

———. "Zur Kritik der Gewalt." In *Gesammelte Schriften,* vol. 2.1, ed. R. Tiedemann, 179–203. Frankfurt: Suhrkamp, 1980.

Bennington, Geoffrey, and Jacques Derrida. *Jacques Derrida.* Translated by Geoffrey Bennington. Chicago: University of Chicago Press, 1993.

Benslama, Fethi. *La guerre des subjectivités en Islam.* Paris: Lignes, 2014.

————. *Psychoanalysis and the Challenge of Islam*. Translated by Robert Bononno. Minneapolis: University of Minneapolis Press, 2009.

————. *Soudain la révolution! De la Tunisie au monde arabe: La signification d'un soulèvement*. Paris: Denoël, 2011.

Blake, Andrew. "Obama-led Drone Strikes Kill Innocents 90% of the Time: Report." *The Washington Times*. Oct. 15, 2015. http://www.washingtontimes.com/news/2015/oct/15/90-of-people-killed-by-US-drone-strikes-in-afghani/.

Bloch, Ernst. *Christian Thomasius, ein deutscher Gelehrter ohne Misere*. Frankfurt: Suhrkamp, 1967 [1953].

Blumenberg, Hans. *Theorie der Unbegrifflichkeit*. Edited by Anselm Haverkamp. Frankfurt: Suhrkamp, 2007.

Brooks, Rosa. "America Tortures (Yawn)." *Los Angeles Times*. Feb. 23, 2007. http://articles.latimes.com/2007/feb/23/opinion/oe-brooks23.

Bryant, Brandon. "'Numbing & Horrible': Former Drone Operator Brandon Bryant on His Haunting First Kill." *Democracy Now!* Nov. 20, 2015. http://www.democracynow.org/2015/11/20/numbing_horrible_former_drone_operator_brandon.

Bureau of Investigative Journalism. "Get the Data: Drone Wars." https://www.thebureauinvestigates.com/category/projects/drones/drones-graphs/.

Burns, Russell. *Communications: An International History of the Formative Years*. Stevenage: The Institution of Electrical Engineers, 2004.

Butler, Judith. *Frames of War: When is Life Grievable?* London: Verso, 2009.

Carlson, Julie. *England's First Family of Writers: Mary Wollstonecraft, William Godwin, Mary Shelley*. Baltimore: Johns Hopkins University Press, 2007.

———— and Elisabeth Weber. "For the Humanities." In *Speaking about Torture,* eds. Julie Carlson and Elisabeth Weber, 1–9. New York: Fordham University Press, 2012.

Carr, David. "With Videos of Killings, isis Sends Medieval Message by Modern Method." *New York Times*. Sep. 7, 2014.

http://www.nytimes.com/2014/09/08/bUSiness/media/with-videos-of-killings-isis-hones-soCIAl-media-as-a-weapon.html?_r=0.

Carrillo Rowe, Aimee. "Be Longing: Toward a Feminist Politics of Relation." *NWSA Journal* 17, no. 2 (2005): 15–46.

Caruth, Cathy. *Literature in the Ashes of History.* Baltimore: Johns Hopkins University Press, 2013.

Center for Constitutional Rights. "Adnan Latif – the Face of Indefinite Detention – Dies at Guantánamo. CCR blames Courts and Obama for Tragedy." Sept. 11, 2012. http://ccrjustice.org/newsroom/press-releases/adnan-latif-%E2%80%93-face-of-indefinite-detention-%E2%80%93-dies-guant%C3%A1namo.

———. "Barhoumi v. Obama." http://ccrjustice.org/home/what-we-do/our-cases/barhoumi-v-obama.

———. "Guantánamo by the Numbers." http://ccrjustice.org/home/get-involved/tools-resources/fact-sheets-and-faqs/guant-namo-numbers.

———. "The United States Tortures before It Kills: An Examination of the Death Row Experience from a Human Rights Perspective." Position Paper. October 11, 2011. https://ccrjustice.org/sites/default/files/assets/files/deathrow_torture_postition_paper.pdf.

Chamayou, Grégoire. *A Theory of the Drone.* Translated by Janet Lloyd. New York: The New Press, 2015.

———. "The Manhunt Doctrine," trans. Shane Lillis. *Radical Philosophy* 169 (2011): 2–6.

Churchill, Ward. *Kill the Indian, Save the Man: The Genocidal Impact of American Indian Residential Schools.* San Francisco: City Lights Books, 2004.

Cockburn, Patrick. *The Jihadis Return: ISIS and the New Sunni Uprising.* New York: OR Books 2014.

Coetzee, J.M. *Waiting for the Barbarians.* New York: Penguin, 1982.

Corngold, Stanley. *The Commentators' Despair: The Interpretation of Kafka's Metamorphosis.* Port Washington: National University Publications, 1973.

Cuthbertson, Anthony. "DARPA Plans Autonomous 'flying insect' Drones with Skills to Match Birds of Prey." *International Business Times*. Jan. 2, 2015. http://www. ibtimes.co.uk/darpa-plans-autonomoUS-flying-insect-drones-skills-match-birds-prey-1481554.

Daoud, Kamel. "Saudi Arabia, an ISIS that Has Made It." *New York Times*. Nov. 20, 2015. http://www.nytimes. com/2015/11/21/opinion/saudi-arabia-an-isis-that-has-made-it.html.

Dayan, Colin. *The Story of Cruel and Unusual*. Cambridge: MIT Press, 2007.

Deleuze, Gilles. *Francis Bacon: Logique de la sensation*. Paris: Éditions de la Différence, 1981.

———. *Francis Bacon: The Logic of Sensation*. Translated by Daniel W. Smith. Minneapolis: University of Minnesota Press, 2002.

Derrida, Jacques. "Autoimmunity: Real and Symbolic Suicides." In Giovanna Borradori, *Philosophy in a Time of Terror: Dialogues with Jürgen Habermas and Jacques Derrida*, 85–136. Chicago: University of Chicago Press 2003.

———. "Avowing – The Impossible: 'Returns,' Repentance, and Reconciliation," trans. Gil Anidjar. In *Living Together: Jacques Derrida's Communities of Violence and Peace*, ed. Elisabeth Weber, 18–41. New York: Fordham University Press, 2013.

———. "Faith and Knowledge: The Two Sources of 'Religion' at the Limits of Reason Alone." In *Acts of Religion*, ed. Gil Anidjar, 42–101. New York: Routledge, 2002.

———. "Force of Law." In *Acts of Religion*, ed. Gil Anidjar, 230–98. New York: Routledge, 2002.

———. "Geopsychoanalysis: … and the Rest of the World," *American Imago* 48, no. 2 (1991): 199–231.

———. *Margins of Philosophy*. Translated by Alan Bass. Chicago: Chicago University Press, 1982.

———. "Nombre de oui." In *Psyché: Inventions de l'autre*, 639–50. Paris: Galilée, 1987.

————. "Poetics and Politics of Witnessing." In *Sovereignties in Question: The Poetics of Paul Celan*, ed. Thomas Dutoit and Outi Pasanen, 65–96. New York: Fordham University Press, 2005.

————. *Politics of Friendship*. Translated by G. Collins. London: Verso, 1997. Originally published as *Politiques de l'amitié*. Paris: Galilée, 1994.

————. "Provocation: Forewords." In *Without Alibi*, trans. Peggy Kamuf. Stanford: Stanford University Press, 2004.

————. "Psychoanalysis Searches the State of its Soul: The Impossible Beyond of a Sovereign Cruelty." In *Without Alibi,* trans. Peggy Kamuf. Stanford: Stanford University Press, 2004.

————. *Rogues: Two Essays on Reason*. Translated by Pascale-Anne Brault and Michael Naas. Stanford: Stanford University Press 2005.

————. *Specters of Marx*. Translated by Peggy Kamuf. New York: Routledge, 1994.

————. *The Animal That Therefore I Am*. Edited by Marie-Louise Mallet and translated by David Wills. New York: Fordham University Press, 2008.

————. *The Death Penalty,* Volume 1. Translated by Peggy Kamuf. Chicago: University of Chicago Press, 2014.

———— and Elisabeth Roudinesco. *For What Tomorrow...: A Dialogue*. Translated by Jeff Fort. Stanford: Stanford University Press, 2004.

Dershowitz, Alan. "Tortured Reasoning." In *Torture: A Collection,* ed. Sanford Levinson, 257–80. Oxford: Oxford University Press, 2004.

Dorfman, Ariel. *Death and the Maiden*. New York: Penguin, 1994.

————. "Foreword: The Tyranny of Terror." In *Torture: A Collection,* ed. Sanford Levinson, 3–18. Oxford: Oxford University Press, 2004.

Dreazen, Yochi J. "The Prison Poets of Guantanamo Find a Publisher." *Wall Street Journal.* June 21, 2007.

DuBois, Page. *Torture and Truth*. New York: Routledge, 1991.

Eisenman, Stephen. *The Abu Ghraib Effect*. London: Reaktion, 2007.

Eshel, Amir. *Futurity: Contemporary Literature and the Quest for the Past*. Chicago: Chicago University Press, 2013.

Esposito, Roberto. *Bíos: Biopolitics and Philosophy*. Translated by Timothy Campbell. Minneapolis: University of Minnesota Press, 2008.

Fair, Eric. "An Iraq Interrogator's Nightmare." *Washington Post*. Feb. 9, 2007. http://www.washingtonpost.com/wp-dyn/content/article/2007/02/08/AR2007020801680.html.

———. "No More: No Torture, No Exceptions." *Washington Monthly*. January–March 2008. https://www.princeton.edu/~slaughtr/Commentary/0801.f.pdf

Falk, Richard. "Report of the Special Rapporteur on the Situation of Human Rights in the Palestinian Territories Occupied since 1967." United Nations, General Assembly, Human Rights Council, 16th session, Agenda item 7, A/HRC/16/72. Jan. 10, 2011.

———. *The Costs of War: International Law, the UN, and World Order after Iraq*. New York: Routledge, 2008.

———. *The Great Terror War*. New York: Olive Branch Press, 2003.

———. "Why Drones are more dangerous than nuclear Weapons." In *Drones and Targeted Killing: Legal, Moral and Geopolitical Issues,* ed. Marjorie Cohn, 29–49. Northampton: Olive Branch Press, 2015.

Falkoff, Marc (ed.). *Poems from Guantánamo: The Detainees Speak*. Iowa City: University of Iowa Press, 2007.

———. "'Where is the World to Save us From Torture?'" In *The Routledge Companion to Literature and Human Rights,* eds. Sophia McClennen and Alexandra Schultheis Moore, 351–60. London: Routledge, 2016.

Felman, Shoshana. *The Juridical Unconscious: Trials and Traumas in the Twentieth Century*. Cambridge: Harvard University Press, 2002.

Feldman, Keith P. "#NotABugSplat: Becoming Human on the Terrain of Visual Culture." In *The Routledge Companion to*

Literature and Human Rights, ed. Sophia McClennen and Alexandra Schultheis Moore, 224–32. London: Routledge, 2016.

Fenton, James. "A Poke in the Eye with a Poem." Review of Paul Muldoon, Horse Latitudes. *The Guardian.* Oct. 21, 2006. http://www.guardian.co.uk/books/2006/oct/21/featuresreviews.guardianreview6.

Fiero, Petra S. *Schreiben gegen Schweigen: Grenzerfahrungen in Jean Améry's autobiographischem Werk.* Hildesheim: Olms, 1997.

———. "The Body in Pain: Jean Améry's Reflections on Torture." *Publications of the Missouri Philological Association* 18 (1993): 26–32.

Finn, Peter, and Anne E. Kornblut. "Obama Creates Indefinite Detention System for Prisoners at Guantanamo Bay." *Washington Post.* March 8, 2011. http://www.washingtonpost.com/wp-dyn/content/article/2011/03/07/AR2011030704871_pf.html.

Fontenay, Elisabeth de. *Le Silence des Bêtes: La philosophie à l'épreuve de l'animalité.* Paris: Fayard, 1998.

Foucault, Michel. *Discipline and Punish: The Birth of the Prison.* Translated by Alan Sheridan. New York: Vintage, 1979.

Franceschi-Bicchierai, Lorenzo. "Revealed: 64 Drone Bases on American Soil." *Wired.* June 13, 2012. https://www.wired.com/2012/06/64-drone-bases-on-US-soil/.

Freud, Sigmund. "Thoughts on War and Death." In *On the History of the Psychoanalytic Movement, Papers on Metapsychology and Other Works.* Vol. 14 of *The Standard Edition of the Complete Psychological Works of Sigmund Freud,* trans. James Strachey. London: Hogarth, 1957.

Gall, Carlotta. "Opium Harvest at Record Level in Afghanistan." *New York Times.* Sep. 3, 2006.

Garoian, Charles, and Yvonne Gaudelius. *Spectacle Pedagogy.* Albany: State University of New York Press, 2008.

Gauger, Hans-Martin: "Er fehlt uns, er ist da: Über Jean Améry." *Merkur: Deutsche Zeitschrift für Europäisches Denken* 59, no. 671 (March 2005): 249–55.

Ghazal, Amal, and Larbi Sadiki, "ISIS: The 'Islamic State' between Orientalism and the Interiority of MENA's Intellectuals." *Jadaliyya*. Jan. 19, 2016. http://www.jadaliyya. com/pages/index/23616/isis_the-islamic-state-between-orientalism-and-the.

Gibson, Jennifer. "Living with Death by Drone." *Lincoln Journal Star*. Oct. 7, 2012. http://journalstar.com/news/opinion/editorial/columnists/column-living-with-death-by-drone/article_1adfa14e-afbd-59f6-a8bb-7115f1150c2c.html.

Goodman, Amy and Juan González. "Exclusive: 2 Air Force Vets Speak Out for First Time on Why They Want the Drone War to Stop," *Democracy Now!* Nov. 20, 2015. http://www.democracynow.org/2015/11/20/exclUSive_2_air_force_vets_speak.

Gorelick, Nathan. "Fethi Benslama and the Translation of the Impossible in Islam and Psychoanalysis." *Umbr(a)* (2009): 188–92.

Greenwald, Glenn. "Extremism Normalized." *Salon*. July 31, 2012. http://www.salon.com/2012/07/31/extremism_normalized/.

Gregory, Derek. "Drone Geographies." *Radical Philosophy* 183 (2014): 7–19.

———. "From a View to a Kill: Drones and Late Modern War." *Theory, Culture & Society* 28, no. 7–8 (2011): 188–215.

Grimm, Jacob, and Wilhelm Grimm. *Deutsches Wörterbuch*. Munich: DTV, 1984.

Gross, Aaron. *The Question of the Animal and Religion: Theoretical Stakes, Practical Implications*. New York: Columbia University Press, 2015.

——— and Anne Vallely (eds.). *Animals and the Human Imagination: A Companion to Animal Studies*. New York: Columbia University Press, 2012.

Gusterson, Hugh. *Drone: Remote Control Warfare*. Cambridge: MIT Press, 2016.

Hajjar, Lisa. "Our Heart of Darkness." *Amnesty Now* 30, no. 4 (Summer 2004).

———. "Drone Warfare and the Superpower's Dilemma." Part 1 and Part 2. *Jadaliyya.* Sept. 21, 2015. http://www.jadaliyya.com/pages/index/22734/drone-warfare-and-the-superpower%E2%80%99s-dilemma-(part-1. http://www.jadaliyya.com/pages/index/22735/drone-warfare-and-the-superpower%E2%80%99s-dilemma-(part-2.

Halliday, Fred. *Shocked and Awed: A Dictionary of the War on Terror.* Berkeley: University of California Press, 2011.

Hartman, Geoffrey. *Scars of the Spirit: The Struggle Against Inauthenticity.* New York: Palgrave Macmillan, 2002.

Haselstein, Ulla. "Vorbemerkungen der HeraUSgeberin." In Ulla Haselstein, *Allegorie. DFB-Symposion 2014, IX–XV.* Berlin: De Gruyter, 2016.

Heidegger, Martin. *Being and Time.* Translated by Joan Stambaugh. Albany: State University of New York Press, 1996.

———. "Building Dwelling Thinking." In *Basic Writings,* ed. David F. Krell, 347–63. San Francisco: Harper, 1992.

———. "The Thing." In *Poetry, Language, Thought,* trans. Albert Hofstadter, 165–86. New York: Harper & Row, 1971.

Hengel, Martin. "Crucifixion." In *The Cross of the Son of God,* trans. Jon Bowden. London: SCM Press, 1986.

Higham, Scott, and Joe Stephens. "New Details of Prison Abuse Emerge: Abu Ghraib Detainees' Statements Describe Sexual Humiliation and Savage Beatings." *Washington Post.* May 21, 2004. A01. http://www.washingtonpost.com/wp-dyn/articles/A43783-2004May20.html.

Hirsch, Marianne. "Editor's Column: The First Blow—Torture and Close Reading." *PMLA* 121, no. 2 (March 2006): 361–70.

Hogan, Michael. "Bugsplat!, Channel 4, Review: 'Current'." *The Telegraph.* May 6, 2015. http://www.telegraph.co.uk/culture/tvandradio/tv-and-radio-reviews/11587892/Bugsplat-Channel-4-review-current.html.

Holdridge, Jefferson. *The Poetry of Paul Muldoon.* Dublin: The Liffey Press, 2008.

Hoppe, Ralf, and Marian Blasberg. "Photos from Abu Ghraib: The Hooded Men." *Der Spiegel.* March 22, 2006. http://

www.spiegel.de/international/photos-from-abu-ghraib-the-hooded-men-a-407263.html.

Hsu, Spencer S. "Judge in D.C. Tosses Suit Challenging Placement of Yemeni Cleric on Terrorist List." *Washington Post*. Dec. 7, 2010. http://www.washingtonpost.com/wp-dyn/content/article/2010/12/07/AR2010120702202.html.

Hubbard, Ben, and Eric Schmitt, "Military Skill and Terrorist Technique Fuel Success of ISIS." *New York Times*. Aug. 27, 2014. http://www.nytimes.com/2014/08/28/world/middleeast/army-know-how-seen-as-factor-in-isis-successes.html.

Human Rights Watch News. "The Legal Prohibition Against Torture." June 1, 2004. http://www.hrw.org/legacy/press/2001/11/TortureQandA.htm.

Hussain, Nasser. "The Sound of Terror: Phenomenology of a Drone Strike." *Boston Review*. Oct. 16, 2013. https://bostonreview.net/world/hUSsain-drone-phenomenology.

Huus, Kari. "Yemen's Rising Radical Star." MSNBC. Oct. 29, 2010. http://www.msnbc.msn.com/id/39914164/ns/US_news-security.

International Human Rights and Conflict Resolution Clinic, Stanford Law School, and Global Justice Clinic, NYU School of Law. "Living Under Drones: Death, Injury, and Trauma to Civilians from US Drone Practices in Pakistan." Sept. 2012. https://www-cdn.law.stanford.edu/wp-content/uploads/2015/07/Stanford-NYU-LIVING-UNDER-DRONES.pdf

Jacobs, Carol. *Skirting the Ethical*. Stanford: Stanford University Press, 2008.

Janouch, Gustav. *Conversations with Kafka*. New York: Praeger, 1953.

Jenkins, Britta. "There, Where Words Fail, Tears Are the Bridge." In *At the Side of Torture Survivors,* eds. S. Graessner, N. Gurris, and C. Pross, trans. J.M. Riemer, 142–52. Baltimore: Johns Hopkins University Press, 2001.

Jennings, Gareth. "DoD Confirms Gorgon Stare to be Operational in Afghanistan." *HIS Jane's Defence Weekly*. Dec.

17, 2015. http://www.janes.com/article/56720/dod-confirms-gorgon-stare-to-be-operational-in-afghanistan.

Johnson, Jenna. "Trump Says 'Torture Works,' Backs Waterboarding and 'Much Worse.'" *Washington Post.* Feb. 17, 2016. https://www.washingtonpost.com/politics/trump-says-torture-works-backs-waterboarding-and-much-worse/2016/02/17/4c9277be-d59c-11e5-b195–2e29a4e13425_story.html.

Johnston, Maria. "Tracing the Root of Metastasis." *Contemporary Poetry Review.* 2007. http://www.cprw.com/Johnston/muldoon.htm.

Kaag, John, and Sara Kreps. *Drone Warfare.* Cambridge: Polity, 2014.

———. "The Moral Hazard of Drones." *New York Times.* July 22, 2012. http://opinionator.blogs.nytimes.com/2012/07/22/the-moral-hazard-of-drones/.

Kadidal, Shayana. "The CIA Inspector General's Torture Report: First Reactions from CCR Senior Managing Attorney Shayana Kadidal." *Center for Constitutional Rights.* Jan. 19, 2010. http://ccrjUStice.org/home/press-center/press-releases/CIA-inspector-generals-torture-report-first-reactions-ccr-senior.

Kafka, Franz. "Die Verwandlung," in *Drucke zu Lebzeiten,* eds. Hans-Gerd Koch, Wolf Kittler, Gerhard Neumann, 113–200. Frankfurt: Fischer, 1994.

———. *Nachgelassene Schriften und Fragmente I.* Edited by Malcolm Pasley. Frankfurt: Fischer, 1993.

———. *Schriften–Tagebücher–Briefe. Kritische Ausgabe: Der Prozeß.* Apparatband, vol. II. Edited by Malcolm Pasley. Frankfurt: Fischer, 1990.

———. *The Metamorphosis.* Translated by Susan Bernofsky. New York: W.W. Norton, 2016.

———. *The Metamorphosis.* Translated and edited by Stanley Corngold. New York: Modern Library Classics, 2013.

———. *The Metamorphosis.* Translated by Joyce Crick. Oxford: Oxford University Press, 2009.

————. *The Trial*. Translated by Willa and Edwin Muir. New York: Schocken, 1995.

Kahn, Paul W. "The Paradox of Riskless Warfare." *Faculty Scholarship Series,* Paper 326. New Haven: Yale Law School, 2002. http://digitalcommons.law.yale.edu/fss_papers/326.

Kamuf, Peggy. "Protocol: Death Penalty Addiction." *Southern Journal of Philosophy* 50 (2012): 5–19.

Kant, Immanuel. *Political Writings*. Edited by H.S. Riess. New York: Cambridge University Press, 1991.

Khorchide, Mouhanad. *Islam ist Barmherzigkeit: Grundzüge einer modernen Religion*. Freiburg: Herder, 2012.

Kittler, Wolf. *The Middle Voice: Steady and Discrete Manifolds in Walter Benjamin*. Center for German and European Studies Working Paper 3.25. Berkeley: University of California, 1996.

Kurnaz, Murat. *Five Years of My Life: An Innocent Man in Guantánamo*. New York: St. Martin's Griffin, 2008.

Lacan, Jacques. *Écrits*. Paris: Éditions du Seuil, 1966.

————. *Écrits: A Selection*. Translated by Bruce Fink. New York: Norton, 2002.

————. *The Seminar of Jacques Lacan, Book II: The Ego in Freud's Theory and in the Technique of Psychoanalysis*. Edited by J.-A. Miller and translated by S. Tomaselli. New York: W.W. Norton, 1991.

————. *The Seminar of Jacques Lacan, Book VII: The Ethics of Psychoanalysis 1959–1960*. Edited by J.-A. Miller and translated by Dennis Porter. New York: Norton, 1992. Originally published as *Le Séminaire Livre VII: L'Éthique de la psychanalyse 1959–1960*. Edited by J.-A. Miller. Paris: Éditions du Seuil, 1986.

Lahbib, Hella. "Entretien avec Fethi Benslama." *La Presse de Tunisie*. Aug. 30, 2014.

Laub, Dori. "Bearing Witness, or the Vicissitudes of Listening." In *Testimony: Crises of Witnessing in Literature, Psychoanalysis, and History,* eds. Shoshana Felman and Dori Laub. 57–74. New York: Routledge, 1992.

Ledé, Jean-Charles. "Fast Lightweight Autonomy (FLA)." *DARPA*. http://www.darpa.mil/program/fast-lightweight-autonomy.

Leithead, Alastair. "Afghanistan Opium at Record High." *BBC News*. Aug. 27, 2007. http://news.bbc.co.uk/2/hi/south_asia/6965115.stm.

Lentes, Thomas. "Der Blick auf den Durchbohrten: Die Wunden Christi im späten Mittelalter." In *Deine Wunden: Passionsimaginationen in christlicher Bildtradition und Bildkonzepte in der Kunst der Moderne,* eds. Reinhard Hoeps, Richard Hoppe-Seiler, and Thomas Lentes, 43–61. Bielefeld: Kerber, 2014.

———. "Der hermeneutische Schnitt: Die Beschneidung im Christentum." In *Haut ab! Haltungen zur rituellen Beschneidung,* ed. Felicitas Heimann-Jelinek, 105–17. Göttingen: Wallstein, 2014.

Leopold, Jason. "How Guantanamo Became America's Interrogation 'Battle Lab.'" *Vice News.* Jan. 12, 2012. https://news.vice.com/article/how-guantanamo-became-americas-interrogation-battle-lab.

———. "Sold Into 'A Piece of Hell': A Death of Innocence at Gitmo." *Truthout.* Oct. 18, 2012. http://truth-out.org/news/item/12171.

Levi, Primo. *Survival in Auschwitz [Se questo è un uomo* (If this is a man)]. Translated by Stuart Woolf. New York: Touchstone, 1996.

Levinas, Emmanuel. *Otherwise than Being, or Beyond Essence.* Translated by Alphonso Lingis. Pittsburgh: Dusquesne University Press, 1998.

———. *Totality and Infinity.* Translated by Alphonso Lingis. Pittsburgh: Duquesne University Press, 1991.

Levine, Michael. *The Belated Witness: Literature, Testimony, and the Question of Holocaust Survival.* Stanford: Stanford University Press, 2006.

———. "The Day the Sun Stood Still: Benjamin's Theses, Trauma, and the Eichmann Trial." *MLN* 126 (2011): 534–60.

———. "The Sense of an Unding: Kafka, Ovid, and the Misfits of Metamorphosis." In *Franz Kafka's The Metamorphosis, New Edition,* ed. Harold Bloom. New York: Bloom's Literary Criticism, 2008.

Lummerding, Susanne. "Signifying Theory_Politics/Queer?" In *Hegemony and Heteronormativity: Revisiting "The Political,"* in *Queer Politics,* eds. M. do Mar Castro Varela, N. Dhawan, and A. Engel, 143–68. Farnham: Ashgate, 2012.

Martelle, Scott. "When Nations Live by the Sword." Review of John W. Dover, *Cultures of War: Pearl Harbor, Hiroshima, 9–11, Iraq* (New York: W.W. Norton, 2010). *Los Angeles Times,* Oct. 24, 2010, E10.

Massad, Joseph. "Psychoanalysis, Islam, and the Other of Liberalism." *Umbr(a)* (2009): 43–68.

Mavridis, Thomas. "'Wer der Folter erlag, kann nicht mehr heimisch werden in der Welt': Vom verlorenen Weltvertrauen Jean Amérys." *Fussnoten zur Literatur* 38 (1996): 70–79

Mayer, Jane. "Whatever It Takes." *New Yorker.* Feb. 12, 2007. http://www.newyorker.com/printables/fact/070219fa_fact_ mayer.

McCans, William. *The ISIS Apocalypse: The History, Strategy, and Doomsday Vision of the Islamic State.* New York: St. Martin's Press, 2015.

McCoy, Alfred. *A Question of Torture.* New York: Holt, 2006.
———. "The U.S. Has a History of USing Torture." *History News Network.* Dec. 6, 2006. http://historynewsnetwork. org/article/32497.
———. "Tomgram: Alfred McCoy, Perfecting Illegality." *TomDispatch.* Aug. 14, 2012. http://www.tomdispatch.com/ post/175582/tomgram%3A_alfred_mccoy%2C_perfecting_ illegality/#more.
———. *Torture and Impunity: The U.S. Doctrine of Coercive Interrogation.* Madison: University of Wisconsin Press, 2012.

McManus, Antonia. *The Irish Hedge School and Its Books, 1695–1831.* Dublin: Four Courts Press, 2002.

McVeigh, Karen. "Drone Strikes: Tears in Congress as Pakistani Family Tells of Mother's Death." *The Guardian*. Oct. 29, 2013. https://www.theguardian.com/world/2013/oct/29/pakistan-family-drone-victim-testimony-congress.

Meddeb, Abdelwahab. *The Malady of Islam*. Translated by Pierre Joris and Ann Reid. New York: Basic, 2003.

Meltzer, Julian Louis. "Zionists Condemn Palestine Terror." *New York Times*. Dec. 24, 1946.

Merback, Mitchell B. *The Thief, the Cross, and the Wheel: Pain and the Spectacle of Punishment in Medieval and Renaissance Europe*. Chicago: University of Chicago Press, 1999.

Miller, Greg. "CIA's Black Sites, Illuminated." *Los Angeles Times*. Aug. 31, 2009. http://articles.latimes.com/2009/aug/31/nation/na-CIA-detainee31.

Mitchell, W.J.T. *Cloning Terror: The War of Images, 9/11 to the Present*. Chicago: University of Chicago Press, 2011.

———. "Echoes Of A Christian Symbol: Photo Reverberates with Raw Power of Christ on Cross." *The Chicago Tribune*. June 27, 2004. http://articles.chicagotribune.com/2004-06-27/news/0406270291_1_torture-humiliation-image.

———. "Sacred Gestures: Images from Our Holy War." *Afterimage* 34, no. 3 (Nov.–Dec. 2006): 18–23.

Mladek, Klaus. "Folter und Scham." In *Wahrheit und Gewalt: Der Diskurs der Folter in Europa und den USA*, ed. Thomas Weitin, 243–265. Bielefeld: Transcript, 2010.

Morrison, Toni. *The Bluest Eye*. New York: Vintage, 2007.

Moynihan, Maura. "Torture Chic: Why Is the Media Glorifying Inhumane, Sadistic Behavior?" *AlterNet*. Feb. 2, 2009. http://www.alternet.org/authors/maura-moynihan-0.

Muldoon, Paul. *Horse Latitudes*. New York: Farrar, Straus and Giroux, 2006.

———. "Out of School and into Summer; Hedge School." *New York Times*. June 26, 2004. http://www.nytimes.com/2004/06/26/opinion/out-of-school-and-into-summer-hedge-school.html.

Mullin, Major James E., III. "The JFA: Redefining the Kill Box." *Fires Bulletin: A Joint Publication for U.S. Artillery Professionals* (March–April 2008).

Murav, Harriet. "The Juridical Unconscious: Trials and Traumas in the Twentieth Century (Review)." *Comparative Literature Studies* 42, no. 3 (2005): 234–37.

Naas, Michael. "The Philosophy and Literature of the Death Penalty: Two Sides of the Same Sovereign." *Southern Journal of Philosophy* 50 (2012): 39–55.

Nakamura, Lisa. *Digitizing Race: Visual Cultures of the Internet.* Minneapolis: University of Minnesota Press, 2007.

Nakashima, Ellen, and Craig Whitlock. "With Air Force's Gorgon Drone 'We Can See Everything.'" *Washington Post.* Jan. 2, 2011.

National Research Council, *Uninhabited Air Vehicles. Enabling Science for Military Systems.* Washington, DC: National Academy Press, 2000.

Nichanian, Marc. *The Historiographic Perversion.* Translated by Gil Anidjar. New York: Columbia University Press, 2009.

Niederland, William G. *Folgen der Verfolgung: Das Überlebenden-Syndrom Seelenmord* [Consequences of persecution: the survivor-syndrome soul-murder]. Frankfurt am Main: Suhrkamp, 1980.

Nossel, Suzanne. "With the Death of Adnan Latif, So Must Come the Death of Guantánamo." *Huffington Post.* Sept. 12, 2012. http://www.huffingtonpost.com/suzanne-nossel/the-death-of-guantanamo_b_1878375.html.

Obama, Barack. "Executive Order 13491 — Ensuring Lawful Interrogations." January 22, 2009. The White House. http://www.whitehouse.gov/the_press_office/EnsuringLawfulInterrogations/.

———. "Letter from the President — Report with Respect to Guantanamo," https://obamawhitehouse.archives.gov/the-press-office/2017/01/19/letter-president-report-respect-guantanamo; https://obamawhitehouse.archives.gov/sites/whitehouse.gov/files/images/Obama_Administration_Efforts_to_Close_Guantanamo.pdf

————. Remarks at the White House Correspondents Association Dinner. May 1, 2010. YouTube video posted by Michael Moore. https://www.youtube.com/watch?v=WWKG6ZmgAX4

Ould Slahi, Mohamedou. *Guantánamo Diary.* New York: Little, Brown and Co., 2015.

Pandolfo, Stefania. "'Soul Choking': Maladies of the Soul, Islam, and the Ethics of Psychoanalysis." *Umbr(a)* (2009): 71–103.

Pareene, Alex. "Obama Threatens Jonas Brothers with Drone Strikes." *Salon.* May 3, 2010. http://www.salon.com/2010/05/03/obama_drone_joke_jonas_brothers/.

Pasternack, Alex. "Life in the Dronescape: An Interview with Madiha Tahir." *Motherboard.* Oct. 29, 2013. http://motherboard.vice.com/blog/life-in-the-dronescape-an-interview-with-madiha-tahir.

Peacham, Henry. *The Garden of Eloquence: Conteining the most excellent ornaments, exornations, lightes, flowers, and formes of speech, commonly called the figures of rhetorike.* London: Field, 1593.

Peters, Edward. *Torture.* New York: Basil Blackwell, 1985.

Pfiffner, James. "US Blunders in Iraq: De-Baathification and Disbanding the Army." *Intelligence and National Security* 25, no. 1 (2010): 76–85.

Pilkington, Ed. "Life as a Drone Operator: 'Ever Step on Ants and Never Give It Another Thought?'" *The Guardian.* Nov. 19, 2015. http://www.theguardian.com/world/2015/nov/18/life-as-a-drone-pilot-creech-air-force-base-nevada.

Priest, Dana. "CIA Holds Terror Suspects in Secret Prisons." *Washington Post.* Nov. 2, 2005. A01. http://www.washingtonpost.com/wp-dyn/content/article/2005/11/01/AR2005110101644.html.

Quintilian. *Institutes of Oratory.* Edited by Lee Honeycutt and translated by John Selby Watson (1856). http://rhetoric.eserver.org/quintilian/index.html.

Rauff, Ulrich. "Interview with Giorgio Agamben—Life, A Work of Art Without an Author: The State of Exception, the

Administration of Disorder and Private Life." *German Law Journal* 5 (May 2004). http://www.germanlawjournal.com/article.php?id=437.

Reifer, Tom. "A Global Assassination Program." In *Drones and Targeted Killing: Legal, Moral and Geopolitical Issues,* ed. Marjorie Cohn, 79–89. Northampton: Olive Branch Press, 2015.

Rejali, Darius. "Speak Frankly about Torture: Exercising International Citizenship." Lecture at Harvard Law School. March 12, 2009.

———. "The Real Shame of Abu Ghraib." *Time.* May 20, 2004. http://content.time.com/time/nation/article/0,8599,640375,00.html#ixzz2sUIPTL2L.

———. *Torture and Democracy.* Princeton: Princeton University Press, 2007.

Reprieve. "Investigations: Drones." http://reprieve.webfactional.com/investigations/drones/.

———. "UN Expert: Lethal Use of Drones Must Be Curbed." June 19, 2014. http://www.reprieve.org.uk/press/2014_06_19_pub_un_expert_drones_must_be_curbed.

Revault d'Allonnes, Myriam. *L'homme compassionnel.* Paris: Éditions du Seuil, 2008.

Richardson, Michael. *Gestures of Testimony: Torture, Trauma, and Affect in Literature.* New York: Bloomsbury, 2016.

Riess, Werner. "Die historische Entwicklung der römischen Folter- und Hinrichtungspraxis in kulturvergleichender Perspektive." *Historia: Zeitschrift für Alte Geschichte* 51, no. 2 (2002): 206–26.

Robinson, Jennifer. "'Bugsplat': The Ugly US drone war in Pakistan." *AlJazeera.* Nov. 29, 2011. http://www.aljazeera.com/indepth/opinion/2011/11/201111278839153400.html.

Ronell, Avital. "Support Our Tropes." In *Finitude's Score: Essays for the End of the Millennium,* 269–91. Lincoln: University of Nebraska Press, 1994.

Rottenberg, Elizabeth. "Cruelty and Its Vicissitudes." *Southern Journal of Philosophy* 50, Spindel Supplement (2012): 143–59.

———. "Review of Shoshana Felman, The Juridical Unconscious: Trials and Traumas in the Twentieth Century." *MLN* 199, no. 5 (2004): 1098–99.

———. "The 'Question' of the Death Penalty." *Oxford Literary Review* 35, no. 2 (2013): 189–204.

Ryan, Klem. "What's Wrong with Drones? The Battlefield in International Humanitarian Law." In *The American Way of Bombing: Changing Ethical and Legal Norms, from Flying Fortresses to Drones,* eds. Matthew Evangelista and Henry Shue, 207–23. Ithaca: Cornell University Press, 2014.

Savage, Charlie, and Julie Hirschfeld Davis. "Obama Sends Plan to Close Guantánamo to Congress." *New York Times.* Feb. 23, 2016. http://www.nytimes.com/2016/02/24/US/politics/obama-guantanamo-bay.html?_r=0.

Scahill, Jeremy, and Glenn Greenwald. "Death by Metadata." In *The Assassination Complex: Inside the Government's Secret Drone Warfare Program,* ed. Jeremy Scahill. New York: Simon and Schuster, 2016, Kindle Edition.

Scarry, Elaine. *The Body in Pain: The Making and Unmaking of the World.* New York and Oxford: Oxford University Press, 1985.

Scelfo, Julie. "Beneath the Hoods." *Newsweek.* July 18, 2004. http://www.newsweek.com/beneath-hoods-130657.

Schröder, Peter. *Christian Thomasius zur Einführung.* Hamburg: Junius, 1999.

Schulman, Miriam, and Amal Barkouki-Winter. "The Extra Mile: The Ancient Virtue of Hospitality Imposes Duties on Host and Guest." *Ethics* 11, no. 1 (Winter 2000): 12–15. http://www.scu.edu/ethics/publications/iie/v11n1/hospitality.html.

Sebald, G.W. "Mit den Augen des Nachtvogels." *Études Germaniques* 42 (July–Sept. 1988): 313–27.

Segev, Tom. *The Seventh Million: The Israelis and the Holocaust.* Translated by Haim Watzman. New York: Hill and Wang, 1993.

Sells, Michael. *Approaching the Qur'an: The Early Revelations.* 2nd Edition. Ashland: White Cloud Press, 2007.

Selz, Peter. *Art of Engagement: Visual Politics in California and Beyond.* Berkeley: The University of California Press, 2006.

Serle, Jack. "Obama Drone Casualty Numbers a Fraction of Those Recorded by the Bureau." *The Bureau of Investigative Journalism.* July 1, 2016. https://www.thebureauinvestigates. com/2016/07/01/obama-drone-casualty-numbers-fraction-recorded-bureau/.

Serrano, Richard A. "Prison Interrogators' Gloves Came Off Before Abu Ghraib." *Los Angeles Times.* June 9, 2004. http:// articles.latimes.com/2004/jun/09/world/fg-prison9.

Shane, Scott. "Acting C.I.A. Chief Critical of Film 'Zero Dark Thirty.'" *New York Times.* Dec. 22, 2012, www.nytimes. com/2012/12/23/US/politics/acting-CIA-director-michael-j-morell-criticizes-zero-dark-thirty.html?_r=1.

———. "The Lessons of Anwar al-Awlaki." *New York Times Magazine.* Aug. 27, 2015. http://www.nytimes. com/2015/08/30/magazine/the-lessons-of-anwar-al-awlaki. html.

Shinkman, Paul. "Obama to Leave 8,400 U.S. Troops in Afghanistan Through to 2017." *U.S. News and World Report.* July 6, 2016. http://www.USnews.com/news/ articles/2016-07-06/obama-to-leave-8-400-US-troops-in-afghanistan-through-2017.

Siddiqui, Sohaira. "Beyond Authenticity: ISIS and the Islamic Legal Tradition." *Jadaliyya.* Feb. 24, 2015. http://www. jadaliyya.com/pages/index/20944/beyond-authenticity_isis-and-the-islamic-legal-tra.

Sierra Nevada Corporation. "Gorgon Stare: Persistent Wide-Area Airborne Surveillance (WASS) System." June 9, 2014.

Singer, P.W. *Wired for War: The Robotics Revolution and Conflict in the 21st Century.* New York: Penguin, 2009.

Sironi, Françoise. *Bourreaux et victimes: Psychologie de la torture.* Paris: Odile Jacob, 1999.

Solomon-Godeau, Abigail. "Torture and Representation: The Art of Détournement." In *Speaking about Torture,* eds. Julie Carlson and Elisabeth Weber, 115–28. New York: Fordham University Press, 2012.

Sontag, Susan. "Regarding the Torture of Others." *New York Times Magazine.* May 23, 2004. http://www.nytimes.com/2004/05/23/magazine/regarding-the-torture-of-others.html.

Stach, Reiner. *Kafka: The Decisive Years.* Translated by Shelley Frisch. Orlando: Harcourt, 2005.

Tahir, Madiha. *Wounds of Waziristan.* Parergon Films. 2013. http://woundsofwaziristan.com/.

Talk Nation Radio. "Jennifer Gibson: Drones Terrorize Populations, Victims Seek Justice at ICC." Feb. 24, 2014. https://soundcloud.com/davidcnswanson/talk-nation-radio-jennifer.

The *New York Times.* "The Guantánamo Docket: A History of the Detainee Population." http://projects.nytimes.com/guantanamo.

The *New York Times* Editorial Board. "A Stark Reminder of Guantánamo's Sins." *New York Times.* Aug. 25, 2016. http://www.nytimes.com/2016/08/25/opinion/a-stark-reminder-of-guantanamos-sins.html.

———. "The Broken Promise of Closing Guantánamo." *New York Times.* June 20, 2016. http://www.nytimes.com/2016/06/20/opinion/the-broken-promise-of-closing-guantanamo.html.

Tholen, Georg Christoph. "Platzverweis: Unmögliche Zwischenspiele von Mensch und Maschine." In *Computer als Medium,* eds. Norbert Bolz, Friedrich Kitter, and Christoph Tholen, 111–38. Munich: Wilhelm Fink Verlag, 1994.

Thomasius, Christian. *Über die Folter: Untersuchungen zur Geschichte der Folter.* Edited and translated by Rolf Lieberwirth. Weimar: Hermann Böhlaus Nachfolger, 1960. Originally published as *De tortura ex foris Christianorum proscribenda, Über die Folter, die aus den Gerichten der Christen verbannt werden muss* (1705).

Tinker, George. "Preface. Tracing a Contour of Colonialism: American Indians and the Trajectory of Educational Imperialism." In Ward Churchill, *Kill the Indian, Save the*

Man: The Genocidal Impact of American Indian Residential Schools. San Francisco: City Lights Books, 2004.

Toorawa, Shawkat. "Poetry." In *The Cambridge Companion to Modern Arab Culture,* ed. Dwight Reynolds, 96–111. Cambridge: Cambridge University Press, 2015.

UN Convention on Torture and Other Cruel, Inhuman or Degrading Treatment or Punishment. http://www.ohchr. org/Documents/ProfessionalInterest/cat.pdf.

U.S. Supreme Court. *Brown v Plata.* Syllabus. 563 U.S. 09–1233. 2011.

Vendler, Helen. "Fanciness and Fatality." Review of Paul Muldoon, *Horse Latitudes. The New Republic Online.* Nov. 9, 2006. http://www.powells.com/review/2006_11_09.html.

Vogl, Joseph. "Kafkas Komik." In *Kontinent Kafka. Mosse-Lectures an der Humboldt Universität zu Berlin,* eds. Klaus Scherpe and Elisabeth Wagner, 72–87. Berlin: Vorwerk 8, 2006.

———. "Technologien des Unbewußten: Zur Einführung." In *Kursbuch Medienkultur,* eds. Claus Pias, Joseph Vogl, et al., 373–76. Stuttgart: Deutsche Verlagsanstalt, 1999.

———. "Vierte Person: Kafkas Erzählstimme." *Deutsche Vierteljahrsschrift für Literaturwissenschaft und Geistesgeschichte* 68, no. 4 (Dec. 1994): 745–56.

De Waal, Frans. *The Age of Empathy.* New York: Three Rivers Press, 2009.

Weber, Elisabeth. *Verfolgung und Trauma: Zu Emmanuel Levinas' Autrement qu'être ou au-delà de l'essence.* Vienna: Passagen Verlag, 1990.

Werckmeister, Otto Karl. *Der MedUusa-Effekt: Politische Bildstrategien seit dem 11. September 2001.* Berlin: Form + Zweck, 2005.

Wesel, Uwe. "Das Fiasko des Strafrechts." *Die Zeit* 49. Dec. 1, 2005. http://www.zeit.de/2005/49/A-Thomasius_neu.

White, Josh. "Army, CIA Agreed on 'Ghost' Prisoners." *Washington Post.* March 11, 2005. A 16. http://www.washingtonpost.com/wp-dyn/articles/A25239-2005Mar10. html.

Williams, George H. "Mercy as the Basis of a Non-Elitist Ecological Ethic." In *Festschrift in Honor of Charles Speel,* ed. Thomas J. Sienkewicz and James E. Betts. Monmouth: Monmouth College, 1997.

Wills, David. "Drone Penalty." *SubStance* 43, no. 2 (2014): 174–92.

———. "The Blushing Machine." *Parrhesia* 8 (2009): 34–42 http://www.parrhesiajournal.org/parrhesia08/parrhesia08_wills.pdf.

Wolf, Siegbert. *Von der Verwundbarkeit des Humanismus: Über Jean Améry.* Frankfurt: Dipa Verlag, 1995.

Wood, Graeme. "What ISIS Really Wants." *The Atlantic.* March 2015. http://www.theatlantic.com/magazine/archive/2015/03/what-isis-really-wants/384980/.

Woods, Chris. *Sudden Justice: America's Secret Drone Wars.* Oxford: Oxford University Press, 2015.

Worthington, Andy. *The Guantánamo Files: The Stories of the 774 Detainees in America's Illegal Prison.* London: Pluto Press, 2007.

Wright, Austin, and Nick Gass, "Obama Announces Plan for Closing Guantanamo Bay Prison." *Politico.* Feb. 23, 2016. http://www.politico.com/story/2016/02/obama-congress-guantanamo-bay-closure-plan-219663.

Wynne, A.S. "Heliography and Army Signalling Generally." *The Journal of the Royal United Service Institution* 24 (1881): 235–58.

Yizhar, S. "The Prisoner," trans. I.M. Lask. In *Midnight Convoy and Other Stories,* 63–88. New Milford: Toby Press 2007.

Zilcosky, John. "Samsa Was a Traveling Salesman." In Franz Kafka, *The Metamorphosis,* trans. and ed. Stanley Corngold, 245–71. New York: Modern Library Classics, 2013.

Zischler, Hanns. *Kafka Goes to the Movies.* Translated by Susan Gillespie. Chicago: Chicago University Press, 2003.

"W. dreams, like Phaedrus, of an army of thinker-friends, think-er-lovers. He dreams of a thought-army, a thought-pack, which would storm the philosophical Houses of Parliament. He dreams of Tartars from the philosophical steppes, of thought-barbarians, thought-outsiders. What distance would shine in their eyes!"

— Lars Iyer

Made in United States
North Haven, CT
29 September 2022